'This pioneering study brings high politics into the analysis of labour emigration. Richly textured and theoretically fecund, it deserves a close reading by scholars of the Middle East, international migration, and authoritarian states.'

David Scott FitzGerald, University of California, San Diego.
Author of Refuge Beyond Reach: How Rich Democracies Deter Asylum Seekers.

'The significance of migration for economic development is indisputable, but its political effects are often overlooked. In this highly original work Tsourapas shows us how population movements drive political change in Egypt and the Middle East, from the rise of Arab nationalism under Nasser to the "Arab Spring" and beyond.'

James F. Hollifield, Southern Methodist University

'The Politics of Migration in Modern Egypt makes a major contribution to the nascent literature on migration states beyond the Global North. Melding analytical insights from immigration and emigration, as well as diasporas and development, Tsourapas provides a framework for thinking about migration policy as a multidimensional set of strategic decisions. His study offers an invaluable benchmark, especially for comparisons to other authoritarian regimes.'

Audie Klotz, Syracuse University

'The Politics of Egyptian Migration provides a valuable contribution on the complex links between political authoritarianism and emigration. The book challenges widely held assumptions about authoritarianism and shows how autocrats use and abuse migration for political ends.'

Fawaz A. Gerges, London School of Economics

'This is an important and insightful book that develops an original argument around the politics and the political economy of migration in modern Egypt. Gerasimos Tsourapas unravels with consummate skill the threads that bind the fate of Egyptian governments to the success or otherwise of Egypt's export of human capital over the course of the past sixty years. In a lucid and highly readable account, he explores the ways in which this phenomenon has been a key factor in Egypt's regional as well as domestic political predicaments.'

Charles Tripp, SOAS

T0382032

'In this book, Gerasimos Tsourapas deeply researches and conceptualises labour emigration policies, bringing out their political rationale over three successive articulations of the Egyptian authoritarian regime between the 1950s and 2011. The primary sources he has used are impressive. The book will be essential material for researchers in migration studies, Egyptian politics and politics of authoritarianism more generally.'

Ibrahim Awad, The American University in Cairo

'A unique book on how the most sedentary people on earth suddenly discovered exodus, and the world's oldest nation its citizens abroad. Tsourapas offers a major contribution to both the history of contemporary Egypt and the scientific study of international migration.'

Philippe Fargues, European University Institute

'A pioneer study theorising across a spectrum of non-democratic regimes and perceptively tracing the relationships in Egypt (1952–2011) between different policies (de)regulating the emigration of workers and professionals and regime legitimation, the policy priority being political survival. This well documented study is enriched by intrepid interviewing in Sisi's Egypt and lightened by abundant cartoons.'

Clement M. Henry, The University of Texas at Austin

'This engaging and superbly researched book convincingly demonstrates how the analysis of emigration policies can provide fascinating insights into the broader domestic and international politics of an authoritarian regime. It is a much-needed and stimulating contribution to a stronger linkage between the research agendas on migration and politics in the Global South.'

Eva Østergaard-Nielsen, Autonomous University of Barcelona

The Politics of Migration in Modern Egypt

In this groundbreaking work, Gerasimos Tsourapas examines how migration and political power are inextricably linked, and enhances our understanding of how authoritarian regimes rely on labour emigration across the Middle East and the Global South. Dr Tsourapas identifies how autocracies develop strategies that tie cross-border mobility to their own survival, highlighting domestic political struggles and the shifting regional and international landscape. In Egypt, the ruling elite has long shaped labour emigration policy in accordance with multiple tactics aimed at regime survival. Dr Tsourapas draws on a wealth of previously unavailable archival sources in Arabic and English, as well as extensive original interviews with Egyptian elites and policy-makers, in order to produce a novel account of authoritarian politics in the Arab world. The book offers a new insight into the evolution and political rationale behind regime strategies towards migration, from Gamal Abdel Nasser's 1952 Revolution to the 2011 Arab Uprisings.

GERASIMOS TSOURAPAS is a Lecturer in Middle East Politics at the University of Birmingham. Prior to this, he was a Senior Teaching Fellow in International Relations at SOAS, University of London, and a Visiting Graduate Scholar at the Centre for Migration and Refugee Studies, The American University in Cairo. He received the 2017 Martin O. Heisler Award of the International Studies Association for work on the politics of migration interdependence in the Middle East. His forthcoming book is entitled *Migration Diplomacy in the Middle East* (2019).

The Politics of Migration in Modern Egypt

Strategies for Regime Survival in Autocracies

GERASIMOS TSOURAPAS
University of Birmingham

CAMBRIDGE
UNIVERSITY PRESS

University Printing House, Cambridge CB2 8BS, United Kingdom

One Liberty Plaza, 20th Floor, New York, NY 10006, USA

477 Williamstown Road, Port Melbourne, VIC 3207, Australia

314-321, 3rd Floor, Plot 3, Splendor Forum, Jasola District Centre, New Delhi - 110025, India

79 Anson Road, #06-04/06, Singapore 079906

Cambridge University Press is part of the University of Cambridge.

It furthers the University's mission by disseminating knowledge in the pursuit of education, learning and research at the highest international levels of excellence.

www.cambridge.org
Information on this title: www.cambridge.org/9781108468640
DOI: 10.1017/9781108630313

© Gerasimos Tsourapas 2019

First published 2019
First paperback edition 2020

A catalogue record for this publication is available from the British Library

ISBN 978-1-108-47554-9 Hardback
ISBN 978-1-108-46864-0 Paperback

To my father, Antonios Tsourapas (1945–2018)

The number of people makes the wealth of states
Frederick the Great

Contents

Figures

Tables

Acknowledgements

In a project that has lasted for almost four years, one incurs many debts to all those who have sacrificed their time in helping make this manuscript a reality. I wish to offer my heartfelt thanks to Laleh Khalili, Charles Tripp, and Gilbert Achcar for the inspiration and advice they provided throughout my time at SOAS, University of London. One could not have asked for a stronger group of senior scholars to see this project to its successful completion. I also owe gratitude to my two mentors, Fiona Adamson and Maria Koinova. Fiona's unfailing encouragement has been instrumental in my academic endeavours. Her energy and dedication to the study of migration made the experience of conducting research infinitely more enjoyable. Maria is also deserving of my warmest thanks for her insightful comments and support, while also encouraging me to find my own voice as I navigated my way through the world of migration and diaspora politics. My thanks to both of you. I remain profoundly grateful, and I hope you find that the end result is worthy of your help. I am also indebted to staff members of the SOAS Department of Politics and International Studies, who have, at various times, shared their feedback on my work, including Reem Abou-El-Fadl, Arshin Adib-Moghaddam, Felix Berenskoetter, Phil Clark, Bhavna Davé, Enze Han, Stephen Hopgood, Salwa Ismail, Mark Laffey, Matt Nelson, Anna Rader, Meera Sabaratnam, Lawrence Saez, Kristin Surak, and Leslie Vinjamuri.

This manuscript was completed at the Department of Political Science and International Studies, University of Birmingham, which has been a welcoming and supportive home since 2016. During the course of writing, there have been many colleagues who have graciously given me their time, energy, and advice. I would like to mention Tereza Capelos, David Dunn, Giuditta Fontana, Tim Haughton, George Kyris, Scott Lucas, Richard North, Adam Quinn,

Asaf Siniver, Eleni Vezirgiannidou, Marco Vieira, Robert Watt, Mark Webber, Mark Wenman, Stefan Wolff, Christalla Yakinthou, and Sotiris Zartaloudis. I have striven to emulate their determination, intellectual vigour, and academic engagement in my own work.

In researching the politics of Egyptian emigration, I benefitted from a variety of funding sources, including a generous three-year SOAS Research Studentship. During my fieldwork in Egypt, I was affiliated with the American University of Cairo and the Netherlands-Flemish Institute in Cairo. I am grateful to both institutions, particularly for the help of Ibrahim Awad and Rudolf de Jong. Additional grants from the University of Birmingham School of Government and Society and the Department of Political Science and International Studies, the SOAS Department of Politics and International Studies, the SOAS Doctoral School, the American Political Science Association, the British International Studies Association, the European University Institute, the Middle East Studies Association, and the Political Science Association have been instrumental in allowing me to present my work, and significantly improve it. James F. Hollifield, Theodore Couloumbis, and Neophytos Loizides have been constant sources of useful advice and guidance. Much gratitude is owed to Philippe Fargues, David Scott FitzGerald, Fawaz A. Gerges, Clement M. Henry, and Audie Klotz. Valuable comments by Walter Armbrust, Michael Farquhar, Sirada Khemanitthathai, Dana Moss, Michelle Pace, Sherene Seikaly have helped strengthen this manuscript in numerous ways. I have had the pleasure of working with exceptional students, including Ahmed Barakat, Hannah Betyna, Noam Chen-Zion, and Ziad Abu Mustafa, who have provided excellent research assistance.

At Cambridge University Press, my thanks are also due to Maria Marsh for believing in this project and seeing it through various stages of publication, as well as to the manuscript's anonymous reviewers for their generous and detailed comments. I am also grateful to Abigail Walkington, Helen B. Cooper, and Natasha Whelan for their indefatigability and expert support. This book builds on previous work published in diverse outlets since 2011, including the *British Academy Review, British Journal of Middle Eastern Studies, International Political Science Review, International Studies Quarterly, Journal of Ethnic & Migration Studies, Journal of Middle East & North African Migration Studies, Mediterranean Politics*, as well as in the *American Political Science Association Migration &*

Citizenship Newsletter. Feedback from journal editors and anonymous reviewers has made a great contribution to my thinking.

I owe my disbelief in the unwritten rule that academic research is a solitary experience to my friends and family. Their enthusiasm and encouragement have been instrumental in so many different ways. Without the help of Tara Buss, this project would have been completely different, and a few lines do not give credit to her enormous contribution. Yoni Abramson, Christian Achreiner, Ahmed Azzam, Hannes Baumann, May Darwich, Emanuele Degli Esposti, Somaia El Sayed, Sarah Garding, Maria Gianniou, Triantafyllos Gouvas, Omar Hammam, Christian Henderson, Janine Hirt, Katie Igras, Dženeta Karabegović, Nancy A. Khalil, Iosif Kovras, Iman Mahdy, Nadejda K. Marinova, Ben Mason, Akanksha Mehta, Covadonga Meseguer, Sruthi Muraleedharan, Kelsey P. Norman, Eleni Papacharalampous, Cathy Purcell, Anna Rader, Mohamed Rahmy, Niamh and Gillian Reoch, Samar Saeed, Ilyas Saliba, Omar Sirri, Jonathan Stephens, Summaiya Zaidi, and Mathilde Zederman have been wonderful sources of camaraderie across different states, countries, and continents. I am grateful to Lachezara Stoeva for her friendship and love of intellectual debate. Alexandros Politis continues to provide unwavering support, through good times and bad. My brother, Dimitris, and my mother, Aikaterini Tsourapa, have always been there for me. Over the past five years, Christine and Torquil Reoch have been an invaluable source of encouragement and bonhomie. Finally, I owe thanks to Fergus Reoch, who has read more drafts on the politics of Egyptian migration than anyone should have to. He has made this book possible with his kindness, enthusiasm, and love for anything Middle Eastern. Here's to many more years of travel and adventure.

Chronology of Key Events

1952   The Free Officers Movement, led by Muhammad Naguib and Gamal Abdel Nasser, overthrows the British-backed Egyptian monarchy, forcing King Farouk into exile in a process known as the *1952 Revolution*.

1954   Nasser places Naguib under house arrest; he becomes prime minister and, in 1956, president.

1954   The Egyptian Ministry of Education is designated the Ministry of Education and Public Instruction, as high-skilled regional emigration is expanded, systematised, and politicised.

1956   Great Britain, France, and Israel's failed attempt to remove Nasser from power during the *Suez Crisis* catapults the popularity of Nasser and Nasserism across the Arab world.

1958–61 Egypt and Syria form a political union, the *United Arab Republic*.

1967   The Six-Day War between Israel and Arab states leads to a humiliating military defeat for Egypt, which loses the Sinai Peninsula to Israel and faces massive socio-economic problems.

1969   Confronted with exorbitant amounts of emigration requests, the Egyptian state suspends all permits.

1970   Nasser dies at 52. He had appointed Anwar Sadat as vice-president only in December 1969.

1971   Sadat purges the Nasserist elements from government and security forces, initiating a sustained process of de-Nasserisation known as the *15 May*, or *Corrective, Revolution*.

1971   Sadat has the new *Permanent Egyptian Constitution* adopted via referendum. Article 52 states that 'Egyptian

	citizens shall now have the right to permanent or temporary migration'.
1973	Egypt launches a surprise attack against Israel that leads to the *October War*. Egyptian forces cross the Suez Canal and regain the Sinai. Sadat becomes the *Hero of the Crossing*.
1973	Detailed state statistics on Egyptian emigration cease to be collected.
1974	Any remaining measures regulating labour emigration are formally abolished, as per Egypt's open-door economic policy, or *al-Infitah*.
1975	Prime Minister Mamduh Salim declares that 'Egypt's policy is to encourage export of its manpower to the Arab world … so that Egyptians can participate in the development plans of sister Arab states'.
1978	Sadat and Israeli Prime Minister Menachem Begin sign the Camp David Accords.
1978–89	Immediately following Camp David, Arab states impose an economic and diplomatic embargo on Egypt.
1980	Egyptian military experts, followed by servicemen and, ultimately, civilians, are recruited by the Saddam Hussein regime during the 1980–88 Iran–Iraq War.
1981	Sadat is assassinated during an annual celebration of the Suez Canal crossing. Hosni Mubarak becomes president, without any changes to state emigration policy.
1981	Presidential Decree 574 establishes a separate Ministry of State for Emigration Affairs.
1983	Law 111 on 'The Emigration and Egyptians' Welfare Abroad', still in use today, formalises the distinction between temporary and permanent Egyptian migrants.
1990–91	More than 0.5 Egyptian migrants forcibly return from Iraq and Kuwait.
1996	Presidential Decree 31 establishes a Ministry for Manpower and Emigration
2011	Mubarak is forced to resign during the *January 25 Revolution*

1 | *Introduction*

> One should never fear there being too many subjects or too many citizens ... being that there is no wealth nor strength but in men.
>
> Jean Bodin, *Les Six Livres de la République* (1583)

'We will continue to meet the manpower requirements of Arab countries.' Anwar Sadat, Egypt's third president, showed no sign of distress when asked, in early January 1977, how he would address the country's extensive technical staff shortages and grave inflationary pressures that followed the deregulation of Egypt's labour emigration policy. Voices urging for a review of Egypt's emigration policy in light of its grave economic effects were ignored. In fact, little has changed in the decades following the 1971 decision to lift any obstacles to citizens' emigration abroad. Existing political economy approaches cannot explain his nonchalant response to the economic repercussions of Egyptian labour emigration: why would the Egyptian regime not attempt to fine-tune a policy that adversely affected the national economy? If labour emigration is solely a tool for economic development, policy-makers would normally be expected to anticipate inflationary pressures or labour market imbalances, and to adjust accordingly. A closer examination of the politics of Egyptian migration reveals why Sadat refused to debate any policy shifts, and why he appeared to prioritise the labour needs of the oil-producing Arab states at Egypt's expense: political survival would not be jeopardised for the sake of economics. The Egyptian regime understood how, as Jean Bodin shrewdly wrote, power lay in citizens' numbers.

This book provides the first attempt to examine how autocracies employ labour emigration policy in order to enhance regime durability. It focuses on modern Egypt, a state that has played a predominant role in Arab politics, continues to be a strategic actor across the Middle

East, and serves as the region's main supplier of migrant labour. *Masr Umm al-Dunya* – 'Egypt is the mother of the world', as the Arabic saying goes – alludes to the country's crucial role in the rise of Arab nationalism and pan-Arabism, as well as to its status as the birthplace of political Islam and the cultural heart of the Middle East. Despite the fact that millions of Egyptians have left the homeland in search of employment abroad since Egypt gained its independence from the British in 1952, labour migration rarely features in the voluminous literature on Egyptian politics. This book demonstrates how cross-border mobility constituted a salient component of the Egyptian ruling regime's survival strategy for more than half a century. From 1952 until the 2011 Arab Uprisings, Egyptian autocrats incorporated labour emigration in their legitimation tactics, their use of repression, and their co-optation of domestic business actors. Labour emigration policy, in other words, sustained a ruling authoritarian regime in multiple ways that have yet to be analysed.

The book examines the importance of labour emigration policy for the Egyptian regime's strategies of legitimation, repression, and co-optation via two case studies: firstly, it analyses the constraining and highly regulated regional emigration policy framework that the Egyptian state developed and implemented under President Gamal Abdel Nasser (1952–70); secondly, it focuses on the deregulated, liberalised regional emigration policy framework that came in place under Presidents Anwar Sadat and Hosni Mubarak (1970–2011).[1] The study will employ qualitative and quantitative methods, drawing on unexamined archival data from British and Egyptian sources, semi-structured interviews with key Egyptian elites, including a former prime minister and former ministers, and statistical data on macroeconomic indicators, remittances inflows, and cross-state migration stocks and flows. It will inductively demonstrate how the ruling Egyptian regime, from 1952 to 2011, employed labour emigration to enhance its durability and withstand pressures for reform. In sketching the different ways through which Egyptian elites benefitted from citizens' cross-border mobility, the book also sheds light on the importance of labour emigration policy for authoritarian regimes on a global scale. But, before outlining the exact nature of the Egyptian ruling regime's strategies, an initial overview of academic research into the politics of migration and a discussion of cross-border mobility within the broader Middle East is required in order to better contextualise the reader.

Researching Population Mobility and Authoritarian Politics

> The promotion of democracy and human rights in Cuba is in the national interest of the United States [and, thus,] measures that decrease dependency of the Cuban people on the Castro regime and that promote contacts between Cuban-Americans and their relatives in Cuba are means to encourage positive change in Cuba. The United States can pursue these goals by … increasing the flow of remittances and information to the Cuban people.
>
> American President Barack Obama (quoted in Badella 2014, 158)

This study theorises the interaction between labour emigration policy, broadly defined as a state's institutional framework regulating citizens' cross-border movement for purposes of employment outside their country of origin, and the durability of a non-democratic regime. Emigration politics cannot be separated from actions taken by political forces within the sending state. Although each citizen has a degree of agency in choosing to emigrate or to remain within a country, this decision is also necessarily filtered through governmental policies that enable or hinder mobility – particularly within non-democratic contexts. At one end of the spectrum, Morocco constitutes a clear example of a state that has developed a policy that includes benefits, pre-migration training, medical insurance, and emergency loans for its migrant population. At the other end, the Democratic People's Republic of Korea considers migration a form of defection and pursues a "shoot to kill" policy for citizens attempting to cross its borders. Surviving would-be migrants face torture and forced labour in "re-education camps". Until 2013, even talk of unauthorised travel abroad carried a six-month prison sentence for Cuban citizens. Ultimately, how do authoritarian regimes regulate cross-border mobility, and how important is labour emigration policy in sustaining non-democratic structures of power?

Historically, scholars of the politics of migration have paid scant attention to the effects of population mobility on political processes within sending states, particularly in non-democratic contexts. Initially, the political science literature on migration suffered from a tendency to marginalise the role of the state altogether. 'The most striking weakness in migration theories drawn from the social sciences', wrote Teitelbaum, 'is their failure to deal in a serious way with government action in initiating, selecting, restraining, and ending

international migration movements' (2001, 26). Two notable exceptions – Aristide Zolberg and Myron Weiner – led an early debate within
political science that highlighted the role of states in managing migratory processes (cf. Talani and McMahon 2015, 19; Hollifield 2012).
This early work initiated a tradition of focusing on liberal democracies,
rather than authoritarian regimes, by espousing the long-standing
claim that non-democracies tend to restrict population mobility
(Hirschman 1993, 179). This was a perspective informed by the Cold
War, when 'communist countries rightly feared a mass exodus of
dissatisfied citizens, while many people living under communist rule
secretly hoped for an opportunity to leave' (Munz and Weiner 1997,
vii; cf. Dowty 1989). Such an approach obscured the intricacies of
communist regimes' emigration practices, including cross-border
population management and, in particular, exchanges of elites between
states of the Warsaw Pact (cf. Babiracki 2015). The Socialist Federal
Republic of Yugoslavia, for instance, was a prime example of
a communist regime that had adopted a permissive emigration policy
since the 1960s (Kosinski 1978). More importantly, this Cold War
perspective paid less attention to non-communist authoritarian
regimes, such as Turkey or Morocco, which had already developed
intricate emigration policies (Adamson 2018; Collyer 2004).
To this day, non-democracies are seen as more likely to restrict citizens'
emigration than either established liberal states (Messina and Lahav
2006, 24–30) or emerging democracies (Massey 1999).

   At the same time, even as the scholarship grew to theorise the
importance of state practices in regulating cross-border mobility
(Hollifield and Brettell 2015; Hollifield 2004; Messina and Lahav
2006; Adamson and Demetriou 2007), it has largely focused on the
politics of immigration. In other words, the sizeable body of research
on the politics of migration suffers from a tendency 'to focus on the
consequences of immigration in wealthy, migrant-receiving societies,
and to ignore the causes and consequences of migration in origin
countries' (Castles, Miller, and De Haas 2014, 26). As Boucher and
Gest argue, 'the most glaring shortcoming of contemporary migration
policy regime typologies is a general reluctance to include non-OECD
countries' (Boucher and Gest 2014, 7). The small group of scholars
examining the politics of emigration tend to focus on liberal democratic
states (Rodriguez 2010; Kapur 2010; Fitzgerald 2009; Naujoks 2013),
at the expense of non-democracies (notable early exceptions include

Østergaard-Nielsen 2003; Brand 2006). Although scholars are gradually shifting focus to how authoritarian regimes engage with population groups abroad (Moss 2016; Glasius 2018; Koinova and Tsourapas 2018), the political importance of such policies for sending states remains under-theorised.

In an effort to amend this, I draw on work by Hollifield and Gamlen (Hollifield 2004; Gamlen 2008), and argue for the need to examine the workings of 'authoritarian emigration states', namely 'the set of institutions, practices, and mechanisms regulating cross-border mobility developed within non-democratic contexts' (Tsourapas 2018a, 403). This study's approach to authoritarianism embraces Linz's classic macro-definition of 'political systems with limited, not responsible, political pluralism, without elaborate and guiding ideology, but with distinctive mentalities, without extensive nor intensive political mobilization, except at some points in their development, and in which a leader or occasionally a small group exercises power within formally ill-defined limits but actually quite predictable ones' (Linz 1964, 255).

How may emigration feature in discussions of authoritarian durability? In terms of the determinants of authoritarian power, Wedeen's argument holds true that 'there are, oddly, few recent writings on authoritarianism in comparative politics and they tend to be concerned primarily with the transition from authoritarian to democratic rule' (Wedeen 1999, 26). For the purposes of this analysis, comparative politics scholarship on the determinants of authoritarianism can be divided into two broad categories, neither of which has yet accounted for the importance of labour emigration. One large group of scholars explains authoritarianism via domestic factors (Schlumberger 2007; Posusney and Angrist 2005). Non-democratic regimes maintain power by developing a strong middle class (Bellin 2004, 2012), ensuring the presence of technocrats (O'Donnell 1973), or a functioning party system (Huntington 2006). Similarly, other scholars highlight the importance of a single-party apparatus (Brownlee 2004, 5), electoral processes (Levitsky and Way 2011), the organisation of political propaganda and the development of "personality cults" (Wedeen 1999; Tripp 2007), or "coup-proofing" strategies across domestic institutions (Quinlivan 1999; Byman and Lind 2010).[2] As will be detailed in the section below, scholars also identify the importance of legitimation, repression, and co-optation in supporting an authoritarian regime's stay in power.

More recently, a second group of scholars has attempted to go beyond the domestic determinants of authoritarian power and theorise the role of international actors in shaping non-democratic politics (Tansey 2016). Ambrosio's work built on Elkins and Simmons in conceptualising the process of 'authoritarian diffusion' as an unintentional process that does not involve 'any collaboration, imposition, or otherwise programmed effort on the part of any of the actors' (cf. Simmons and Elkins 2005, quoted in Ambrosio 2010, 378). For some, this constitutes a process of 'authoritarian learning', as in Heydemann and Leenders' work (2011), which examined such processes of policy adaptation among non-democratic regimes following the post-2011 Arab Uprisings. Empirical evidence supports this research agenda, given that authoritarian regimes also rely on each other for economic, military, and diplomatic support. They provide vetoes in the United Nations Security Council, offer bilateral and multilateral aid in military and security issues, exchange ideas on developmental strategies, or engage in ideational and material support (Erdmann et al. 2013, 5). This literature continues to be 'highly fragmented' and its empirical and conceptual bases are found lacking (Erdmann et al. 2013, 27), as the international dimension of authoritarian regimes 'remains an under-theorised field of study' (von Soest 2015, 628). At the same time, similar to the comparative politics literature on the domestic context of authoritarian rule, labour emigration does not feature as an instrument of cross-regime interaction (Alemán and Woods 2014).

Going beyond comparative politics research on authoritarianism and the literature on the politics of migration, three strands of research are relevant in theorising the importance of labour emigration in autocratic contexts, namely the literature on "rentier states", on developmentalism, and on mobility as a "safety valve". In terms of the first, research on economic remittances has engaged most fruitfully (albeit indirectly) with the importance of labour migration in sustaining non-democratic regimes. Theorists have argued that economic remittances constitute a form of unearned income for the sending states' governments – or, a form of 'rent' (cf. Mahdavy 1970). According to Beblawi and Luciani's political economy analysis, 'with virtually no taxes, citizens are far less demanding in terms of political participation', as per the 'no taxation without representation' demand that contributed to the modern European nation-state system (Beblawi and Luciani

1987, 53–54; cf. Tilly 1992). In examining migrants' remittances as a source of unearned income for sending states, or rent, scholars have argued that emigration ultimately supports incumbent regimes' stay in power. Ahmed argued that unearned foreign income, such as remittances, 'reduces the likelihood of government turnover, regime collapse, and outbreaks of major political discontent', because governments are able to divert expenditure from the provision of welfare goods to 'patronage goods' (Ahmed 2012, 146, 148). In fact, certain non-democracies, such as Cuba or Eritrea, appear to be sustained to a significant extent by workers' remittances (Byman and Lind 2010).

The rentier state argument has been widely discredited from a number of different perspectives (Waterbury 1997; Dunning 2008; Haber and Menaldo 2011). The underlying theory has been rightly accused of being rather ahistorical, given that non-democratic practices in numerous cases existed well before the emergence of rentier resources. The theory also suffers from reducing regimes' strategies to a purely economic rationale (see Birks and Sinclair 1979, for an example of such an account), while bypassing the fact that many rentier states in Northern Europe and Latin America are, in fact, liberal democracies. Importantly, remittances cannot be considered a form of rent, given that they are not transmitted directly into governmental or state coffers, but to households. In many cases, remittances are poorly tracked, or even untaxed, by sending-state governments (de Luna-Martinez 2005; Chami et al. 2008). Boix and Stokes argue that remittances, as they are received by households, create greater financial security that is expected to produce conditions necessary for liberalisation, rather than authoritarianism (Boix and Stokes 2003; cf. Lipset 1959). In Mexico, remittances are used for infrastructure projects that allow for individual political mobilisation (de la Garza and Hazan 2003). Such findings are corroborated by more recent research on the impact of remittances on processes of democratic transitions (Escribà-Folch, Meseguer, and Wright 2015). At the same time, an influx of remittances can have secondary macroeconomic repercussions, from heightened inflation to altered consumption patterns that might increase, rather than decrease, social inequality and political tensions within the sending state (Castles and Wise 2008).

A second, historically dominant paradigm has been the developmentalist approach, in which emigration policy is shaped by a state's developmental needs (see debate in De Haas 2010; Faist 2008). This has been a debate that has adopted various phases over the decades: an initially positive take on labour migration as allowing developing countries to take-off built on neoclassical approaches and modernisation theory, approaching migration as mobility from capital-poor, labour-abundant areas to capital-rich, labour-scare ones (Todaro 1969; cf. Rostow 1960). Wage differentials drive migration processes that will, ultimately, result in wage convergence and equilibrium. Once economic conditions in sending and host states become similar, the incentive for migration is expected to decrease. This view was challenged by a number of critical scholars working through dependency theory, world systems theory, or globalisation theory frameworks. These scholars argued that individuals are fundamentally constrained by structural forces; they highlighted issues of "brain drain", and focused on migration's importance for the 'development of underdevelopment' (Frank 1966; cf. Bhagwati 1976), by examining the contribution of cross-border mobility to uneven trade relations between 'developed (migration receiving) and less-developed (migration sending) countries' (Hollifield 2012, 366; cf. Sassen 1988). In recent years, the pendulum has swung back to a renewed faith in the importance of remittances for the development of sending states, particularly in the Global South; remittances and, by extension, migration constitute 'mother's milk for poor nations' (Kapur and McHale 2003, 49).

There is little doubt that the developmental paradigm has influenced states' migration policies, in both democratic and autocratic contexts. Furthermore, it has been instrumental in highlighting how migration features in the broader patterns of inequality across world politics, as well as the importance of "push" and "pull" factors in understanding economically driven, cross-border mobility flows. While an elaborate macroeconomic analysis of the benefits and drawbacks of this paradigm is beyond the scope of this study, developmentalism nevertheless allows us to identify how these debates have affected autocratic regimes' policies. On the one hand, some regimes have discursively linked a restrictive emigration policy with their broader developmental strategy, which includes preventing brain drain: most notably, the German Democratic Republic's construction of the Berlin Wall functioned as a symbol of the regime's wish for economic development that specifically prevented the emigration of their most able citizens. On the other hand, there have also been attempts by autocracies to discursively link a permissive emigration policy to 'brain gain', as part of popularising a broader developmental strategy: the post-1978 shift in Chinese emigration policy, for instance, framed labour migration as a positive phenomenon, and was employed to popularise the developmental shift towards the market by Deng Xiaoping. Yet, the extent to which emigration policy (in particular, arguments on brain drain or brain gain) may feature in such strategies of autocratic regimes has not been fully explored as a separate field of inquiry.

Beyond economic remittances as rent and developmentalist approaches, social scientists have also approached labour migration as a 'safety valve' that allows sending states to artificially reduce their unemployment rates, or to tackle demographic problems by allowing citizens to migrate abroad (Castles and Wise 2008; Weiner and Teitlebaum 2001). This line of thought builds on Albert Hirschman's key work on "voice", "exit", and "loyalty". The German economist noted that customers may respond to a firm's deteriorating performance in two ways: they can either exit by choosing a different product or voice their complaints to the management about the product's decline in quality, with loyalty constituting an additional barrier to exit. Beyond economics, he identified in passing how this would be relevant in authoritarian contexts: 'Competition does not restrain monopoly but comforts and bolsters it by unburdening it of some of its more troublesome customers ... those who hold power in the lazy monopoly may actually have an interest in creating some opportunities for exit on the part of those whose voice might be uncomfortable' (Hirschman 1970, 59–60). By importing this framework into authoritarian contexts, scholars have argued that migration can serve as a safety valve against unemployment, overpopulation, or other socio-economic problems. It may even promote a wish among return migrants to maintain the illiberal status quo, as in the case of 1970s Portugal (Brettell 1979). Scholars have identified notable cases of authoritarian emigration states where citizens were encouraged to emigrate in order to minimise grievances against a non-democratic regime, such as Haiti, Morocco, and Zimbabwe (De Haas 2005). Hirschman (1993) applied his model into the demise of the German Democratic Republic. Already in 1978, he had been arguing that exit, more broadly, enabled the silencing of voice across nineteenth-century Europe: 'the ships carrying the migrants contained actual or potential anarchists and socialists, reformers and revolutionaries. [That] Emigration of dissenters will strengthen an authoritarian regime in the short run is obvious; not content with allowing emigration, many such regimes have taken it upon themselves to deport or ban their political enemies' (Hirschman 1978, 102–3).

Discussions of socio-economic and political safety valves are problematic. Despite its attractiveness, Hirschman's framework is rather abstract and, at times, self-contradictory: for example, travel restrictions have been shown to decrease regimes' repression costs and, thus, add to their stability (Alemán and Woods 2014). At the same time, the exit of a country's citizens can also produce destabilising effects for an authoritarian regime when done en masse. In cases when citizens are able to 'vote with their feet', to use Lenin's famous phrase, the regime is threatened with breakdown, as in East Germany: the German Democratic Republic collapsed after more than 13,000 citizens left for Hungary in August 1989, or crossed into West Berlin three months later (Brubaker 1990; Pfaff 2006). In other instances, however, even mass migration did not destabilise the regime – such was the case, for instance, in French West African colonies, which underwent massive waves of 'protest migration' (Herbst 1990, 186). Thus, the breaking point between migration as a stabilising and as a disruptive force remains unspecified. Furthermore, exit does not necessarily imply the absence of voice. Migrants can also seek to influence their sending states' domestic politics from abroad (Glasius 2016). In fact, 'since emigrants often have greater access to important resources, ranging from remittances, skills-transfer through returns, and networks, as well as symbolic and cultural capital, they may well enhance their voice in the country of origin' (Kapur 2010, 42). Finally, if migration occurs as a response to "quality decline" (in this case, increased authoritarianism), then are we assuming that citizens prefer a democratic polity versus a nondemocratic one, and that this preference forms the reason for their emigration?

The Politics of Authoritarian Emigration States: A Framework of Repression, Co-Optation and Legitimacy

In order to comprehend the interplay between labour emigration policy and authoritarianism, this study proposes a framework that builds on aforementioned debates on population mobility within social sciences. Its framework rests on two key assumptions. First, labour emigration policy operates within a continuum between two endpoints: at one end, labour emigration policy can be restrictive, namely curtailing citizens' free movement beyond state borders; at the other end, state policy can be permissive, namely lacking any obstacles impeding citizens' free movement beyond state borders. European and North American states today, for instance, generally pursue permissive labour emigration policies, while the German Democratic Republic and the Soviet Union historically adopted restrictive labour emigration policies. Many states fall between these two extremes, adopting policies that allow the emigration of certain groups (for instance, low-skilled labourers) while restricting the emigration of others (for instance, high-skilled professionals). Often, these policies are gendered: a 2014 decision by the Indian government restricted women's emigration to the Gulf except via government agencies, aiming to curtail harassment abroad. As will be seen in the section below, Egypt under Nasser adopted a restrictive labour emigration policy, aiming to prevent citizens' emigration in the 1952–70 period. Under Sadat and Mubarak, Egypt would shift to a permissive labour emigration policy.

A second assumption refers to a key rationale of non-democracies, which is the prioritisation of regime survival at the expense of other state goals. An authoritarian regime is more likely to develop policies that produce short-term political gains that enable ruling elites to remain in power. In other words, given that an authoritarian regime does not need to enact state policies with a view to re-election, it will evaluate potential measures primarily with regard to their impact upon its consolidation and survival. For example, the Castro regime in Cuba has habitually refused American humanitarian aid since its installation into power. Even though aid would have been a welcome relief to the Cuban state budget, it would undermine the political ideology of the Castro regime and shed doubt upon its capacity to govern Cuba. A similar mentality governs the Democratic People's Republic of Korea's attitude towards international aid. A more extreme example is Bashar al-Assad's strategy in post-2011 Syria, where the need to secure the regime's position constitutes the ruling elites' main objective even at the expense of the survival of the Syrian state. This is not to argue that economic calculations are not part of a regime's calculus, be it autocratic or not; economic prosperity and the well-being of a state's citizens is capable of promoting regime durability. However, an autocratic regime is expected to opt for short-term policies with a distinct political benefit, even if that comes at an economic cost, rather than long-term policies with distinct economic benefits and political costs.

With these assumptions in mind, the study puts forth the argument that non-democracies develop labour emigration policies – restrictive, permissive, or a combination of both – in order to enhance their durability, defined as a regime's 'capacity to survive crises' rather than the length of its stay in power (Levitsky and Way 2012, 870). Analytically, durability needs to be distinguished from duration, for 'duration alone is not the best measure of regime durability since it tells us little about the stability of the regime, or its ability to meet and overcome potential crises' (Grzymala-Busse 2011, 1279). The study theorises that labour emigration policies are aimed towards enhancing regime durability along two axes: domestically and internationally. Domestically, labour emigration policy is employed to bolster regime durability in three ways: through repression, through co-optation, and through internal legitimation (for a discussion on these three aspects, see Gerschewski 2013). Beyond the state's borders, labour emigration is employed to enhance regime durability through external legitimation. The discussion that follows will highlight each of these aspects.

Labour Emigration Policy and Regime Repression Tactics

Firstly, authoritarianism relies upon opposition repression, or the 'actual or threatened use of physical sanctions against an individual or organization, within the territorial jurisdiction of the state, for the purpose of imposing a cost on the target as well as deterring specific activities' (Davenport 2007, 2). This can be 'high-intensity', based upon the use of violence, or 'low-intensity', focusing on more subtle forms, such as surveillance or opposition management (Levitsky and Way 2011). As Gerschewski describes, 'high intensity coercion can be defined as visible acts that are targeted either at well-known individuals like opposition leaders, at a larger number of people, or at major oppositional organizations. Concrete measures include the (violent) repression of mass demonstrations, (violent) campaigns against parties, and the attempted assassination or imprisonment of opposition leaders' (Gerschewski 2013, 21). On the other hand, lower intensity coercion would then aim at groups of minor importance, is less visible, and often takes more subtle forms. Concrete measures can be the use of (formal and informal) surveillance apparatus, low intensity physical harassment and intimidation, and also non-physical forms such as the denial of certain job and education opportunities as well as the curtailment of political rights like the freedom of assembly. (Gerschewski 2013, 21)

Labour emigration policy may facilitate either type of repression. A restrictive labour emigration policy prevents political dissenters from crossing state boundaries and operating beyond the limits of the ruling regime, thereby enabling high-intensity repression: the construction of the Berlin Wall, for instance, was partly aimed at preventing defection of East German dissenters and reinforced the German Democratic Republic's ability to quell opposition within its borders. Similar attempts to limit the emigration of political opposition members, often via tight 'exit visa' policies, have been implemented in Cuba, Tunisia, and elsewhere. On the other hand, a permissive labour emigration policy complements the low-intensity management of political opposition that is reminiscent of Hirschman's framework. This occurs frequently, according to an "out of sight, out of mind" approach to repression. In the aftermath of the 1979 Iranian Revolution, for instance, the Khomeini regime did not prevent the emigration of 'two to 4 million entrepreneurs, professionals, technicians, and skilled craftspeople' (Kanovsky 1997, 4). The absence of organised political opposition during this transitional period facilitated the domestic consolidation of the Islamic Republic.

Labour Emigration Policy and Regime Co-Optation Strategies

Authoritarianism is not able to survive based solely on the state's repressive apparatus. Non-democratic regimes also rely upon co-optation, or upon 'persuading [individuals] to not exercise [their] powers to obstruct', but 'to use the resources in line with the ruling elites' demands' (Bertocchi and Spagat 2001, 592). A very familiar tactic across authoritarian regimes, this may include the promise or disbursement of favours to specific individuals or population groups in return for political support. In other words, co-optation refers to a regime's 'capacity to tie strategically-relevant actors (or group of actors) to the regime elite', including military and business elites

(Gerschewski 2013, 22). Co-optation of key actors usually occurs within political parties, elections, or parliaments; but there are other ways to tie actors into a regime, including patronage, clientelism, and corruption (Gerschewski 2013).

Arguably, a state's labour emigration policy plays a key role in supporting the economic interests of business elites, in particular: a regime's policies on how to manage its labour force may strengthen its linkages with economic actors, if these decisions take these actors' interests into account. A permissive labour emigration policy would reflect the interests of business elites that depended on workers' mobility: a regime might co-opt economic elites that desired a high-skilled labour force by allowing emigration for the purposes of training abroad; similarly, a permissive policy would also co-opt important economic actors that sought to employ a state's workers in locations outside the nation-state. A restrictive labour emigration policy would be more likely to reflect the interest of business elites that sought to prevent labour mobility in the interests of lowering competition or in support of import substitution industrialisation. In both permissive and restrictive contexts, the adoption of labour emigration policies that benefit the interests of strategic actors make the latter less likely to obstruct the regime's workings – in other words, such policies facilitate processes of co-optation.

Empirical examples allow for a better illustration of labour emigration and elite co-optation in non-democratic contexts: the permissive labour emigration policy of the Socialist Federal Republic of Yugoslavia, for instance, mirrored the needs of key business interests within Yugoslavia, particularly elites associated with the Yugoslav engineering and construction firm, *Energoprojekt*. A permissive labour emigration allowed *Energoproject* to recruit Yugoslav workers abroad, expanding its workings across Libya, Kuwait, Zambia, and elsewhere, and facilitated the co-optation of local economic elites into the Yugoslav ruling regime (Woodward 1995, 222–59). The Chinese state's 'Four Modernizations' programme, enacted by Deng Xiaoping from 1978 onwards, promoted short-term emigration abroad as part of the regime's attempt to end the country's isolation from the international scientific community. Through this process, the Chinese ruling regime was able to tie strategically relevant economic actors into its workings, who came to rely upon the recruitment of Chinese return migrants that had received professional training abroad (Wang and Hu

1999, 212–15). A restrictive labour emigration policy, on the other hand, may also serve as an instrument of co-optation: historically, this has been most common in Third World states that adopted developmentalist policies, characterised by high tariffs and aiming to develop self-sufficiency, thereby protecting domestic economic elites' interests from foreign competition. Emigration in that sense was restricted because it contradicted the aim of economic autarchy in numerous Latin American and East Asian countries, but also supported the interests of strategic economic actors. More recently, until Portugal's transition to democracy in 1974, the country's constitution also stipulated that 'the state has the right and the obligation to coordinate and regulate the economic and social life of the Nation with the objective of populating the national territories, protecting emigrants, and disciplining emigration' (Baganha, 2003, 2–3).

Labour Emigration Policy and Regime Legitimation Processes

Finally, labour emigration facilitates, beyond repression or co-optation, a regime's legitimation processes. For the purposes of this study, legitimation constitutes an attempt to 'guarantee active consent, compliance with the rules, passive obedience, or mere toleration within the population' (Gerschewski 2013, 18; cf. Weber 2009). Legitimacy refers to a regime's relations with the broader social body, whereas co-optation refers to a regime's relations with specific, strategically important actors. A range of debates has evolved since Max Weber proposed this aspect of political rule, both on its nature and on its applicability to non-democratic contexts (Lipset 1959; Hudson 1977; Dawisha 1985). It can be argued that authoritarian regimes aim to construct a set of beliefs that would 'legitimise' their stay in power, similar to democratic ones (March 2003). Building on Weatherford and others, Sedgwick's work provides a useful empirical analysis of the term within the Egyptian context, and differentiates between internal and external legitimacy. Internal legitimacy consists of output legitimacy and descriptive legitimacy: output legitimacy refers to a regime's ability to respond to the 'objective needs' of its constituents, and highlights material issues; descriptive legitimacy 'relates more to process than to product', and refers to traditional, religious, ideological, and charismatic legitimacy (Sedgwick 2010, 253). Importantly, the use of labour emigration policy as an instrument of material and descriptive legitimation requires a solid economic base that can support it: for a permissive labour emigration policy, there needs to be sufficient economic opportunities available beyond the borders of the sending state, whereas a similar degree of domestic economic opportunities need to exist in order to legitimise a restrictive labour emigration policy.

On the one hand, Moscow's restriction of citizens' labour emigration to the West was firmly embedded within the ideological framework of the Cold War: restricting labour emigration provided output legitimacy by aiming to minimise the phenomenon of *brain drain*. At the same time, these restrictions were imperative in order to provide descriptive legitimacy to the anti-Western, socialist framework of the Soviet Union. Those who were denied permission to emigrate – the 'refuseniks' – would face employment discrimination or unemployment (Peretz 2015). But this may only be successful in the presence of domestic economic opportunities: the Berlin Wall, for instance, initially legitimised the East German regime and underlined its wish to combat brain drain, but it could no longer function as an instrument of regime legitimation in the absence of employment opportunities within the German Democratic Republic. On the other hand, autocracies that favour labour emigration may also employ it as a legitimation instrument, particularly with regard to output legitimacy, emphasising issues of economic remittances as well as *brain gain* from their citizens' emigration and return. This is the rationale behind a number of autocracies' engagement with emigration, for instance in Turkey (Martin 1991), or in North Africa (see Brand 2006). But permissive policies may also give descriptive legitimacy to an autocratic regime. In this context, the end of the Soviet Union's restrictive policy on the 'refuseniks' under Mikhail Gorbachev in the 1980s is tied to the broader attempt of abandoning the anti-Western rhetoric of previous Soviet leaders, and legitimising the twin processes of perestroika and glasnost.

The development of a permissive labour emigration framework also strengthens the durability of a ruling authoritarian regime on the international level, supporting its external legitimacy. This reflects the fostering of cross-regime interaction and the development of linkages between non-democratic regimes in the host and sending states, as per the aforementioned literature on the international aspect of authoritarianism. Within a permissive labour emigration policy framework, an authoritarian regime is able to link the supply of migrant labour to receiving socio-economic or political benefits. For instance, China has linked its supply of high-skilled migrants engaged in development projects across sub-Saharan Africa to the strengthening of military or diplomatic relations with ruling non-democratic regimes, such as Mugabe's Zimbabwe. Historically, states pursuing restrictive labour emigration policies also develop certain frameworks of limited labour emigration, frequently involving high-skilled professionals, in order to create, and strengthen, cross-regime relations with other non-democracies. During the Cold War, Bulgaria developed a scheme of dispatching professionals to Gaddafi's Libya for distinctly political purposes linked to external legitimation strategies (cf. Cooley 1982). A key Soviet Union strategy involved the short-term emigration of high-skilled Russian professionals across the Eastern bloc, with the aims of strengthening the two sides' economic and developmental linkages (Babiracki 2015).

This study's theoretical framework is based upon certain scope conditions, namely that it focuses exclusively on states' labour emigration policies within authoritarian contexts. There is a need for precision for, as globalisation deepens, authoritarian regimes develop complex strategies aimed at controlling populations from afar. The Syrian regime, for instance, has attempted to thwart political activists abroad by employing a variety of repression and intimidation tactics (Moss 2016). Historically, non-democracies have resorted to violence and targeted assassinations of dissenters who resided abroad; most recently, the Putin regime has been implicated in the murder of Alexander Litvinenko in London (Emsley 2008) and the attempted murder of Russian former military intelligence officer Sergei Skripal and his daughter in March 2018 (Tsourapas 2018c). Other regimes, particularly North African ones, have employed surveillance strategies on populations living in Western Europe (Brand 2006). However, these policies do not operate within the framework of *labour emigration*. They are either developed and implemented post hoc once a citizen or a group has crossed a country's boundaries and settled abroad, or they target second-generation descendants of emigrants – in either case, they form part of states' *diaspora management* policies, and therefore remain outside the scope of this study.

In sum, this study theorises that labour emigration policy is employed in order to enhance the durability of authoritarian regimes on two levels: the domestic, and the international (Table 1.1). Domestically, it is

Table 1.1 *A framework of labour emigration and authoritarian regime durability*

Type of Emigration Policy	Level of Analysis	Influence on Regime Durability
Restrictive	Domestic	High-Intensity Repression Labour Force Co-Optation Internal Legitimation
	International	External Legitimation
Permissive	Domestic	Low-Intensity Repression Labour Force Co-Optation Internal Legitimation
	International	External Legitimation

employed to bolster a regime's internal legitimation strategies, enhance its high- or low-repression tactics, and co-opt the labour force into its developmental agenda. Internationally, labour emigration policies are linked to the strengthening of an authoritarian regime's external legitimation strategies via interactions with other non-democracies, within both a restrictive and a permissive context. The following section introduces the study's two case studies on Egypt: firstly, a restrictive emigration policy framework under Nasser (1952–70), and secondly, a permissive emigration policy framework under Sadat and Mubarak (1970–2011). In both cases, the ruling regime employed labour emigration to enhance its durability on both the domestic and the international levels. But first, an initial overview of the politics of migration within the broader Middle East is required in order to better contextualise the reader.

The Politics of Labour Emigration in the Middle East: The Case of Egypt

> Egyptians have the reputation of preferring their own soil. Few ever leave except to study or travel; and they always return.
>
> Wendell Cleland (1936, 36)

As a region, the Middle East has been particularly rich in population mobility (Hourani 2013). Historically, while some restrictions were put in place under the Ottomans, nomads or pilgrims would not hesitate to cross the (often arbitrary) state boundaries of the time. It was during the period of European colonialism that barriers to migration were more firmly imposed upon the region, while the subsequent disruption of accommodation between Muslims and Christians has been credited for the first major wave of emigration to the West. In the late nineteenth century, Christians left Mt. Lebanon in order to settle in North America, later to be joined by a few thousand Muslims in the 1900–14 period (Khater 2001). Palestinian emigration to the West similarly increased in light of their continuing struggle with the British authorities over the influx of Jews that abandoned Europe in the aftermath of World War I. Even during the colonial era, modest population movements across the Arab world persisted, notably in the historic region of the *bilād al-shām* (Syria, Lebanon, Palestine, and Jordan), in the Sinai Peninsula, and in Western Libya, as well as in parts of the Arabian Peninsula (the Hejaz, Yemen, and Oman).

Two events have shaped the migration trajectory of the Middle East since World War II: firstly, the 1948 Arab–Israeli War, which resulted in the exodus of more than 710,000 Palestinians that sought refuge mostly in neighbouring states. Known as *al-Nakba* (the catastrophe), the displacement of the Palestinians and the negotiations over the return to their homeland have plagued Arab–Israeli relations to this day. The unresolved question of Palestine has been a perennial international issue ever since, rendered more complex by the 1967 Six-Day War, which produced a second major wave of Palestinian emigration (Morris 2004; Pappe 2007). A second watershed event was the discovery of oil, attracting an unprecedented number of labourers to the Gulf (and other oil-rich countries in the region), particularly following the 1973 Arab–Israeli War and the ensuing oil embargo (Kapiszewski 2001a; Seccombe 1983). Migrants numbered around 800,000 before 1973, while by 1974 they had reached roughly 4,000,000. This is not to imply that all these workers were employed in the oil industry; in fact, most worked in construction, services, or education. Since the mid-1980s, South Asian workers, believed to be cheaper and less politically active, have gradually replaced Arab labour as the most populous migrant group in the oil-exporting countries (Kapiszewski 2006). This was accentuated by the expulsion of large numbers of Arab workers in the aftermath of the Gulf War: as punishment for the Palestinian and Yemeni political leadership's support of the Iraqi invasion of Kuwait, the Gulf states expelled roughly 800,000 Yemeni workers. The vast majority of Palestinian migrants were also forced to leave from Kuwait, where they had sought shelter following the 1948 and 1967 Wars (Van Hear 1998). At the same time, oil-producing states have developed policies directed towards reducing the number of migrant workers, in favour of providing more employment opportunities to their national populations. The regional instability of the early 1990s also led to the repatriation of more than 700,000 Egyptians and roughly 200,000 Jordanians.

The Arab Republic of Egypt is the Arab world's most populous state, with a population of more than 94 million in the 2017 census (Iraq, the second most populous Arab state, has fewer than 33 million inhabitants). The development of Egypt in the early nineteenth century – when Muhammad Ali seized control from the Ottoman Empire and embarked on an extensive project of modernisation – predates the creation of other states in the Middle East or Africa. As a result, Egypt has often been regarded as a trend-setter and a political, social, and cultural hub of the Arab world. The 1952 overthrow of the British-backed King Farouk (the great-great-grandson of Muhammad Ali) by a group of Egyptian military men, the Free Officers, was one of the first military coup d'états in the region. One of the group's leaders, Gamal Abdel Nasser, rose to become a symbol of and inspiration for the Arab world until his death in 1970. Anwar Sadat, the successor to the presidency of Egypt, initiated a period of controversial structural reforms and economic liberalisation processes in Egypt that have been emulated across the Arab world to this day. Finally, the ousting of Egypt's fourth president, Hosni Mubarak, in February 2011 has arguably inspired the regional process of the ongoing 'Arab Spring'. From 1952 to 2011, Egypt was continuously ruled by members of a military elite – starting with Nasser, who selected Sadat to be his successor, who, in turn, chose Mubarak.

In terms of labour emigration, Egypt has also been the largest supplier of migrant labour in the Middle East – currently, it is estimated that more than 6.5 million Egyptians reside outside the country, not including emigrants' descendants. The reader should take two issues into account when discussing Egyptian emigration: firstly, there exists a long-standing policy distinction between 'temporary' and 'permanent' migration. While the political importance of this will be clarified in Chapters 4 and 5, the reader needs to keep in mind that, in practice, this differentiation is determined by migrants' country of destination: Egyptians living in Arab countries are invariably considered temporary workers even when they have lived there for decades. All those emigrating to Australia, Europe, North America, or elsewhere, on the other hand, are considered permanent migrants by the state, even if they just arrived in their host countries (Zohry and Harrell-Bond 2003, 34). Unavoidably, the realities of labour migration render this a false dichotomy, yet one that has determined policy-making for the past half-century. This study focuses on the politics of labour emigration, rather than the politics of Egyptians' 'permanent' migration, or diaspora politics (on the latter, see Tsourapas 2015b).

A second issue that invariably arises when examining Middle East migratory processes is the absence of available data on migrant stocks and flows (Birks and Sinclair 1980, 44; Feiler 1986), and 'fuzzy lines' around categorisation processes (Fargues 2014). Researchers lack access to reliable data both from the sending state (i.e. emigration statistics) and from the main Arab host states (i.e. immigration statistics). Importantly, Egypt formally abandoned any efforts to keep track of emigration in the early 1970s, while official figures from Arab host states tend to underestimate the number of foreign workers (Kapiszewski 2001b). Table 1.2 demonstrates how data on Egyptians working abroad are either inflated, if one employs Egyptian sources, or reduced, if one considers Arab host states' statistics, both for political reasons (on this, see Chapter 5). This is complicated by the difficulties in conducting research on authoritarian regimes within non-democratic contexts, as well as by the fact that migration is typically regarded as a 'security issue' within the Egyptian regime and across the Middle East (Tsourapas 2014). As a key textbook on Middle East political economy argues:

Severe issues with the accuracy of data plague all estimates of the magnitude of migration. For labor migration, the data typically count inflows, not outflows. They usually enumerate work permits rather than persons, making no allowance for multiple entries. They also suffer from a variety of other difficulties, including the underreporting of unauthorized migration, which all analysts agree is substantial. Moreover, different countries use different definitions for 'visitor', 'short-term migrant' and 'long-term resident foreigners'. The distinction between 'temporary' and 'permanent' migrants is contentious, as is that between 'economic migrant' and 'refugee'. Although some of these problems bedevil EU statistics on MENA immigrant labor, they are especially severe in the data on labor migration to the major oil-exporting countries of the Persian Gulf. In that area, where some of the problems are due to imprecise definitions, labor force numbers are lower than total migrant population numbers. (Cammett et al. 2015, 500)

Broadly, we identify two main periods of Egyptian emigration: firstly, the pre-1952 monarchical period and the rule of Nasser between the 1952 Free Officers' Revolution and his death in 1970; and, secondly, the post-1970 period under Sadat and Mubarak, which ends in 2011. Research on migration in pre-Nasserite Egypt has long identified

Table 1.2 *Stock of Egyptian migrants abroad, 2012*

Egyptian Consular Data				
Country of Residence	Number of Temporary Migrants	Country of Residence	Number of Permanent Migrants	Host State Data
Libya	2,000,000	United States	776,000	203,932
Saudi Arabia	1,300,000	Canada	141,000	41,700
Jordan	525,000	United Kingdom	250,000	31,000
Kuwait	480,000	Italy	190,000	92,001
United Arab Emirates	260,000	France	160,000	26,825
Qatar	88,500	Greece	80,000	9,461
Oman	45,000	Germany	30,000	13,316
Lebanon	38,000	Netherlands	30,000	12,038
Iraq	15,000	Other (Europe)	48,645	39,481
Bahrain	12,000	Australia	106,000	34,838
Yemen	10,300	Others	8,518	166,175
Syria	10,000			
Total Temporary Migrants	4,783,800	Total Permanent Migrants	1,681,163	629,067

Source: Migration Policy Centre, 2013

Egyptians' hesitation to abandon their land: Cleland's famous 1936 study of Egyptian demographics noted that 'Egyptians don't migrate' (Cleland 1936, 52), a statement that obscured the qualitative wealth of population movements that occurred before 1952 (cf. Hourani 1947). Student missions were organised for France and elsewhere as early as 1826 (Silvera 1980), while Egyptian population mobility increased in response to the growing popularity of Egyptian Arab nationalism in the early twentieth century (Coury 1982), and the discovery of oil (Seccombe 1983). At the same time, Egyptian professionals were increasingly dispatched across the Arab world in a show of solidarity – an important political process that will be examined in more detail in Chapter 3.

The study of population mobility out of Egypt in the Nasserite era is overshadowed by the post-1970 period, and the 1952–70 period is frequently identified as one when emigration was non-existent, in accordance with the state-sponsored socialist policies of the Free Officers regime (Dessouki 1982). Nasserite Egypt is characterised as 'a land of immigrants not emigrants' (Sell 1988, 89). This is surprising because the 1952 creation of the modern Egyptian state, and Nasser's subsequent ascent to power, coincided with a rise in diverse forms of movements (voluntary or otherwise), despite various institutional restrictions, that will be discussed in Chapter 2. The exodus of Egyptian Jews was coupled with the emigration of political dissenters – royalist supporters of the *ancien régime*, communists, Muslim Brotherhood members – and foreigners, primarily Greeks, Italians, and Syrians. More than 40,000 Egyptians were dispatched to the Yemen Arab Republic, as were a few thousand to Syria during its short-lived unification with Egypt. Thousands of high-skilled Egyptians would pursue temporary work across the Middle East and Africa, under the aegis of the Egyptian Ministry of Education.

Egyptian emigration under Sadat and Mubarak has attracted the bulk of social scientists' attention, but this strand of literature has focused largely – if not exclusively – on identifying the economic rationale behind Egyptian emigration and the state's emigration policy. This was perhaps driven by the historical conjecture of the post-1973 rise in oil prices that encouraged millions of Egyptians to pursue employment abroad, at a time when Egypt was facing severe economic problems (Milton-Edwards 2011, 80–98; Cammett et al. 2015, 484–93). It could also be due to the relative abundance of data on migrant remittances (as opposed to a dearth of information on migration stocks and flows). Irrespective of the reasons, this has led to an overly economistic approach to these processes: 'In retrospect, labour migration can be seen as the main way in which oil revenues from the oil-exporting countries have been redistributed to the oil-importing countries, to the great benefit of millions of households', Cammett et al. argue. 'Whether this redistribution strategy reduced the incentives of regimes to reform their own economic structures earlier remains a matter for debate' (Cammett et al. 2015, 510). Sika argued that:

Egyptian policy makers saw the importance of easing restrictions on migration, as far back as the mid 1970s. The government favoured migration flows from Egypt to the GCC [Gulf Cooperation Council states] for various reasons: the Egyptian market's inability to absorb the growing numbers of workers seeking employment; the government's need to use remittances to reduce [the] deficit in the balance of payments; and the oil boom of the 1970s. (Sika 2015, 158)

Research and Data Collection in Precarious Environments

This study is based upon two case studies within a single-country context, for theory development purposes (George and Bennett 2005, 32–33). 'Inferring and testing explanations that define *how* the independent causes the dependant variable are often easier with case-study than large-n methods', Van Evera argued. 'If case-study evidence supports a hypothesis, the investigator can then explore the case further to deduce and test explanations detailing the operation of the hypothesis' (Van Evera 1997, 54). The two cases are selected in a 'most different' approach, with the first (Egypt under Nasser, 1952–70) constituting a case of a restrictive labour emigration policy, whereas the second (Egypt under Sadat and Mubarak, 1970–2011) refers to a permissive labour emigration policy. I employ process-tracing methodology, where qualitative data are examined sequentially to draw descriptive and causal inferences inductively, and to disconfirm rival explanations (Beach and Pedersen 2013). A key element of this process is a careful selection of the timeframe and the individual stages in the analysis. 'To characterize a process, we must be able to characterize key steps in the process, which in turn permits good analysis of change and sequence' (Collier 2011, 824).

For the purposes of this analysis, the ruling regime is approached as the main actor in shaping the Egyptian state's emigration policy. This is not to suggest that there do not exist pressures aiming to constrain the regime's decision-making process. A rich literature has evolved detailing multi-level negotiations on emigration policies within liberal democratic states that discount the understanding of the state as a unitary actor, and its role as the natural unity of analysis (cf. Fitzgerald 2006). However, the extent to which such debates exist, or are able to produce policy outcomes within authoritarian contexts, is limited (Messina and Lahav 2006). By default, non-democratic regimes aim to curtail – with varying degrees of success – other political actors' ability to set debates on emigration or to affect government policies. While this study is conscious of non-regime actors, its focus rests primarily upon Egyptian elites' strategies. That said, it pays particular attention to domestic and international registers, highlighting the complexity of negotiations around states' emigration policies, but continues to focus on the ruling regime for analytical purposes.

This study primarily draws on eleven months of continuous fieldwork in Cairo (2013–14). Fieldwork in societies undergoing lengthy socio-political transitions, such as post-2011 Egypt, entails specific pre-planning and on-site considerations that are different from the preparation one would make for research in more ordinary times. I realised the necessity of maintaining a flexible fieldwork schedule during the events of summer 2013, particularly once the Egyptian army had violently dispersed the largely pro-Muslim Brotherhood protesters in *al-Nahda* Square and the *al-Rabaa* Mosque, on 14th August. Almost immediately, the military re-imposed a state of emergency and strict evening curfews in fourteen Egyptian governorates that were not lifted until November. Practically, this meant that greater Cairo's more than 15 million residents were confined to their homes from 7pm until 6am each day – a policy that the state enforced strictly at first, but gradually relaxed over the following months. While infrastructural problems traditionally abound in Egypt, the new situation on the ground put additional constraints on fieldwork. Research centres, for instance, kept erratic working hours, if any. The curfew limited the window for interviews dramatically, meaning it was no longer possible to meet subjects outside central Cairo as I had to conclude all meetings in time to beat the heavy afternoon traffic and be home on time.

Renewed caution and a heightened sense of awareness have become imperative because of the changing security circumstances, although this fieldwork was conducted before the brutal murder of Giulio Regeni in early 2016, at a time when foreign researchers had not been specifically targeted. Yet, I avoided carrying a camera in public, in part to reduce the chances of being mistaken for a member of the press, and I followed the usual advice for people in potentially hostile environments, such as maintaining a low profile, and keeping clear of demonstrations and areas of conflict. In order to keep abreast of developments on the ground, besides following local and international news reports, I registered with different embassies or consulates, and maintained a research affiliation with the American University of Cairo and the Netherlands-Flemish Institute. I received multiple text messages each day from the American and Greek embassies, as well as frequent emails from the American University of Cairo, alerting me to the situation on the ground, not to mention constant updates from news websites, and from anxious friends and relatives abroad. I had to postpone research both at Cairo University, which was adjacent to the protest site of *al-Nahda* Square, and in neighbourhoods that play host to large migrant communities, such as *Madinat Nasr*, because they were targeted by the state as Muslim Brotherhood strongholds. Avoiding such areas was not only crucial for my safety, but also for that of my interviewees, whose security could be jeopardised if they were accused of consorting with foreigners. In terms of access to experts, Cairo University was still recovering from bombing attacks in early April 2013, while certain university faculties, such as its *Dar al-Ulum* Faculty Cairo or *al-Azhar* University, which historically attract pro-Muslim Brotherhood students, had been transformed into both long-term protest centres against military rule and sites of police violence.

Beyond fieldwork security, conducting interviews in post-revolutionary Cairo also carried certain challenges, particularly once the situation on the ground grew more unpredictable and a sense of urgency developed. The speed with which the Muslim Brotherhood was ousted from power, for example, implied that any elite interviews with key Islamist actors had to be scheduled fast, if one were to be fortunate enough to secure a discussion with a high-ranking member of the Brotherhood's Justice and Development Party. More often than not, my calls went unanswered; since July 2013, Egyptian friends I have made over the years have been incarcerated due to their affiliation with the Muslim Brotherhood. But it is not only the Brothers that have been caught in this. One of the most poignant moments of my fieldwork came after an interview in Dokki, an upper-middle class Cairo neighbourhood, in October 2013. My interviewee and I had been discussing the emigration of Egypt's Coptic Christian population, reported to be fleeing the country due to heightened tensions with Muslims. As I came out onto the street, the first thing I saw was the shell of a local Coptic church, having been set on fire a few hours earlier. It quickly became clear that the linkages between emigration and domestic politics, which this book attempts to track in the 1952–2011 period, persisted in the post-Mubarak era.

These linkages became even more clear through the perceived national security implications of my research, which further complicated fieldwork. One of the primary issues I have encountered is the view that emigration constitutes a 'security issue' for the Egyptian state. This is not a novel phenomenon in the literature – in Egypt, the tendency to obscure data on migration can be traced back to the early 1970s, when the complete deregulation of emigration processes under President Sadat signalled the total retreat of the state from any attempt to keep track of Egyptians abroad. Similar processes have been observed elsewhere in the region, such as in the Gulf states. Yet, in the post–2011 period, new waves of politically minded, Egyptian population movements have reinforced that view. There has been a reported increase in the stream of Egyptian Copts seeking refuge in Europe and North America since the toppling of President Mubarak in 2011. At the same time, in the aftermath of President Morsi's ousting and the institution of military rule in June 2013, Muslim Brothers abandoned Egypt for Qatar, Tunisia, and Turkey, to avoid imprisonment and persecution. Egypt is also experiencing a growing influx of Syrian refugees, while the political and economic elite that had risen during President Mubarak's 30-year reign (1981–2011) was fleeing the country. Practically, this contributed to my interlocutors' tendency to treat research in this matter as, somehow, suspicious. Researchers not accustomed to such an environment should not be surprised to encounter, firstly, the surprise of their interviewees at an ostensibly 'odd' choice of research subject and, following that, a degree of hesitation in revealing information. I attempted to overcome such obstacles in a number of ways. I took extra care in building a relationship with various 'gatekeepers' – i.e., Egyptians who have worked on such issues in the past and were able to recommend my work and vouch for my integrity to some extent. A research affiliation proved very useful in that respect as well. I also developed carefully crafted responses to various introductory questions I expected to be asked, which aimed at gauging my identity or personal politics. While I never misrepresented my motives, I was conscious of the fact that interview research in Egypt has often meant that I am being interviewed by my subjects as much as I interview them; discussions of the current political situation led up to 'Why are you interested in this topic?' and, invariably, 'Where are you from?' While warm-up conversations are customary and expected, I was unprepared for the extent to which my nationality mattered in my interlocutors' decision to be interviewed, and have since made a note of mentioning this early on in any contact with potential subjects. The question of one's gender also bears reflection – my position as a male researcher allowed access to specific groups of Egyptians (and arguably hindered access to others); a female researcher working on such topics would have a completely different take on the challenges of fieldwork in the Egyptian setting.

Overall, this analysis includes thirty-one semi-structured expert and elite interviews conducted in Cairo, including extensive interviews with former Prime Minister Abdel Aziz Muhammad Hegazy, the current and former Ministers of Migration, a number of ministers of the Sadat and Mubarak periods, as well as high-ranking government officials, based on the snowball method, for the purposes of triangulation. I examine these against a variety of elites' published memoirs and oral history archives in English and Arabic, which I also approached critically, for many of these (auto)biographies have been accused of blurring the line between fact and fiction.[3] At the same time, the adoption of data collection from multiple sources aims to overcome the difficulties in conducting research on authoritarian regimes within non-democratic contexts (Tsourapas 2014). It also aimed to address the well-established secrecy that characterises the upper echelons of Egyptian policy-making circles.[4] The emphasis on regime elites reflects an understanding about policy-making in Egypt (and, it can be argued, across non-democracies), where policy decisions are taken by the higher echelons of the regime – frequently by the president and his entourage – rather than filtered through bureaucratic mechanisms or other institutions (cf. Owen 2012).[5]

Finally, a number of unforeseen problems arose to complicate archival research during fieldwork: loss of archival data is frequent in conflict zones, and Egypt was no exception. The bombing of part of the National Library and Archives of Egypt, the *Dar al-Kutub wa'l-Watha'iq al-Qawmiyya*, on 24 January 2014, put a halt to all research activities in that building, while staff repaired the extensive damage caused. This came only two years after the complete destruction of Cairo's Institute of Egypt. Only 30,000 of the Institute's books, from a collection of more than 190,000 volumes, survived a devastating fire. In turn, I decided to resort to smaller collections of archival material, located within individual ministries, once I had built an initial network of contacts across the Egyptian bureaucracy. There are advantages and drawbacks to this solution: ministerial sources tend to contain more recent (going back to the 1970s) and more detailed emigration-related data; sometimes they also (accidentally) contain material that would not have made its way to the National Archives due to its sensitive nature. Having said that, such collections lack the comprehensiveness of the National Archives. Access to them invariably entails tactical difficulties, such as obtaining official sanctions at the ministerial levels. At the same time, I have had to resort to non-Egyptian archival sources for pre-1970 material, such as the National Archives and the LSE Archives and Special Collections in London, as well as the Middle East Centre at St Anthony's College, Oxford, which has further lengthened my fieldwork time.

As a result, I rely on diverse primary and secondary material in Arabic, French, and English. Through archival research, I have created a dataset of all emigration-related articles, analyses, and op-eds published in the three major, semi-governmental daily newspapers in Egypt (*al-Ahram, al-Akhbar, al-Gomhuria*) between 1952 and 2011. The three main Egyptian dailies are referred to as semi-governmental because they were, at various points, formally nationalised media instruments of the regime, or loosely affiliated with various officials, operating under strict censorship (Sakr 2013). Formal censorship of print media had been lifted in 1952 (only to return later), but each newspaper had to accept a governmental representative on its staff, who would ensure that editorial policy did not veer too far from the governmental line (Nutting 1972, 298). For instance, *al-Gomhoriya*'s first editor, in 1954, was Sadat himself. Thus, these sources are treated as broadly reflecting government views, and provide the main solution to the lack of official data on emigration. Similarly, newspaper cartoons or published images are often able to clearly depict, and elucidate, elites' views. They are included throughout the study for this reason. Sometimes, they provide particularly incisive commentary on Egyptian politics – much like anecdotes, or political jokes, which are also employed throughout the analysis. I have also examined non-Egyptian Arab sources, and Western media sources. Non-Egyptian sources are also approached critically (particularly British and American sources), given that they are shaped by shifting Cairo–London and Cairo–Washington relations. In terms of my approach to data collection, I initially engaged in a detailed reading of the coverage of emigration in the Egyptian press in order to gain a strong understanding of the precise shifts of Egypt's emigration policy over the 1952–2011 period. This was necessary because existing knowledge on the subject has been lacking. This was also important because careful description is key in process-tracing approaches. I also attempted to circumvent the problem of the unavailability of numerical data on migration by collecting statistical information published in state newspapers or tracing unpublished doctoral dissertations within Egyptian universities by students who had access to such data in the 1952–1970 period.[6] In order to assess the accuracy of views and information presented in media sources, I conducted semi-structured elite and expert interviews.

What Lies Ahead

The study is organised in a chronological order. It aims to take the reader through the intricacies of Egypt's labour emigration policy from 1952 to 2011 and identify its importance for the authoritarian emigration state. Chapters 2 and 3 focus on the Nasserite era, from the 1952 Free Officers Revolution to President Nasser's death in 1970, while Chapters 4, 5, and 6 focus on the Sadat and Mubarak years until the January 25 Revolution of 2011, which forced President Mubarak to step down. In terms of the Nasserite period, Chapter 2 identifies the restrictive labour emigration policy that the Free Officers regime implemented, and highlights how it served three domestic regime survival strategies: internal legitimation, high-intensity repression, and the co-optation of key business elites. It also discusses the economic tensions that this emigration policy produced. Chapter 3 focuses on the sole exception within the Free Officers' policy, namely the short-term, regional dispatch of high-skilled Egyptian professionals. It describes the intricacies of the policy and links it to the Egyptian regime's external legitimation tactics, which used emigration in order to 'export' the Egyptian revolution abroad and aid in the development of the Arab world in the immediate postcolonial era.

Nasser's death signalled a shift in Egypt's emigration policy, as Sadat implemented a fully permissive labour emigration policy from 1971 onwards. Similar to the analysis of the domestic political aims of Nasser's policy, Chapter 4 examines how this policy shift contributed to internal legitimation, low-intensity repression, and the co-optation of strategic actors. At the same time, reminiscent of Nasser's policy, Egypt's emigration policy under Sadat and Mubarak also had external legitimation aims. Chapter 5 demonstrates how a permissive emigration policy served the regime's pursuit of external legitimation through a rapprochement with the oil-producing states of the Arab world, and how it enabled the ruling regime to overcome the decade-long crisis in its regional foreign policy following the 1978 Camp David Accords. How successful was this strategy? Chapter 6 concludes this study's main body by underlining how Egypt's labour emigration policy under Sadat and Mubarak failed to improve a number of socio-economic indicators. It details how emigration policy was employed as an instrument of short-term political gain for the ruling regime, rather than of long-term socio-economic development. This was not without political consequences: the expulsion of Egyptians from a number of Arab host states, as well as the gradual tightening of immigration in the Gulf states, in combination with the deteriorating domestic political economy situation in Egypt, served as one of the factors paving the way for the fateful events of the January 25 Revolution.

2 | 'Egyptians Don't Emigrate'
The Domestic Politics of Migration Restriction

- When will Egyptians ... be permitted to travel freely abroad [?]

- When we have a surplus of foreign currencies, which we can spend on luxury and on summer vacations in Europe and America.

Gamal Abdel Nasser
(Interview with *Columbia Broadcasting System*; 7 April 1958)

The 1952 Free Officers Revolution ushered a new socio-economic and political era for Egypt, during which a group of nationalist officers from the armed forces seized power from the British-backed monarchy and ruled uninterrupted until the 2011 Arab Uprisings. The Nasserite era, between 1952 and 1970, is particularly interesting from a labour emigration point of view. It is characterised by a broad, restrictive policy for unskilled and skilled labourers wishing to emigrate, particularly to Western states, with a sole exception specifically for high-skilled Egyptian professionals seeking short-term positions across Africa, the Middle East, Asia, and Latin America, which the regime employed as a strategy of external legitimation. Following a brief introduction into the political economy of post-1952 Egypt, Chapter 2 focuses on how the restrictive policy implemented in the 1952–70 period was employed in order to enhance the domestic durability of the Free Officers regime, in three ways. Firstly, it aimed to strengthen the regime's legitimation and co-optation strategies. The rejection of labour emigration projected an image of an affluent, self-sufficient state that could afford to take a political stance by not engaging in labour migration with either the First or the Second World. A restrictive labour emigration policy buttressed the regime's economic policy of state developmentalism and import substitution industrialisation (ISI), and facilitated the co-optation of business elites within Egypt towards large-scale industrial projects that depended upon ample manpower. Secondly, it facilitated the regime's repressive tactics against opposition movements, notably the Muslim Brotherhood, whose members were generally unable to avoid imprisonment by escaping abroad. However, the legitimation benefits of a restrictive labour emigration policy dissipated once the Egyptian state became unable to economically sustain this policy: from the early 1960s onwards, overpopulation and urbanisation problems heightened as rising levels of unemployment and the creation of a bloated, ineffective Egyptian public sector undermined the legitimation appeal of a restrictive emigration policy.

In order to understand the political rationale behind Egypt's restrictive emigration policy under Nasser, a brief discussion of state economic policy is needed (for a more extensive discussion, see Wahbah 1994). At the time of the Free Officers Revolution, Egypt was primarily an agrarian country, as the bulk of its foreign exchange came from the production and export of cotton, while industry only accounted for 10 per cent of its Gross National Product (GNP). It was a fairly liberalised economy (irrigation and the railway system were the only two sectors in which the state was directly active), but also a deeply unequal one, with foreign residents controlling much of its financing and trading institutions and with indirect taxation driving a large percentage of government revenue (Amin 1989). In the first few years in power, the Free Officers regime was more concerned with the political consolidation of their rule, focusing on the negotiations over the remaining British forces' evacuation from Egypt. As a result, with the exception of some attempts at encouraging the industrial sector, the country's economic policy involved 'holding down expenditures and inflation', and was broadly 'a continuation of the pre-1952 free enterprise system' (Vatikiotis 1991, 395).

Yet, the radicalisation of Egypt's economic policy towards a statist model that favoured public ownership at the expense of private initiative was underway. The 1952 Agrarian Reform Law, which limited the holding of agricultural land to 200 *feddans* (or 300, if the owner had children), ensured the gradual transfer of any surplus land to the state. While a detailed discussion of the sequestration processes that the Free Officers regime engaged in would be beyond the scope of this study, it is important to note that ownership of foreign banks and companies (around 15,000 establishments in total) were gradually transferred to the control of the state. Marked by this wave of nationalisation, initiated in 1956 with the French-owned Suez Canal Company, the Egyptian economy experienced relatively high rates of growth and significant industrial development. The elimination of foreign interests gave way to new opportunities for Egyptian capital, and the public sector expanded massively under the various expropriations organised by Aziz Sidki, the Minister of Industry and a long-time Nasser associate. The private sector was steadily being put under increased state authority through a variety of regulations, such as Law 28|1958 that granted the Ministry of Industry the responsibility to provide licences to any new industrial establishments (Dekmejian 1971, 126–27; Waterbury 1983, 69–70). In the decade following the 1952 Revolution, all industry, finance, transport, and trade institutions were nationalised, while the property of the 600 wealthiest families in Egypt was duly sequestered by the state.

Economic nationalism was also reflected by the regime's ideological shift towards an anti-Western stance that paved the way for Nasser's espousal of the Non-Aligned Movement, characterised by a deep distrust against both Cold War superpowers (Abou-El-Fadl 2015). This was particularly evident with regard to Egypt's relationship with the United States, which vacillated significantly in the first twenty years of the 1952 Revolution (Hahn 1991; Mufti 2012). Initial American support for the Free Officers' overthrow of King Farouk, perceived in Washington as a corrupt and largely ineffective leader, was replaced with alarm as the new regime developed closer ties with the Soviet Union. That said, the early 'intimacy' in the relationship between Washington and the Free Officers is well documented (Gerges 2012, 42). In fact, one of Nasser's early nicknames had been 'Colonel Jimmy' because of his perceived pro-American stance (Jankowski 2002, 24). As will be detailed in Chapter 3, the Free Officers regime was not initially concerned with the effects of decolonisation outside of Egypt. But this early phase of introspection and preoccupation with expelling the British gradually gave way to a more cautious – albeit at times openly hostile – rhetoric towards the West. A gradual reorientation became evident once Nasser embedded himself firmly in control of Egypt by 1954, followed by his participation in the 1955 Bandung Conference of the Non-Aligned Movement (Sayyid-Marsot 2007, 132; cf. Abou-El-Fadl 2015).

By the mid-1950s, the Egyptian regime had experienced a 'shift in revolutionary action from the domestic to the international stage [that] was accompanied by a parallel redirection of ideological development'

(Dekmejian 1971, 405). The Free Officers regime adopted an Egypt-centred, anti-Western, and anti-colonial rhetoric that has been termed 'Nasserism' (Dekmejian 1971, 108–18; James 2006). In terms of Egypt's position vis-à-vis the Cold War, it highlighted the president's distrust of both the United States and the Soviet Union, and his favouring of the Non-Aligned Movement. As a result, Americans decided to freeze any possibility of funding Nasser's Aswan High Dam project, and Egypt sought Soviet weaponry from Czechoslovakia, a move that paved the way for the nationalisation of the Suez Canal and the 1956 Suez Crisis. The joint intervention of France, Great Britain, and Israel against Nasser failed spectacularly once the Eisenhower administration forced the colonial powers to abandon hopes of recapturing the Suez Canal, where they had been dispatching military parachutists.

Nasser duly appropriated the fortuitous results of the 1956 Suez Crisis as a national victory for both Egypt and the Arabs against colonialism which would now be explicitly targeted by the regime's nascent foreign policy. 'Only after the signing of the Suez Agreement our people began thinking in strategic terms', Nasser told *The Sunday Times*; '[u]ntil then we had concentrated only on Egypt' (*Sunday Times*, 1 August 1954). Egyptian opposition to American policies increased with the creation of the Baghdad Pact (Gerges 1994, 24–28). Overnight, following Egyptian resistance in the Suez crisis, Nasser became a symbol of anti-colonial and anti-Western resistance for the Arab world. It is in this context that the Free Officers regime began aiming for full control over all sectors of the national economy:

The radicalisation of the State's economic policy occurred on a large scale after the Suez War. It reflected the decision of the regime to acquire greater control of the economy simultaneously with its commitment to state planning. It also reflected the new political orientation of the regime to break away from the West in favour of a closer economic and political relationship with the Soviet bloc and certain states in Asia and Africa. (Vatikiotis 1991, 396)

The emphasis on state-led economic development deepened in the 1958–61 period, as Egypt 'witnessed a qualitative change, from an economy largely dominated by the private sector, both local and foreign, to one dominated by the state'. As the first Five-Year Plan (1960–65) came into operation, it aimed to use industry and large industrial and construction projects – such as the Aswan Dam – to double national income by 1970. Wahbah argues that 'the years 1958–61 can be seen as a period when the etatist system, already triumphant in ideology, was finally put into practice' (Wahbah 1994, 86–87). However, economic development was short-lived, as a number of issues also contributed to *al-inkimāsh* (economic shrinkage). Egypt's costly involvement in the Yemeni Civil War (1962–70) – which will be detailed in Chapter 3 – amounted to roughly $60 million annually. The failure of the 1961 cotton crop also dealt a considerable blow to domestic production, particularly if one keeps in mind the post-1965 suspension of American food for peace shipments following the worsening of bilateral relations (Amin 1995). Through his decision to sever diplomatic relations with West Germany, Nasser had also jeopardised some $290 million in aid. Egypt's domestic debt exceeded $1.5 million, while its foreign debt was estimated at more than $2.5 billion (Gerges 1994, 205).

Furthermore, the devastating result of the 1967 Arab–Israeli War, in which Israel seized control of the Sinai Peninsula, marked Egypt's economic decline: GNP growth reached –3.1 per cent in the 1967–68 fiscal year, as the closure of the Suez Canal, which had been in Egyptian hands since the events of 1956, deprived the state of another valuable source of revenue. On top of this, 80 per cent of military equipment had to be replaced, and Nasser continued prioritising the war effort during the 1967–70 'War of Attrition' with Israel. 'The military struggle', Nasser told Egyptians, 'will have to be fought not only by the armed forces but by the whole nation' (quoted in Hopwood 1991, 79). 'Egypt thus ended the sixties devoting almost as low a share of GDP to investments as it had in 1947', argue Hansen and Nashashibi. 'But public consumption had more than tripled [to almost 25%] while that of private consumption had shrunk by one fourth [to about 65%]. A largely unchanged payments deficit persisted' (quoted in Waterbury 1983, 83).

Finally, the 1960s were marked by an exacerbating balance-of-payments deficit for Egypt. Not only had the strategy of ISI not boosted exports, it required heavy capital and intermediary goods imports. Despite its trade with Soviet and Eastern European markets, Egypt was unable to forego imports from Western markets, which were denominated in convertible currencies. Given that its exports to the West were dwindling, Egypt was unable to generate substantial foreign exchange reserve earnings, which created a serious balance-of-payments problem for Egypt (Waterbury 1985, 66). Its foreign exchange reserves were depleted, given both the cessation of American economic aid and a decline of public savings: from less than 2 per cent of GNP in 1962–63, they became negative in 1964–65 and 1965–66 (Beattie 2000, 6). At the same time, the multiple wars waged against Israel (and the continuous mobilisation required) burdened state coffers. As Sadat puts it:

> Since the 1950s, Egypt has been subjected to many economic pressures, which have resulted in its present economic position. It suffices to note the four wars waged by Egypt to protect Arab rights and the rights of the Palestinian people. They required a huge increase in general military expenditures, which resulted in an inability to renew and strengthen the fundamental utilities in line with the population increase. (quoted in Brand, 2014, 81)

It is within this shifting economic climate of the 1950s and 1960s that the Free Officers developed, and implemented, Egypt's restrictive emigration policy. The following two sections examine the political effect of this policy on regime legitimation and co-optation, as well as high-intensity repression, respectively; the final section highlights elite resistance to amending state policy in the face of rising economic hardship. Overall, a close analysis of the rationale behind Egyptian emigration policy under Nasser paints the picture of a regime that appears more concerned about short-term political survival, rather than long-term economic prosperity.

Nasser's Co-Optation and Internal Legitimation Strategies

> I have chosen to spend the past days thinking. I thought about our people everywhere ... I wanted my choice to be theirs, and my attitude to be an expression of theirs. I say to you now that I have chosen ... and my choice was that the road of revolution should be our road. To proceed with all force towards revolutionary acts is the only answer to all demands of our national struggle. Our responsibility is to reconstruct the homeland and to liberate it.
>
> Gamal Abdel Nasser, 16 October 1958

For most of Nasser's rule, labour emigration was not an option for Egyptians. Theoretically, Egyptians' emigration under the Free

Officers' regime was not forbidden, but the regime discouraged such movements both discursively and substantively. Nasser supported the long-held view that Egyptians are loathe to emigrate, as per the traditional attachment of the *fallāhīn* (farmers) to the land. This 'state of apathy' towards emigration traces its roots to the nineteenth century (Baer 1964, 28; Choucri 1977, 5–6; Feiler 1986, 4–7). For Issawi, Egyptians are some of 'the most sedentary people in the world' (Issawi 1963, 82). One of the most-cited sources on this is Cleland's study of population dynamics, according to which 'Egyptians have the reputation of preferring their own soil. Few ever leave except to study or travel; and they always return ... Egyptians do not emigrate' (Cleland 1936, 36, 52). 'External migration plays a very small part in recent Egyptian demographic history', argued Mountjoy. 'Few Egyptians leave their country for good, and the numbers of foreigners entering and residing in Egypt is small' (Mountjoy 1972, 297). This has been a feature that ruling elites traditionally put forth as a proud element of national identity: as Sadat himself wrote, 'our Egyptian civilization – which dates back 7,000 years – has always been inspired by man's love of, and attachment to the land' (Sadat 1978a). The Orientalist overtones of such a stereotype have been played up by Western sources: the *New York Times*, for instance, argued that 'since the days of the Pharaohs, Egyptians have been loath to migrate from the fertile valley of the Nile, which they considered the centre of the world' (*The New York Times*, 29 August 1969).

In the aftermath of the 1952 Free Officers Revolution, the expectation that Egyptian citizens would reject the option to emigrate served the Nasserist rhetoric of the ruling regime, and formed part of its legitimation strategy, aiming for both material and descriptive legitimacy. With regard to the former, Egyptians' rejection of labour emigration supported the socialist framework of the Free Officers regime by highlighting citizens' rejection of Western capitalism in particular. As the chapter's epigram suggests, the idea of emigration became, thus, linked to capitalism and Western preoccupation with the pursuit of wealth; the rejection of emigration augmented the regime's material legitimacy, given that its macroeconomic policy relied on socialism and the rejection of Western-style capitalism. The Free Officers regime ensured that Egyptians realise how labour constitutes a political instrument, as Nasser addressed a rally in Minia: 'Brethren, we have an appointment with destiny to build up ... a strong nation which feels independent and every member of which feels that he works for himself, his brothers, sons and every man and woman and not for foreigners, imperialists, zones of influence or aggressive domination from within or without' (13 November 1958, quoted in Sadat 1975, 247). Furthermore, Nasser applauded practices that discouraged consumerism, thereby aiming to delineate Egyptian citizens' fields of action within specified parameters of socio-political disposition. At the same time, the president repeatedly demonised cases of greed or corruption, discouraging the self-interested pursuit of profit in favour of collective concern for the state. The regime also highlighted the potential dangers of 'brain drain' for its developmental strategy, providing additional legitimation to its restrictive emigration policy (Amin 2011). After all, a citizen who wished to seek better economic conditions abroad contradicted the oft-stated principles of autarky, frugality, and equality, upon which the regime relied – not unlike the policies of other socialist regimes at the time. According to Nasser:

There are certain notions [that] should be discarded like extravagance and luxury. Today I would like to say a thing or two about extravagance. Every pound we save in constructing a factory contributes to the national wealth and, by increasing these savings, we can build another factory and thus provide, for example, one hundred individuals with work ... No one should think only of himself. Those of us who lead a comfortable life do so at the expense of others. (quoted in United Arab Republic Information Department, 1958: 246–7)

At the same time, the regime's legitimation strategy depended on the state's ability to continue the ongoing struggle against the Israeli state. Throughout the 1950s and 1960s, and particularly after the 1956 Suez Crisis, there was a pressing need to support the military struggle against Israel, with which Egypt had been in a state of war since 1948. Nasser's Egypt was seen by both regional and international actors, as well as ordinary Egyptians, as the main Arab country leading the fight, given its size and geographical proximity to Israel. Naturally, the ongoing military operations on Egypt's eastern borders relied on maintaining Egypt's demographic strength. For former Minister Ali E. Hilal

Dessouki 'prohibiting emigration was logical because Egypt needed a strong military, and that was a national goal' (*personal interview*). In this sense, a restrictive emigration policy tied into the ruling regime's legitimation strategy, a necessary measure given the need to defeat Israel, and complemented Egyptians' "rallying around the flag" in support of the Nasserite regime's regional foreign policy. 'Egypt', after all, 'was a country at war, and it viewed its manpower as a much needed resource' (Roy 1991, 554).

But beyond an ideological and political opposition purpose, the restrictive labour emigration policy that the Egyptian state adopted under the rule of Nasser also corresponded to the need to co-opt key elites into the economic model of the Egyptian state, namely ISI and state developmentalism. Even though Nasser had turned against most *ancien régime* capitalists, his stay in power depended on the ability to forge close relations with a new group of elites that had risen following the wave of nationalisations and sequestrations. Ample domestic skilled manpower was needed in order to support Nasser's statist economic programme: the Five-Year Plan that Nasser launched for 1960–65 had the motto of 'from the needle to the rocket', suggesting the range of industrial activity that Egypt aimed to embark upon to become self-sufficient (Waterbury 1983, 80). Beyond legitimation, therefore, the Free Officers also employed the state's restrictive emigration policy in order to co-opt key elites into the Nasserite ruling, given that such constraints ensured ample skilled manpower for large-scale industrialisation projects. Concerned about brain drain, the Egyptian regime attempted to develop domestic training programmes for skilled workers, rather than allow them to be trained abroad: it established the Institutes of Vocational Training and Personnel Management, as well as a Vocational Training and Productivity Centre with the support of the United Nations and the International Labour Organisation (Mansfield 1965, 157). 'The vision of Nasser and Sedky, the industrialisation of Egypt, would not happen if we just let everyone go' recalled former Prime Minister Abd El Aziz Muhammad Hegazy (*personal interview*).

Mansfield, for instance, identifies how Egypt at the time '[was] short both of skilled top-level managers and of trained foremen in the inter-mediate range' (Mansfield 1965, 156). A widely distributed report by the Institute of National Planning highlighted the broader economic circles' anxiety of deficits across most kinds of labour (see Table 2.1): it predicted a major rise in high-skilled workers (in terms of technicians,

Table 2.1 *Projected labour supply in Egypt*

	1965	1970	1975	1980	1985
Managers and	207,920	281,880	369,500	466,660	595,970
Professionals	(+1.1%)	(−11.9%)	(−18%)	(−28.1%)	(−41%)
Technicians	295,480	323,370	356,850	419,690	510,130
	(−28.9%)	(−87.5%)	(−144.4%)	(−192.8%)	(−251%)
Clerks	297,030	340,830	393,690	462,280	559,580
	(+20.6%)	(−1.1%)	(−24.5%)	(−44.9%)	(−65.6%)
Skilled Workers	940,400	1,140,200	1,369,200	1,651,295	1,916,320
	(−12.9%)	(−29.9%)	(−45.2%)	(−58.7%)	(−89.3%)
Unskilled Workers	6,366,170	7,577,720	8,920,760	10,333,075	11,868,000
	(+3.9%)	(+8.9%)	(+18.3%)	(+24.6%)	(+31.3%)
TOTAL	8,107,000	9,664,000	11,410,000	13,333,000	15,450,000

Source: Hamdy 1964, 11

for instance, it expected a 251 per cent deficit by 1985). While the veracity of these calculations is questionable, they had a significant impact on policy-making at the time. In fact, Egyptian elites were deeply concerned about potential labour shortages (both low- and high-skilled) in the late 1950s affecting the process of industrialisation, and a restrictive emigration policy constituted one of the regime's solutions to this issue (Waterbury 1972). In this sense, a restrictive emigration policy was a main way of preventing labour deficits, and catered to the needs of the economic elites, co-opting them into the ruling regime: 'the private-sector capitalists working in contracting were ... co-opted by Nasser's regime', Tarouty notes (Tarouty 2016, 41) due to the fact that 'during this period [of the late 1950s] the public sector had a shortage of personnel'.

One such individual was Osman Ahmad Osman, who headed the Arab Contractors, and benefitted from Egypt's restrictive policy. A key public works project that highlights the Free Officers' intent on state-led economic growth was the construction of the Aswan High Dam, the construction of which lasted from 1960 to 1970, headed by Osman. It was a massive project that depended upon abundant work force: it involved more than 25,000 Egyptian engineers and workers. With an overall cost of LE 560 million (or, roughly $1 billion in today's rates), it diverted the waters of the Nile and gave the state the ability to control the river's annual floods, provide water for irrigation, and generate hydroelectricity (Mossallam 2014; Fahim 2015). Waterbury describes the political importance of the High Dam within the Nasserite context, highlighting how it functioned as an instrument of legitimation: 'The political decision (to build a dam) frequently embodies a symbolic package that is designed to catch people's imagination at home and abroad, to arouse the populace, to set collective goals and thus to find in motivational terms a substitute for war' (Waterbury 1979, 247). It had a 'massive international visibility, both physical and symbolic, that represented the regime's will to assert its sovereignty in the face of neo-imperialism'. More concretely, the project's completion was linked to a number of state-led industrial projects that had to await the High Dam's completion for power – the High Dam, in other words, 'was to be vital for the success of the "hard" phase of ISI, during which the state would have to develop crucial backward linkages in the stead of the private sector' (Waterbury 1983, 66).

Given these factors, it is unsurprising that the regime placed a variety of substantive restrictions on citizens' migration, particularly for high-skilled professionals. All things considered, allowing Egyptians to emigrate after the state had trained them for several years, and at considerable cost, appeared illogical and confirmed the fears of massive brain drain (Ayubi 1995; Mountjoy 1972, 310–13). These were common concerns across Third World countries at the time.[1] 'Given the revolutionary aura of the early sixties and the emphasis on socialist development and self-reliance', Dessouki argued, 'there was little room for migration issues' (Dessouki 1982, 55). As a result, early voices urging consideration of emigration as a solution to Egypt's problem of 'astronomical' overpopulation went largely unheard (al-Ahram, 25 November 1966 and 31 October 1967). As Ibrahim described:

This was the period in which central planning, the public sector, workers' participation in management, land reform, and rent controls were all in vogue. The share of industry in Egypt's GNP was steadily rising, and the transformation of Egypt's labour force to modern sectors looked irreversible. With such socioeconomic forces at work, the thought of massive labour transfer to other countries was unthinkable. (Ibrahim 1982, 65)

The Free Officers' regime did not construct the state's emigration policy solely based on such discursive means. Behind Nasser's public assertions that 'everybody knows that Egyptians do not like to emigrate' (quoted in *al-Ahram al-Iqtisadi*, 7 January 1963), lay an extensive bureaucratic network that delayed the process of leaving Egypt as much as possible: for instance, in Cairo, passports were only issued via a single office, which prevented the fast processing of any citizen wishing to travel abroad. But even in order to gain permission to apply for a passport, an Egyptian citizen would need to be authorised by the work supervisor, as well as the relevant security department. In some cases, for those employed as civil servants, this would require the formal approval of the relevant minister (Dessouki 1982, 62). In multiple instances throughout this long process, those wishing to travel abroad would be subject to 'abnormal and suspicious looks' (Atrouzi 1970).

In addition to measures detailed earlier, Egypt developed a rigid system of exit visas that relied on *al-taklīf* (mandatory work programme), which forbade migration of specific professions until one had been employed within Egypt for a set number of years. Egyptian doctors, pharmacists, dentists, nurses, and medical technicians were considered critically important for the state, and were explicitly forbidden to emigrate (*al-Ahram*, 6 December 1961 and 9 September 1969). As seen earlier in this chapter, 'obtaining an "exit visa" would prove to be one of the most difficult attainments of any Egyptian seeking to leave the country' (Choucri 1977, 6). This policy was expanded by the regime over time, effectively managing the flow of labour across a number of professions that the regime considered important. Corresponding to Egypt's industrialisation efforts and the state developmentalism that characterised the country during the 1950s and 1960s, engineers were denied the right to emigrate according to *Decret-loi* No. 296|1956, a law that coincided with the creation of the Ministry of Industry. Other professions would also be forbidden from emigrating according to state needs – from aerospace engineers to technical high-school graduates.

A wide variety of additional measures were implemented in order to dissuade prospective emigrants. This includes, for instance, the fact that exit visas required two months, at the very least, to be processed. While this was partly due to the extensive bureaucratic apparatus of the Egyptian state, it also aimed to add to the psychological stress of applicants, as applications went back and forth through a multiplicity of departments and agencies that lacked

Table 2.2 *Work permits for employment abroad, 1966–1969*

Year	New Work Permits	Renewed Work Permits	Total
1966	3,497	1,748	5,245
1967	4,314	2,275	6,589
1968	4,336	4,833	9,169
1969	–	N/A	N/A

Source: CAPMAS, 1969

coordination (Atrouzi 1970). To be successful, an exit visa required that the emigrant only travel by the state-owned air carrier, 'Misr Air'. The applicant must have purchased a round-trip ticket in advance, which could not be transferred to any other airline company – an extravagant cost, given Egyptian wages in the 1950s and the rarity of air travel. Finally, even when an Egyptian was issued a passport, a variety of restrictions would be placed on its use: in most cases, passports were only valid for Arab countries, and in some cases only valid for a single one, usually Libya or Syria.

Population Immobility and High-Intensity Repression under Nasser

> If Gamal Abdel Nasser should die, each of you shall be Gamal Abdel Nasser.
>
> Gamal Abdel Nasser, 24 October 1954

At the same time, the restrictive labour emigration policy that the Egyptian state implemented served purposes beyond legitimation and co-optation of business elites. It also facilitated the ruling regime's management of political opposition, primarily via repression. Despite his popular appeal, Nasser was infamous for the repressive tactics he espoused and his insistence on political control (Kandil 2012; Abdel-Malek 1968; Ansari 1986): 'Egypt under Nasser was a very repressive state that was willing to combat perceived enemies of the right and the left. Nasser built a massive network of intelligence agents and a formidable policy apparatus [as the regime] wanted all social forces under its control' (King 2009, 58). In the process, the feared Egyptian secret police (*al-Mukhābarāt*) was given a free hand (Sirrs 2010), as 'torture and police sadism became commonplace' (Waterbury 1983, 342). The president's insistence on political control reached the level of 'paranoia'. As Sayyid-Marsot recounts, 'Nasser spied on his own associates and even had their houses bugged so he could be kept informed of everything they said and thought' (Sayyid-Marsot 2007, 146).

Initially, the Free Officers regime allowed political opponents' move abroad, as a means of punishment and an instrument of domestic political consolidation, in an 'out of sight, out of mind' approach. This is also understandable given the fact that the Free Officers needed time to consolidate their rule across the Egyptian state's repressive institutions; the British had not fully evacuated Egypt until 1956, four years after the July 23 Revolution. King Farouk, for instance, was sent into exile in Italy, along with his entourage. On the day of his departure, 'Anwar, along with Gamal Salem and Muhammad Naguib, two other revolutionaries ... had gone to deliver an ultimatum to the King', recounts Sadat's wife. 'If Faruq did not leave the country by six that night [26 July 1952], the Free Officers would not be responsible for the consequences. Faruq took only five minutes to accept' (Sadat 2002, 130). Interestingly, Nasser reportedly insisted that the King be exiled, rather than killed, in order to help consolidate the 1952 Revolution. He argued that

once blood started to flow, there might be no way of stopping it. Moderation would improve the image of the revolution, and the sight of the gross monarch in the nightclubs of Europe would, if anything, tend to justify it. In the end, a vote was taken. Six of the revolutionary council voted that Faruq should hang, seven that he should be exiled. (Flower 2011, 183)

Over the months and years that immediately followed the 1952 Revolution, royalists, collaborators with the British and, generally, supporters of the *ancien régime* managed to flee abroad. This also included many Egyptians, who managed to flee abroad despite restrictions being gradually implemented in order to avoid mandatory military conscription. This is not to say that restrictions on emigration were not enforced; rather, it suggests that maintaining full control of Egyptian borders (particularly the porous desert border with Libya) was complex and not always fully effective. Interestingly, a process of forced exile was also developed for military dissidents within the regime itself:

Those [military dissidents] who made trouble would spend some time in prison or exile, after which they would be released and given civil service positions. The first test of this strategy – one that proved successful – came in March 1954, when the regime released the artillery officers jailed in January 1953 in order to boost morale in the wake of a strike in the armor corps. (Joel Gordon 1992, 116)

However, the largest waves of permanent emigration involved the communities that had vested interests in the economic life of pre-1952 Egypt. Sequestration and nationalisation encouraged the departure of the foreign communities from Egypt. This included the Greek community, numbering more than 25,000, and more than 60,000 Italians (Sayyid-Marsot 2007, 137; Kazamias 2009; Dalachanis 2017). These communities had existed, and flourished, in Egypt for decades under the monarchical rule. In addition to purely economic reasons, foreigners were compelled to leave Egypt given the Free Officers' rising nationalist, anti-Western rhetoric that materialised after the 1956 Suez Crisis. One of the first communities that felt compelled to leave for Israel or the West was the Egyptian Jews, faced with sequestration processes but also direct or indirect threats by the Free Officers regime, 'forced out by the considerable anti-Jewish feeling in the country' (Hopwood 1991, 57). A once-thriving community would be transformed, by 1956, from 'a national asset into a fifth column' (Beinin 2005, 22; Achcar 2010), again serving within the regime's legitimation strategy. Numbering more 75,000 in the late 1940s, the Egyptian Jewish community was reduced to a few hundred by the end of Nasser's rule, and less than forty currently. As Gordon recounts: 'Jews, Syrians, Greeks, Italians, and Armenians left in droves for Europe, Israel and the Americas: usually voluntary but sometimes under duress and always with tight restrictions imposed on what they could take with them' (Gordon 2012, 52). The forced exodus of Western communities from Egypt also arguably served as an instrument for the legitimation of the Free Officers regime, as discussed in the previous section.

As the Free Officers regime consolidated its power, it was able to implement a restrictive emigration policy with more success. Most prominently, the regime employed its restrictive emigration policies in order to reduce the mobility of members of the Egyptian Muslim Brotherhood (*al-Ikhwan*), a religious group founded by Hassan al-

Banna in 1928, that had evolved in the pre-1952 period into one of the key socio-political movements in Egypt (on their historical development, see Mitchell 1969). While the *Ikhwan* initially supported the Free Officers movement, the two groups' interests split and Nasser formally dissolved the organisation in January 1954, imposing travel restrictions on its members. The presence of common enemies – namely the British and the ruling monarchy – had allowed the two groups to unite in opposition to them; however, upon assuming power, Nasser decided that the Brotherhood's religious agenda could not be reconciled with the Free Officers' goals (see Wickham 2013). Following an assassination attempt against Nasser in October 1954, for which the Muslim Brotherhood was blamed, the regime initiated a long process of imprisonment for around 400 members, together with the Supreme Guide (Dekmejian 1971, 27; Wickham 2013, 27; Jankowski 2002, 23). They were incarcerated in the *Liman al-Tura* prison outside Cairo and in the *al-Wahat* prison camp in the Western Desert (Zollner 2007).

Despite the crackdown and restrictions on travel, during this period hundreds of Muslim Brothers managed to flee to Saudi Arabia, Kuwait, Bahrain, or elsewhere – Yusuf al-Qaradawi, for instance, relocated to Qatar; 'Abd al-Latif Mikki fled to Syria (Kandil 2015, 65). Once abroad, members of the *Ikhwan* became embedded in host states' educational systems and contributed to conservative religious teaching, particularly in Saudi Arabia (Farquhar 2017). Many of those who defied travel restrictions and fled Egypt, such as Sa'id Ramadan, 'Abd al-Hakim 'Abidin, Sa'd al-Din al-Walili, Muhammad Najub Juwayfil, and Kamil Isma'il, were accused of 'treason to the [Egyptian] nation', stripped of their nationality, and forbidden from returning to Egypt (Mitchell 1969, 141). Processes of domestic repression against the *Ikhwan* were repeated in the mid-1960s: after evidence of a second conspiracy in 1965 (or, as it was termed, 'Organisation 1965') the regime incarcerated about 2,000 supposed members, including Sayyid Qutb (Heikal 1983, 126–27; Wickham 2013, 28). Only a few of them managed to escape abroad.

A similar fate awaited members of the Communist movement in Egypt, which included a number of groups whose creation had preceded the 1952 Revolution. After a period of accommodating the Marxist movement within state borders in the early to mid-1950s, the Free Officers regime engaged in an open campaign of imprisonment and repression, starting on 1 January 1959. 'Hundreds of communists were arrested and imprisoned and a campaign of sustain repression was implemented whose goal was the complete destruction of Egyptian Marxism' (Botman 1988, 143). Egyptian Marxists, prevented from fleeing abroad, were arrested by border authorities and subject to a 'harsh crackdown'. This enabled the Free Officers to virtually eliminate any political opposition from the various communist groups until Nasser decided, in 1964, to release them from prison (Ismael and El-Sa'id 1990, 121–23). Naturally, much like the case of the *Ikhwan*, there were always party members that were able to escape – one of the most prominent Egyptian Marxists who fled Egypt was Henri Curiel, who was able to continue his political activity in Europe through the "Rome Group". The multiple linkages between leftist movements within Egypt and abroad have been extensively researched (Beinin 1992, 1990).

The Limits of Legitimation in Nasser's Emigration Policy

> To build factories is easy; to build hospitals and schools is possible; but to build a nation of men is a hard and difficult task.
>
>   Gamal Abdel Nasser, National Assembly Speech, 1957

The extent to which a restrictive emigration policy may serve its internal legitimation functions relies on a state's economic ability to absorb would-be emigrants domestically. In the first few years following the 1952 Revolution, the state's economic capacity was able to support strategies of emigration restriction. However, the first signs that this system of rigid control was unsustainable began to appear in the mid-1960s, as an increasing number of graduates sought to emigrate in response to the worsening economic situation within Egypt and the rise of unemployment (Table 2.3). State statistics during this period are not entirely helpful in understanding the magnitude of the phenomenon, as they estimated unemployment at 1 or 2 per cent nationally – an artificially low figure by most accounts. According to the 1960 census, there were only 308,000 unemployed Egyptians across the entire country, out of a total population of roughly 28 million, divided evenly between rural and urban areas; only 23,600 of those were females, as any woman without work who claimed to be a housewife or occupied domestically was not considered to be part of the work force. Dr Abdel-

Table 2.3 *Number of emigrants by country of immigration, 1962–1970*

	1962	1963	1964	1965	1966	1967	1968	1969	1970
United States	31	51	38	41	68	266	1,046	3,282	2,132
Canada	527	968	942	972	1,407	1,322	1,449	947	439
Australia	56	541	549	404	836	936	803	1,423	1,535
Brazil	115	115	68	25	42	52	357	75	12
Other Countries	140	112	48	37	11	14	31	8	8
Total	869	1,787	1,645	2,079	2,365	2,690	3,686	5,645	4,126

Source: al-Najjar, 1972; based on CAPMAS data

Maguid al-Abd, the Head of Egypt's Central Training Organization, estimated that about 1.5 million Egyptians were actually unemployed in 1960, with about 20 per cent of the active work force in disguised unemployment, and only 14 per cent of the workforce in full employment (Al-Abd 1971, 52).

Statistics aside, it is widely accepted that, by the mid- to late-1960s, Egyptians had become increasingly unconvinced by Nasserite ideals, and the regime's legitimation strategy began to crumble. The policy of state-led economic growth, ISI, and sectoral monopolies stopped bearing fruit by the mid-1960s, with GNP growth falling from 6.4 per cent (1963–64) to 4.4 per cent (1965–66) to 0.3 per cent (1966–67). This became prominent as it accentuated the negative effects of Egypt's demographic imbalances and overpopulation, which plagued the country well before the Free Officers' Revolution.[2] Most economic analyses of time subscribed to orthodox demographic theory doctrines that highlighted the dangers of high population growth, particularly due to its potential to impede processes of modernisation. In particular, they stressed Egypt's status as a labour surplus country, which was expected to become even more so in the coming decades (Waterbury 1972, 1; Fargues 1997). Already in 1953, the first twenty family planning clinics had been set up across Egypt. 'We have to work twice as fast ... to provide work for the 350,000 persons who are born to us each year', Nasser announced in 1958 (quoted in Abdel-Malek 1968, 121). But efforts to curtail the population through family planning were soon abandoned: 'instead of teaching people how to exercise birth control, we would do better to teach them how to increase their land production', Nasser told the *Christian Science Monitor* in 1959 (quoted in Gadalla 1978, 212). By May 1962, the regime put forth *al-mīthāq al-watanī* (the National Charter), a policy document stating that population growth 'constitutes the most dangerous obstacle that faces the Egyptian people in their drive toward raising the standards of production in an effective and efficient way' (*al-Ahram*, 22 May 1962). A new family planning programme was put into place in 1965, aiming to reduce the country's crude birth rate from 41 per 1,000 citizens in 1966, to 30 per 1,000 by 1978 (Wisensale and Khodair 1998, 505). Overall, however, Nasser acknowledged that he had not managed to tackle what he termed 'a growth of population which could be counted in the millions ... and which had (in the past) afflicted the productive apparatus with a paralysis that was virtually total' (quoted in Nutting 1972, 300).

The inability to economically sustain a restrictive emigration policy increasingly undermined the regime's internal legitimation tactics. The measures the regime put forth to prevent emigration came to be seen less as complementing the Egyptian society's rejection of Western capitalism or a necessary sacrifice for national development, and more as autocratic rule. In mid-1966, *The New York Times* ominously highlighted the tensions between a restrictive state policy and the wishes of the social body through its reporting that 'Nasser is Seeking to Hold Students' from pursuing educational opportunities abroad (*The New York Times*, 28 August 1966). Under the prime-ministership of Zakariyya Mohieddin, the state first 'open[ed] the floodgates of emigration' as thousands of trained Egyptians departed for North America and Europe (Vatikiotis 1978, 182–83; cf. Talani 2010, 65). 'Colleagues would look at those who had been able to be granted state permission to emigrate to the United States with envy', recalled Professor Ibrahim Awad (*personal interview*). Even then, however, Egyptian emigration has been estimated to be quite low, with the caveat that statistical data on the levels of pre-1967 Egyptian emigration is incomplete. *Al-Akhbar* reported emigration flows of 10,733, mainly to North America, in the entire 1962–67 period (*al-Akhbar*, 14 January 1969).

Instead of reconsidering its emigration policy towards a more sustainable model, the Egyptian regime under Nasser attempted to tackle the problem of unemployment primarily by expanding the Egyptian public sector (Ayubi 1980, 157–86; Owen and Pamuk 1999). Nasser's *siyāsat al-taʿyīn* (Graduate Appointment Policy),

Table 2.4 *Comparative growth rates: Cairo & Egypt, 1897–1972*

Year	Cairo Population	Growth Rate (%)	Egyptian Population	Growth Rate (%)
1897	590,000	–	9,591,000	–
1907	678,011	1.4	11,136,000	1.5
1917	791,000	1.6	12,670,000	1.3
1927	1,071,000	3.0	14,083,000	1.1
1937	1,312,000	2.1	15,811,000	1.2
1947	2,091,000	4.8	18,806,000	1.8
1960	3,353,000	3.6	26,085,326	2.38
1966	4,964,004	4.13	30,075,858	2.54
1970	5,900,000	4.1	33,329,000	2.54
1972	6,170,000	4.0	35,000,000	2.24

Source: Waterbury 1973a, 1

established by Decree 185|1965, stipulated that the state would provide public sector employment for every Egyptian citizen who graduates from university. The Egyptian state would now serve as an instrument for job creation in a manner that was palatable to the Free Officers' ideological leanings (Baker 1978, 197–217). This complemented the regime's 1962 decision to make university education free for all Egyptians. It is important to note that the Free Officers considered these measures to be deeply political, rather than merely socio-economic: for Hegazy, the *ta'yin* policy corresponded to Nasser's wish to minimise political risks out of massive Egyptian unemployment (*personal interview*). Ibrahim Hilm 'Abd al-Rahman, Nasser's Minister of Planning, recalled that:

In its early history, the *ta'yin* policy was a political measure. The number of graduates was small at the time. The decision involved no one except those at the apex of the government. It was a decision made by the inner circle, because it was regarded as politically sensitive. The *ta'yin* policy was motivated by a fear of political agitation. At the time we were very afraid of graduate unemployment. Nasser was conscious of this potential problem and considered it very serious, because he understood it as a potential source of political instability. After a while, the *ta'yin* policy lost its initial rationale. But once you offer it, it is hard to take back. It becomes a fact' (Wickham 2005, 27).

The Free Officers regime's attempt to fight the issue by placing Egyptians on the public payroll proved to be a short-term solution. By 1968, the civil service would contain some 1,050,900 Egyptians, with another 635,000 employed in public enterprises (Waterbury 1972, 12; see also Figure 2.1). The state employed virtually all of the country's engineers, scientists, and agronomists, more than three-quarters of its physicians, and two-thirds of its lawyers (Ayubi 1980, 242, 355–66). This resulted in a bloated state bureaucratic apparatus of educated, but non-specialised, personnel. At the same time, given the concentration of government agencies in Cairo, this added to the country's urbanisation problem: 'migration from the countryside to the city increased dramatically because of the expansion of education and new development projects, as well as the growth of government bureaucracy, the public sector, and the army' (Amin 2011, 89–90, see also Table 2.4). Kerr describes the situation aptly:

[T]housands of non-so-bright young men in their soiled collars and cheap suits eke out a shabby and insecure but desperately respectable existence on ten pounds a month as minor clerks, bookkeepers, schoolteachers, and journalists. They are assured from time to time in the press and in the President's speeches that as educated men they are the 'vanguard' of the nation's progress, but they are impotent to fashion even their own progress and they can only listen anxiously to the officially propagated theme of equal and widening opportunities under the new socialist economic development plan which ambitiously pledges to double the national income in ten years. (quoted in Wickham 2005, 32)

Beattie provides a sober description of the Egyptian socio-economic state at the time of Nasser's death, in September 1970:

[Since 1952, Egypt's] population had grown from over 21 million to slightly more than 33 million, a 54 percent increase ... Job prospects for the country's burgeoning masses, educated and uneducated alike, were growing increasingly bleak. One palliative was to cram many educated youth into the civil service and public sector companies. Thus, the civil service grew from 325,000 employees in 1952 to an army of 1.2 million in 1970 ... Cairo, a city set up to accommodate the needs of three million, had become home to nearly three times that number [and] most basic services were strained literally to the breaking point. Water pipes and sewage systems exploded, flooding sections of the city.... Cars clogged the streets, and public buses and trams were bursting at the seams ... On top of all this, there was still a war to be fought to liberate the Sinai Peninsula and restore Egypt's national pride. The war effort was costing the state some LE 700 ($1.5 billion) in annual military expenditures, more than twice the sum of Egypt's total exports at the turn of the decade. (Beattie 2000, 13)

This issue was not solely limited to urban areas: Sayyid Marei, Egypt's Minister of Agrarian Reform, estimated that Egypt's rural labour force needs are no more than 1.8 million workers, out of a total rural population of 18 million, and that their marginal productivity was approaching zero by the mid-1950s. A third of Egypt's rural population, according to Issawi's calculations, constituted a surplus (Issawi 1963, 299–303). But it

Figure 2.1 The Ministry of Transport (*al-Ahram*, 3 December 1975)
    'Don't you know which building this is ... ?
    That's the Ministry of Transport!'

was the major urban centres that concerned the Egyptian regime the most, as internal migrants flocked to the cities looking for employment opportunities. The mass exodus from the countryside to Egyptian cities in the post-World War II period attested to this, as about a million Egyptians left the countryside for the cities in the 1947–60 period. Of Cairo's inhabitants in 1960, 37.9 per cent were internal migrants (INP Research Report on Employment Problems in Rural Areas, 1965). The fact that Nasser considered closing Cairo to any new migration in 1967 – a solution

Figure 2.2 'Liberate the Canal!' *(al-Ahram*, 4 October 1972)

Hamdy Ashur, the new governor of Cairo, ponders the best way to end migration into the city.

'Do you want me to tell you the best solution of all? . . . Liberate the Canal!'

quickly abandoned as impractical – reveals the regime's fear of this problem (Al-Tali'a, 1969).

The problem of urbanisation was also exacerbated following the 1967 War, the occupation of the Sinai by Israel, and the subsequent mass evacuation of the civilian populations in canal cities – Suez, Port Tawfiq, Ismailiya, Port Said. Evacuees were moved into urban centres, predominantly Cairo (LaTowsky 1984, 12; see also Figure 2.2). By mid-July 1967, some 96,000 people had left the affected areas (*al-Ahram*, 15 July 1967; *New York Times*, 5 October 1967). 'Ali Sabri, who was appointed Resident Minister for the Canal Zone, made the evacuation of civilians a government policy by granting financial assistance and evacuating around 1,500 people per day from Suez City. By October 1967, more than 350,000 people had moved into urban areas. By November, 90 per cent of the population had departed from Ismailiya and Port Said – estimated, by Waterbury in 1975, to over a million citizens (Waterbury 1975, 6). The fact that the state was demobilising thousands of soldiers stationed in Yemen did not help Egypt's urbanisation problems, which were also complemented by a shortage of housing. In the early 1970s, the state was constructing about 30,000 dwelling units annually across all Egypt when Cairo alone needed 62,000 a year (Lippman 1989, 165).

The 1967 defeat, which for most analysts marked the 'twilight' of Nasserism (Hinnebusch, 1985, 35), intensified pressures towards a more permissive emigration policy. The post-1967 economic, military, and moral bankruptcy of the Nasserite system served as a significant push factor for prospective Egyptian migrants. It diminished any descriptive legitimacy of the Free Officers' restrictive policies, and contributed to the 'realization by Egyptians of the hollowness of the regime's fifteen-year-long claims to military prowess, economic and social reform, not to mention political change' (Vatikiotis 1991, 411). Not incidentally, the regime began considering the pursuit of a more permissive emigration policy as a solution against domestic political agitation: amidst strong student protests erupting across Egypt, Nasser debated how emigration can serve as a "safety valve", exploring the signing of labour agreements with other Arab states (Abdalla 2008). The president put through the 30 March 1968 Manifesto, 'Mandate for Change' (Vatikiotis, 1991, 410; Dekmejian, 1971, 257–62), and, faced with increasing popular demands for emigration, designated Hegazy with communicating with Arab states that could absorb surplus Egyptian labour (*personal interview*). CAPMAS published a 1969 report arguing that 'migration in general was beneficial to Egypt since the country was overpopulated' (quoted in Saleh 1979, 14–15).

Yet, these attempts did not amount to much. A variety of initiatives attempting to liberalise emigration controls were put forth, but the Free Officers resisted their adoption, fearing the implications of such shifts for regime legitimacy. Nasser, for instance, considered dispatching Egyptian workers to West Germany and to Switzerland, although these thoughts never materialised (Sell 1988, 90). Similarly, migration to the United States, Canada, and Australia was perceived, at some point, as one way of tackling the overpopulation problem (Dessouki 1982, 55). A number of Egyptian Copts were granted permission to emigrate to North America and other Western countries, particularly in the post-1956 period. But the Egyptian regime under Nasser was never politically comfortable with employing emigration as a tool for economic development: 'Abd al-Salam 'Arif al-Jumayli, the president of Iraq, had made a request to Nasser for the dispatch of Egyptian farmers in 1963, only to be quickly turned down (Ishow 1996, 189–95). A few years earlier, in 1958, Syrian President Shukri al-Quwwatli had begun discussing the move of 1,000 Egyptian *fallāhīn* families into Syria, but the dissolution of the United Arab Republic put an end to that plan (Feiler 1986, 6). Nasser's thoughts of dispatching a few thousand farmers into Sudan also failed to lead to concrete policies (Vatikiotis 1991, 435), as was a similar post-1967 attempt, which was not ratified by the Sudanese parliament. 'Everyone knew that if [Nasser] agreed to relax emigration, that would be a sign of weakness', confessed Hegazy (*personal interview*). Beyond domestic repercussions, Egyptian experts involved in the early 1970s family planning programmes declared that 'politically it is unwise for large scale emigration [to be adopted, as it] would only arouse the fears of Egypt's neighbours' (Waterbury 1973b, 3).

Meanwhile, pressure for migration policy reform increased exponentially. By June 1969, thousands of requests were being submitted weekly for emigration to the United States (whereas only 151 visas for immigration to the United States were issued in Egypt in 1963, for instance). Hundreds of Egyptians would 'line up each morning in growing numbers' outside the United States Consulate, which operated as a part of the Spanish Embassy due to the 1967 severance of diplomatic ties – a far cry from the regime's discourse that Egyptians would reject emigration to the capitalist West. *The New York Times* reported comments from an immigration officer of the Australian embassy, stating that 'until about the middle of the nineteen-sixties, nearly all the emigrants we processed from here were foreign residents – Greeks, Italians, Armenians and so forth … The Egyptians just were not interested' (*The New York Times*, 23 June 1969). Yet, by July 1969, approximately 28,000 requests for emigration were submitted to the Egyptian authorities, in contrast to a sum total of 15,500 for the six preceding years (*al-Ahram*, 4 July 1969). Inundated with requests for emigration, the Egyptian state decided to suspend all emigration permits on 9 September 1969 (*al-Ahram*, 5 July 1970).

A few months before Nasser's death, Egyptian elites put forth proposals for a new, regulated emigration policy, which identified critical occupations for which restrictions on emigration were to be put in place. These included medicine, dentistry, nursing, pharmacology, architecture, statistics, engineering, and high school teaching. Graduates of any other degree programme would be free to emigrate. This quota system was to be reviewed every six months, according to Gamal Askar, the head of the Central Agency for Public Mobilization and Statistics (CAPMAS), and revised according to supply and demand. A Ministerial Committee of Manpower would individually review any graduate with an advanced degree that wished to emigrate (*al-Ahram*, 18 March 1970). Therefore, the state aimed to begin encouraging migration of certain occupations, primarily as a solution to the country's socio-economic problems; at the same time, it would control and regulate individual migration, which was seen as potentially harmful to the state's needs and its development. It appeared that the Egyptian regime was seriously exploring a gradual shift in labour emigration policy towards a regulated, economically sustainable framework. However, Nasser's sudden death, in September 1970, put this process on hold. It was Anwar Sadat, Nasser's unexpected successor to the presidency, who would spearhead a radical shift in Egypt's emigration policy.

Conclusion

This chapter allowed an initial foray into the interplay between labour emigration and non-democratic politics in the context of modern Egypt, immediately following the 1952 Free Officers

Revolution. It focused in particular on how the state's restrictive emigration policy, as it was implemented in the 1952–70 period, aimed to enhance the rule of President Nasser and the Free Officers regimes, in three ways. Firstly, it strengthened the regime's material and descriptive legitimation strategies. The rejection of labour emigration fed into elements of Nasserism, and projected an image of an affluent, self-sufficient state that could afford to take a political stance by not engaging in labour migration with either the First or the Second World. The restrictive labour emigration policy also enhanced the co-optation of Egyptian business interests by buttressing the regime's economic policy of state developmentalism and ISI. Finally, a restrictive labour emigration policy facilitated the regime's violent crackdown on opposition movements, notably the Muslim Brotherhood, whose members were generally unable to avoid imprisonment by escaping abroad.

Before proceeding to Chapter 3, which will examine the politics of Egypt's secondment policy across the Arab world, it is worth noting that the regime's labour emigration policy choices lend credit to the earlier observation that authoritarian regimes tend to prioritise short-term political gains over long-term economic goals. Despite a rising level of unemployment from the early 1960s onwards, an expanding foreign accounts deficit, and the phenomena of overpopulation and urbanisation that were straining the country's infrastructure and resources, the regime did not contemplate a sustained reform of its emigration policy until a few months before Nasser's death. A variety of pleas towards a policy shift were not heeded, while isolated suggestions for reform were not followed through by Nasser in fear that they would undermine the regime's domestic legitimacy. In particular, elites worried that the impact of a permissive emigration policy would contradict basic tenets of the Nasserite ideology, undermine the regime's repressive efforts on political opponents, and undoubtedly shake the statist foundations of the Egyptian economy. Chapter 3 builds on this point by highlighting the policy of Egyptian secondment, a high-cost policy of regional emigration that also served political, rather than economic, objectives.

3 | Exporting the Free Officers' Revolution

Migration and External Regime Legitimation under Nasser

> We cannot stupidly look at a map of the world, not realising our place therein and the role determined to us by that place. Neither can we ignore that there is an Arab circle surrounding us and that this circle is as much a part of us as we are a part of it, that our history has been mixed with it and that its interests are linked with ours. These are actual facts and not mere words.
>
> Gamal Abdel Nasser, *Philosophy of the Revolution* (1955)

> We should differentiate between Egypt as a state,
> and Egypt as a revolution.
>
> Mohamed Hassanein Heikal (*al-Ahram*, 29 December 1961)

Beyond the domestic political effects of labour emigration policy lies the question of how it affected the Free Officers' standing beyond Egypt's borders, particularly within a changing Middle East. Chapter 3 details how the Egyptian regime under President Nasser successfully employed thousands of Egyptian professionals abroad in order to support the developmental needs of a number of Third World countries. The state-administered short-term labour emigration of high-skilled Egyptians, under a revamped policy entitled *nizām al-i'āra li-l-khārij* (policy of secondment), was the sole exception to an otherwise restrictive emigration strategy. As Egyptian professionals traversed the Arab world, in particular – parts of which had recently been granted independence or, in the case of the Gulf and Africa, were undergoing transition to independence – they engaged in anti-colonial, anti-Western, and pro-Nasserite rhetoric. In this sense, Egyptian regional migration became firmly embedded in the Free Officers' attempt to establish itself between 1952 and 1970 and served as an instrument of external legitimation. This dimension of Egyptian labour emigration policy allows us to analyse an under-examined aspect of authoritarian emigration states' soft power strategies, also evident in the post-1917 Soviet regime or the Cuban Communist Party strategy under Castro – namely, elites' effort to enhance their rule by engaging in revolutionary internationalism, and sponsoring like-minded political structures abroad.

This chapter firstly situates Egypt's regional emigration policy historically, within the colonial and decolonial context, in order to underline the heightened developmental needs of the Third World. As Nasser developed a keen interest in leading the Non-Aligned Movement, Egyptian professionals were dispatched across Latin America and Yugoslavia, as well as to sub-Saharan Africa – in the latter, Egypt became embroiled with Israel's own attempts at soft power via the dispatch of Israeli professionals across newly independent African states. But it was primarily in the Middle East that Egyptian professionals filled a much-needed vacuum, given the growing inability of the British and French colonial powers to continue providing for the region, as well as the massive needs of post-independent Arab states. The chapter continues to account for how the Free Officers regime grasped the opportunity to develop its internationalist ideology, and to sponsor political movements elsewhere in the Arab world, in accordance with the principles of the 1952 Revolution. In order to do so, Egyptian elites expanded, systematised, and politicised Egypt's policy of secondment, which had existed since the nineteenth century. This allowed the regime to project its ideology across the Arab world, as Egyptians across North Africa, the Levant, and the Arabian Gulf worked towards 'exporting the revolution' between 1952 and Nasser's death in 1970.

Decolonisation, Development, and Egyptian Regional Leadership

Because we had a common religion and for the most part, a common language, we felt we were dealing with friends not foes. In the case of our [Egyptian] neighbours, we shared the same Arab perspective on life and the world. Or so we believed. Unfortunately, we found to our dismay that it took more than such commonalties to build a solid foundation for trustworthy relationships.

Mohammad Al-Fahim (1995, 160)

The 1952 Free Officers' Revolution coincided with a time of massive developmental needs across the Arab world, as the process of decolonisation and the 'triumph of nationalism', evident in the Levant, the Arabian Gulf, and North Africa, highlighted the need for an educated, trained bureaucracy (Hourani 2013, 381). While the colonial powers were traditionally suspicious of expanding access to education across the Arab world (Reid 1990), indigenous elites, some empowered with increasing oil revenues, would seek the development of education: 'mass popular education was one of the first tasks which the new governments set themselves, and to which they devoted a high proportion of their revenues', argued Hourani (2013, 389). In this immediately decolonial moment, newly independent Arab states yearned to develop, but lacked the resources and skilled professionals to do so. Paris and London, tasked with providing trained labour across the Middle East, were unable to do so. 'Almost everywhere schools were opened on a large scale, in poor quarters of the towns and in some villages'. Britain's post-World War II 'exhaustion in the economic field' and impeding withdrawal from the Middle East, in particular, did not allow London to satisfy these countries' need for trained labourers (Balfour-Paul 1991, 8).

Initially, as discussed in the previous chapter, the Free Officers regime was not concerned with decolonisation outside of Egypt. But an initial phase of introspection and preoccupation with expelling the British gradually gave way to a 'shift in revolutionary action from the domestic to the international stage [that] was accompanied by a parallel redirection of ideological development whereby Egyptian nationalism evolved into Pan-Arabism' (Dekmejian 1971, 405). Nasserism, as noted in Chapter 2, contained within it key anti-Western elements. At the same time, its pan-Arab rhetoric, namely the belief in the ideal of 'an Arab political union' in the form of a single, united Arab nation, reverberated across the Middle East (Dekmejian 1971, 108–18; James 2006). In other words, Nasserism contained not merely anti-Western, anti-colonial, and anti-Zionist ideas, but also distinct references to *al-waḥda al-'arabiyya* (Arab unity). These references would materialise in Egypt's 1958 merger with Syria, and the creation of the United Arab Republic (Jankowski 2002, 27–39).

Arab masses' enthusiasm for the ideas of Nasserism, however, was not always shared by ruling elites in the Middle East. King Faisal, in particular, who had replaced his brother Saud on the throne of Saudi Arabia in 1964, saw 'Nasser's pan-Arabism as a direct threat to the survival of the Sa'udi ruling group' (Al-Rasheed 2010, 113), and for good reason: given Nasser's popularity, Arab unity would come at the expense of established leaders elsewhere in the region. This rivalry between the Arab revolutionary republics and the Arab monarchies – the so-called Arab Cold War (Kerr 1978) – lends further justification to Egypt's desire to 'export' the 1952 Revolution abroad. It also created multiple moments of bilateral tension, as Egyptian professionals would be deported by host states for engaging in political propaganda; yet, they would always be invited back. Even staunch anti-Nasserite regimes, such as the Saudi regime, relied on Egyptian high-skilled labour throughout the 1950s and 1960s. Overall, in this precise moment in the history of the Middle East, where the Arab world yearned for development and Nasser yearned for regional leadership, Egypt's regional emigration policy gradually became a central component of realising Egyptian leaders' aspiration to become *primus inter pares* within the Arab world.

Broadly, Egypt's policy of secondment traces its roots to Muhammad Ali's attempts at modernisation and state reform in the early nineteenth century. Once he seized control of Egypt from the Ottoman Empire in 1805, Ali prioritised the development of an extensive bureaucratic capacity across the country. The process of reform and educational advances continued under the rule of Ali's grandson, Khedive Ismail, until 1879, and led Egypt to a different developmental trajectory from the rest of the Arab world, which would remain under Ottoman rule until the post-World War I era, or even later. Despite the fact that illiteracy continued to be a major problem, and the introduction of obstructionist policies by Earl of Cromer, once Egypt came under British rule after 1882, state educational facilities catered to an increasing number of students (Vatikiotis 1991, 467–71). At the same time, the 1871 founding of *Dar al-Ulum*, a Training College for Teachers of Arabic, and a separate Teachers' Training College in 1886 substantially increased the number of trained teaching staff within Egypt (Vatikiotis 1991, 476).

As Arab nationalist intellectual trends came to dominate political discourse in Cairo under British rule (Coury 1982), the Egyptian state decided to extend various forms of educational assistance to its Arab neighbours, from welcoming non-Egyptian Arab students into *al-Azhar* and the newly established Cairo University to providing funding for the construction of schools abroad. Aside from primary schools, Egypt established a model secondary school in Rabat in 1956; Alexandria University opened a branch in Beirut, in 1961 (Qubain 1966). In their landmark study of Arab educational systems in the mid-twentieth century, Matthews and Akrawi argue that 'Egypt's educational system has a considerably longer history than that of [the rest of the Arab world]. Whereas the other Arab countries ... started afresh after World War I, the Egyptian educational system in general dates back more than a century' (Matthews and Akrawi 1949, 3). Although still not a well-defined set of policies, the dispatch of Egyptian professionals abroad becomes prominent in the early twentieth century. In addition to welcoming Arab students into its educational system and funding the construction of schools abroad, the Egyptian state developed a policy of secondment in order to address Arab shortages in educational staff. This policy earned Egypt the affectionate name *al-Shaqīqa al-Kubrā* (The Big Sister) of the Arab world, for its contribution to the region's development. The early dispatch of small numbers of high-skilled Egyptians abroad supplanted a growing sense of distinction amongst Egyptian elites on their country's position within the Middle East. Echoing a common sentiment in terms of the domestic perception of Egypt's educational role in the region, Egyptian historian Hussein Fawzi al-Najjar recounted:

It was no coincidence that Egypt should outpace its brethren Arab states in civilization, for when Muhammad Ali embarked on the building of the modern state in Egypt and sent out academic missions to Europe, the Middle East had not yet awakened from their slumber. When those countries started their own civilization at last and began liberating themselves rapidly from the yoke of the Middle Ages, they found only Egypt to supply their needs of schoolteachers and higher education professors. (*al-Ahram*, 17 July 1976)

Gradually, Egypt began dispatching small numbers of other trained professionals in neighbouring countries under the helm of King Farouk (Dekmejian 1971; Doran 1999). Beyond teachers, Egyptian administrators and legal scholars were particularly sought-after abroad: one notable example is 'Abd al-Razzaq al-Sanhuri, who drafted the Egyptian Civil Code. Al-Sanhuri travelled to Baghdad to found the city's School of Law in the mid-1930s, and drafted the Iraqi Civil Code in 1943 (Saleh 1979). More than any other professions, however, teachers were commonly dispatched to countries that were developing their national educational systems: Egyptians were recruited to work in Kuwait's first two public schools, *al-Mubārakiyya and al-Aḥmadiyya*, from the mid-1930s onwards, and in Iraqi schools from 1936 onwards (The National Archives (TNA) – FO 141/660/12–1937). These teachers, nominated by the Ministry of Education, would receive double the salary of their Egyptian counterparts, according to a 1919 decision by the Council of Ministers (*al-Ahram*, 20 October 1936). In fact, in the pre-1956 period, secondary school students across the Arab world would receive the *Tawjīhiyya* (the Egyptian Secondary School Certificate) upon graduation (Misnad 1985, 91).

In the Gulf, while the reign of Sheikh Abdullah Qasim al-Thani in Qatar prevented the dispatch of Egyptian teachers due to his distrust of modern education, Kuwait was able to use profits from oil, which increased massively from 1946 onwards, to found a number of boys' schools (Misnad 1985, 34). In Bahrain, Sir Charles Belgrave, an adviser to the Sheikh of Bahrain, recounted in his memoirs:

In 1945, owing to the dearth of suitable schoolteachers, for teaching was an unpopular profession, it was decided that a few Egyptian masters should be employed ... There was an urgent demand for better education, the number of students was increasing, and a Secondary School had been opened, but the local masters were not capable of conducting secondary education. Twelve experienced schoolteachers were seconded by the Egyptian Ministry of Education for service in Bahrain. The public welcomed their employment, for the Bahrainis are inclined to regard anything from abroad as being superior to the local article, and ... realised that the Egyptians were better qualified than themselves. (Belgrave 1960, 145)

Eventually, the dispatch of teachers helped pave the way for the conforming of most school curricula across the Arab world to the Egyptian system. In the case of Bahrain, as elsewhere, the dispatch of Egyptian teachers coincided with arrangements for local Arab students to receive advanced education in Egypt (Belgrave 1960, 145). This supplanted local aspirations that Egyptian-style education would enable graduates to continue higher education in Egypt (al-Najjar 1972, 18–19), again given the Egyptian state's longer tradition in education. But the importance of Egypt was also highlighted by the fact that textbooks produced in Cairo were acknowledged as the only quality ones available in the

Arab world. A 1940 British report from Kuwait on the textbooks used in schools around the Gulf notes how 'most of them [are] produced in Egypt' (National Archives: R/15/5/196).

Overall, the long history of Egypt's educational system endowed the state with the capacity to cater to its Arab neighbours' needs through the dispatch of trained professionals. This was also buttressed from the perception of Egypt's position as 'the intellectual and cultural centre of the Arab world. In a certain sense', Qubain argued, 'whatever happens in Egypt in the field of education affects the entire Arab world, for it is emulated and looked to for guidance and its educational influence radiates into every corner of the area' (Qubain 1966, 197). Egypt's policy of secondment reinforced this belief through the promotion of Egyptian textbooks, the spreading of Egyptian-style educational system, and the admission of Arab students trained by Egyptians into Egyptian universities. Yet, the largely sporadic nature in which the pre-1952 Egyptian state responded to these needs implies that secondment did not yet constitute a state "policy" in the sense of a well-defined set of state actions. It was only following the Free Officers Revolution and Nasser's rise to power that the expansion and politicisation of educational missions abroad occurred, within a distinct revolutionary agenda.

External Legitimation and Egypt's Regional Labour Emigration Policy

> I am an Arab. Yes, I say it with all pride and happiness. I am not alone. Every Arab is my brother in language, religion, feeling and nationhood ... Yes, I am an Arab from Libya.
>
> Excerpt from Egyptian textbook used in 1950s Libya
> (quoted in Obeidi 1999, 37)

Early on, the Free Officers' regime understood the importance of education in sustaining the momentum of the 1952 Revolution, and incorporated high-skilled emigration into the regime's external legitimation strategy. Domestically, following Nasser's rise to power, efforts were taken to rewrite school and university textbooks and adapt them to fit Egypt's perceived socio-political position within the Arab world (United Arab Republic 1964; Nasser 1955). Law 213|1956 made education free for all Egyptians, while the regime also began changing the syllabi and curricula in order to make education 'relevant to national goals and aspiration' (Vatikiotis 1991, 399). In 1956, for instance, it was decided that, by the fifth grade, 'the Egyptian child begins to study politics and reads about "The Arab World," "The New Army," "The Games of Workers," "The Dam," and "The Arab Hero"' (Szyliowicz 1973, 280; Vatikiotis 1991, 478–79). While little archival material exists to allow a full understanding of these processes, the work of Louis Awad, who had been forced to resign from the position of Chairman of the Faculty of Letters at Cairo University in 1954, is significant. In his 1964 critique of the Egyptian educational system's evolution (quoted in Szyliowicz 1973, 280), he highlights a poem that primary school students were expected to memorise:

> I am an Arab, I love the Arabs.
> My father is an Arab, he loves the Arabs.
> My brother is an Arab, he loves the Arabs.
> Long live the Arabs. Long live the Arab.

The political urge to provide for the developmental needs of Egypt's Arab neighbours during the process of decolonisation should be seen in this light. As discussed in the previous chapter, Nasser himself rarely acknowledged Egyptians' regional migration in his speeches. Yet, by 1954, as Cairo became 'the base and capital of the Arab struggle from Oman to Algeria' (Cremeans 1963, 44), formal rules on secondment policy were established and the Egyptian Ministry of Education was re-designated as the Ministry of Education and Public Instruction. The shift was evident across the Arab world: in Bahrain, 'the first group of Egyptians [arriving in 1945], men of mature age, did much to improve the standard of education and their conduct was exemplary', wrote Charles Belgrave, who served as adviser to the Bahraini Shaikh in the 1940s and 1950s. But, under Nasser, 'they were replaced, later, by men who were not so satisfactory and several of the younger masters had to be sent back to Egypt because they indulged in political propaganda' (Belgrave 1960, 145). In this process of politicisation, the role of the Free Officers regime was instrumental.

By the mid-1950s, new rules were introduced governing the process, and ensuring the political oversight of professionals' actions abroad by the regime: aspiring Egyptians were now required to have at least three years' experience, appropriate letters of reference, and to have completed their military service (if they were male). In later years, as the secondment programme gained in popularity, successful applicants were also expected to be under 50 years of age, and to possess a degree qualifying them to serve as schoolteachers. The Ministry of Education would then decide who to select, and where they should be sent (*al-Ahram al-Iqtisadi*, 15 December 1967). The final step involved obtaining a work permit to leave the country, which was granted for a period of three years, renewable for a total of five. In order to obtain one, prospective Egyptians needed not to have a criminal record, and to indicate that they would 'not work with an agency openly hostile to Egypt or its national interest [or] undermine the development goals of Egypt' (Dessouki 1982, 62).

The desire to tie Egyptians' employment abroad with the regime's international priorities was also evident in terms of those who were employed abroad on individual contracts. A separate process was introduced for the latter: they had to apply for a non-paid leave of absence from their place of work after obtaining a contract to work abroad for a specific time period, usually granted for two years and renewable for a maximum of four. At the personal request of the relevant Ministry, such time periods could be extended to six years, in cases where the Minister believed that national interest was involved (Mohie-Eldin and Omar 1978). While statistics do exist on officially seconded Egyptians, there are only estimates for those employed on individual contracts, who were reported to habitually exceed the number of seconded staff. In the 1956–57 period, for instance, 500 teachers were officially seconded to Saudi Arabia, but more than 600 were estimated to be employed on individual contracts with the Saudis (*al-Gomhuria*, 8 June 1957).

Under Nasser, the Egyptian authorities enjoyed a central role in coordinating the secondment process, particularly since the lack of administrative resources in host countries prevented them from having any say in the types of teachers they would receive. This was officially conducted by the Ministry of Education's Department of Secondment (see Table 3.1), but the process by which host countries were to receive seconded Egyptians was frequently opaque, and filtered through a variety of Free Officers' channels. The logistics and intricacies of this have never been publicly released by the Egyptian state, yet through archival material, interviews, and statistical information the politics of this can be broadly delineated. A British diplomatic report explains how Egyptian authorities

Table 3.1 *Egyptian teachers in Arab and other countries, 1953–1964*

Year	Teachers in Arab States
1953–54	580
1955–56	1,198
1958–59	2,696
1961–62	2,948
1962–63	3,512
1963–64	4,615

Source: Arab Republic of Egypt, Ministry of Education and Technical Education, 2014

approached neighbouring countries, in this case Sharjah's ruler, Sheikh Saqr:

[The Sheikh] had received a letter from a member of the Egyptian Council of the Revolution offering to send a number of school teachers and doctors to Sharjah at the Egyptian Government's expense ... It turned out that the letter, which he showed me, was a private one, in manuscript and without any official heading, from a Colonel Abdel Hamid, whom Saqr had apparently met during his visit to Egypt last year, and who now wrote offering to show him the sights of Alexandria if he paid a further visit this year, and going on to suggest that the Egyptian Government should send to Sharjah six school teachers for the primary school there, and in addition, three engineers who would train students in mechanical and electrical engineering, also a doctor and a lady doctor. He said that the Egyptian Government would pay all expenses except accommodation. ('Egypt's Campaign to Spread its Influence by Dispatch of Egyptian Teachers Abroad', *Elizabeth Monroe Collection*, Middle East Centre Archive; St. Anthony's College, Oxford)

Saqr's experience was not unique, for the Ministry of Education typically provided the salary and relocation expenses for these seconded Egyptian teachers. In numerous cases, Egypt agreed to finance the employment of its emigrants abroad, a fact that further points to their instrumentalisation by the Egyptian state: implied in such arrangements is that emigrants reported directly to Egypt and that host states had little choice but to accept the teachers that the Egyptian state chose to second, a process that favoured politically minded teachers, as British reports and other first-hand accounts indicate: Charles Cremeans, who worked as a teacher in the Arab world, claimed that Egyptian teachers 'are indoctrinated before going to their foreign posts and are instructed to act as representatives of their country and its policies' (Cremeans 1963, 41). Details of such training remain unknown, but according to official archival sources, 'the Ministry prepares training seminars' for selected teachers, in order to 'acquaint them with the countries where they will be serving' and 'to enlighten them' (United Arab Republic 1964, 5). In 1957, *The New York Times* somewhat alarmingly reported that Egyptian teachers 'had received special training in propaganda and sabotage in Egypt' (*The New York Times*, 17 May 1957), while *The Times* identified that teachers employed in Libya had been 'seconded from the Egyptian army' (*The Times*, 25 November 1958).

It can be further argued that the harsh living and working conditions for Egyptians in the Arab world in the mid-1950s led to the recruitment of those teachers eager to undertake secondment appointments, and to 'take with them the flame of Nasser-type nationalism' (Wynn 1959, 137). 'You must keep in mind that these teachers set off from Cairo with notebooks and pencils, blackboards and chalk – most of the places [they were sent to work in] had nothing', Dessouki recalled (*personal interview*). In an effort to strengthen the identification of seconded Egyptians with the Egyptian state, teachers' participation in the secondment programme was valorised through the publication of annual lists of secondees across the main state newspapers (*al-Ahram*, 11 July 1956). In fact, the degree to which these professionals represented foreign policy interests of the Egyptian regime cannot be underestimated. This is evident from the fact that the policy of secondment was pursued at the expense of Egypt's own educational development at a time when the state was suffering from a lack of qualified teaching staff: 'the export of teachers was a sacrifice to Egyptians', noted Wynn. 'Up and down the Nile valley, it is common sight to see Egyptian schoolrooms empty for lack of teachers' (Wynn 1959, 136). Yet, the official state line remained that 'Egypt believes that it is her duty to help her sister Arab states to develop their education and learning', according to an *al-Gomhuria* report, 'and that this development will not be achieved unless Egypt supplies these states with their needs for teachers at any cost' (*al-Gomhuria*, 8 June 1957). Behind such rhetoric, one can clearly identify the desire of the Free Officers regime for external legitimation.

Egypt also directed its professionals to numerous African states. According to the *New York Times*, 'the Egyptians [made] themselves heard everywhere in Africa and play[ed] the part of self-chosen leaders' (*The New York Times*, 1 March 1956). Indeed, as regime stalwart and Nasser confidant Mohamed Hassanein Heikal declared: 'Egypt must send selected missions of experts in science, religion, politics, economics, commerce and social services to aid the African peoples, to support them, to collaborate with them and light the path before them' (Heikal 1956). Again, the foreign policy aspect is prominent, for two reasons: firstly, Egypt believed it stood to gain potential support at the United Nations from the newly independent African nations' votes on issues related to the Arab-Israeli conflict (Cremeans 1963); secondly, and perhaps more importantly, it aimed to contain the involvement of Israel in the continent. In 1965, Nasser wrote:

The struggle of the Asian and African peoples is not waged in isolation from the struggle of the Arab nation. In addition to the responsibilities of the development of the African continent following its liberation call for gigantic efforts so that imperialism should not infiltrate and return to it under the pressure of under-development or behind a deceptive mask, such as the Israeli mask, which imperialism tries actively to make use of in Africa. (Nasser 1966, 12)

Thus, targeted, temporary Egyptian migration to African states expanded into a distinctly political tool under Nasser, with an aim to curtail the influence of Israel, under a broader discourse of anti-colonialism (see Figure 3.1). In effect, Egyptian policy was modelled after Israeli strategising. As Heikal notes:

The day a newly independent African country celebrates its independence, a delegation arrives from Israel bringing with it a deep and detailed study of the problems of the country. While all other delegations are offering their congratulations the Israeli delegation is speaking about the problems [that] the newly independent country faces. Most delegations return home after the celebrations but the African ruler keeps the Israeli envoy because he can discuss post-independence problems with him ... In many cases, an Israeli mission returns bearing with it economic, technical and/or cultural agreements. Israel usually chooses one or two fields and concentrates its activities on these. For example, construction is considered the easiest and profits are positive. Any building [that] rises in any African country continues to be a symbol of Israel's activities. After comes trade and maritime companies, then agricultural centres. Also, Israel chooses her men in Africa very carefully. And its embassies in Africa are comprised of the most efficient men from the foreign ministry. (*Arab Observer*, 216, August 1964)

Figure 3.1 African liberation (*Arab Observer*, 10 July 1960)

To allow for a sufficiently in-depth discussion of the rationale, logistics, and effects of Nasserite efforts at "exporting" the Free Officers Revolution abroad, the following section will focus on the nature of Egyptians' political activism across the Arab world.

The Free Officers Revolution and the Arab World

> The Egyptians write, the Lebanese publish, the Iraqis read.
>
> Arabic saying

Egypt's secondment programme gradually became a main component of the Nasserite regime's support of pro-Egyptian movements across the Arab world. This came to complement a variety of other tactics, from radio broadcasts of the *ṣawt al-ʿarab* (Voice of the Arabs) programme disseminating anti-Western and anti-colonial rhetoric to the distribution of Egyptian newspapers abroad within the context of the Arab Cold War (James 2006; Kerr 1978). Nasser himself, in fact, made the connection between political influence and education by calling the *Voice of the Arabs* 'an open university' that provided 'education in national consciousness' (quoted in Abou-El-Fadl 2015, 232). A British report on Sudan details how 'Egypt's cultural leadership in the Arab world is unrivalled and her present

Government exploits it to the full in pursuit of political aims. Egyptian teachers are sent to the Sudan; Sudanese teachers are trained in Egypt' (TNA – FO 407/237, 1957). But, if these accusations stand, why did Arab regimes continue to employ Egyptian teachers?

First, there was an overall lack of trained, local labour force: countries such as Iraq, Jordan, and Libya simply did not have enough skilled and unskilled national workers to meet their needs, and Egyptians, as native speakers of Arabic, were the main alternative solution (Wynn 1959, 136). 'Throughout the Middle East', writes Belgrave on the Nasserite years, 'there is a shortage of teachers and only Egypt, with its long-established system of education, is willing to send its teachers to work in other Middle East states' (Belgrave 1960, 145). For instance, the Saudi Arabian Bureau of Experts, created by the Saudi Council of Ministers in 1954 in order to advise King Saud, had to be staffed almost exclusively by Egyptians, as there were no Saudi lawyers at the time (Barsalou 1985, 134). In fact, it was estimated that the entire country had no more than twenty doctors throughout the 1950s (Lackner 1978, 81), while a 1960 United Nations survey estimated that 95 per cent of Saudi civil servants only had elementary school education (Huyette 1983, 197). Furthermore, the discovery of

Figure 3.2 The first girls' school in Sana'a, run by Egyptian teachers (Schmidt 1968, 154)

oil lured local graduates away from teaching positions towards more lucrative ones. This was particularly true in Saudi Arabia: 'the trouble remains that Egyptian teachers are available and that local young men have no reason to enter teaching as a career', argued a British report. 'These young men feel that they can do better by staying in Jiddah, Mecca, or Riyadh where the pay may be smaller but the opportunities are greater' ('Egypt's Campaign', *Monroe Collection*). 'Even before Saudi Arabia was unified as a state, the Saud regime was dependent on foreign workers: Ibn Saud's advisers, as well as the area's doctors and teachers in the few existing schools, came from Syria and Egypt (Lackner 1978, 191).

Second, Egyptian teachers were affordable, frequently provided for free by the Egyptian state, while Great Britain was unable to subsidise the costs of seconded British teachers in the Middle East. As a result, British professionals working in newly independent Arab states invariably had their contracts terminated as too costly, and were replaced by Egyptians, despite frequent, disquieting warnings from British diplomats against this (*The Sunday Times*, 28 March 1954). At the twilight of Britain's moment in the Middle East, London was financially unable to provide alternatives: 'we cannot ask the Persian Gulf Rulers to give up employing Egyptian teachers', reads a British report, 'because they cannot obtain a sufficient number of qualified Arabic-speaking teachers from any other source' (TNA – BW 114/3, 1956). In Yemen, Egypt covered all its teachers' expenses (see also Figure 3.2). In Lebanon, which had little demand for teachers of Arabic, 'the Egyptian government paid salaries of Egyptian teachers supplied to private Muslim schools which otherwise would have been unable to support a teaching staff' (Wynn 1959, 136). Saudi Arabia was only responsible for an allowance to seconded Egyptian teachers, whose salary was still provided for in full by the Egyptian state, although the Saudis paid all teachers individually contracted in the country (Egypt's Campaign', *Monroe Collection*). Libya traditionally relied on Egypt for teachers' expenses during this period: 'I've never been so rich in my life', one seconded Egyptian administrator said to a *Sunday Times* reporter in Tripoli. 'I'm seconded by the Egyptian Government, who pay my salary at home in addition to my salary here; they fly me home free for my annual leave' (*Sunday Times*, 28 March 1958).

Third, the recruitment of seconded Egyptian teachers often served as a signal of a regime's pro-Egyptian stance and its desire to strengthen ties with the Free Officers (Takriti 2013). For instance, shortly after Sudanese independence the new government was accused by opposition forces of 'encouraging Egyptian infiltration and propaganda' because of its recruitment of Egyptian doctors and teachers. In Yemen, the tense relations between the ruling Imam and Nasser during 1956 translated into 'Egyptian offers of irrigation engineers, who would be extremely useful in the coastal plan, [being] refused', as the British reported. 'Egyptian teachers went on leave from Sana'a several months ago and are not being encouraged to return ' (TNA – FO 464/12). In Iraq, the 1958 Revolution ousted King Faisal II and allowed for a gradual rapprochement with Egypt once 'Abd al-Karim Qasim withdrew Iraq from the pro-Western Baghdad Pact. Yet, the dispatch of Egyptian teachers to Iraq was aborted due to the 1959 split between Qasim and Nasser over Iraq's potential participation in the UAR, which the Iraqi prime minister was not supportive of. However, by 1961 Egypt agreed to provide Iraq with additional teachers, including a number of professors for the Basra medical college (*al-Gomhuria*, 27 May 1961).

Last but not least, some Arab governments perceived the risks of the politicised nature of Egyptian professionals to be outweighed by the benefits of development that high-skilled immigration would produce. Indicatively, the Kuwaiti Minister of Education rebuffed British criticism of seconded Egyptian teachers' political activism by arguing for the importance of education:

Suppose that we want to follow the logic of the writer, what conclusions will his premises lead us to? He says that schools should not be built in, say, Kuwait unless there are enough Kuwaiti teachers to staff them and adds that the Kuwaitis are not keen on the profession of teaching and that the numbers of the Kuwaiti teachers are on the decrease. Does it not follow, then, according to this remarkable piece of reasoning, that a state like Kuwait should indefinitely stop building schools out of her tremendous income from the oil which has revolutionalised all aspects of life in the country? How can we ever get out of this vicious circle except by inviting teachers from the Arab countries to start the process of supplying the country with her need of professional men? ('Egypt's Campaign', *Monroe Collection*)

The expansion of Egypt's secondment policy was accompanied, just as the British had warned, with a politicisation of migration. In an attempt to understand the nature of seconded Egyptians' politicisation, this section examines their activities in Libya, Syria, Yemen, and the Arabian Gulf countries (see Table 3.2 for a detailed breakdown of Egyptian teachers seconded abroad). The Libyan case underlines the

Table 3.2 *Egyptian teachers seconded to Arab states by destination,*
1953–1962

Country	1953	1954	1955	1956	1957	1958	1959	1960	1961
Saudi Arabia	206	293	401	500	454	551	727	866	1,027
Jordan	-	8	20	31	56	-	-	-	-
Lebanon	25	25	39	36	75	111	251	131	104
Kuwait	114	180	262	326	395	435	490	480	411
Bahrain	15	15	18	25	25	25	26	28	36
Morocco	-	-	-	20	75	81	175	210	334
Sudan	-	-	-	-	580	632	673	658	653
Qatar	-	1	3	5	8	14	17	18	24
Libya	55	114	180	219	217	232	228	391	231
Yemen	-	12	11	8	17	17	17	14	0
Iraq	76	112	121	136	63	449	-	-	-
Palestine	13	32	34	37	46	120	166	175	165
Somalia	-	-	25	23	57	69	90	109	213

Source: Arab Republic of Egypt, Ministry of Education and Technical Education, 2014

main reasons why Nasser's policy of secondment was a success across
the Arab world, complementing the Egyptian regime's wish to undermine the pro-Western elements within the ruling Libyan monarchy and
to spread pan-Arab ideas in the neighbouring state. Sir Alec Kirkbride,
Britain's ambassador to Libya, reported that:

The most important means by which Egyptian influence is spread is through the
activities of the numerous Egyptian officials who are employed by the Libyan
authorities. It is not unnatural that, in the absence of trained Libyan candidates
for a vacancy, resort should be had to the engagement of Egyptians. Egypt is the
nearest source of supply for Arab officials, many part of the Libyan administration are modelled on the Egyptian pattern and lastly the Egyptian Government
continues to pay the salaries of Egyptian civil servants seconded to Libya and
allows them to draw, in addition, the Libyan salaries attached to their posts.
These Egyptians are, therefore, less costly to the Libyan Government than British
personnel or than unsubsidised Arabs from other Middle Eastern countries.
The most damage to British interests is being done by the considerable number
of Egyptian teachers who are employed in the Libyan schools. These people are in
a position to poison the mind of the rising generation of Libyans against the
Western Powers in general and against Great Britain in particular. (TNA – FO
371/108687, 1954)

Egyptian involvement in Libya extended beyond the administering classes: seconded professionals drafted the Libyan labour code (essentially the Egyptian labour code, with minor alterations), while the Libyan University, established in 1955, was initially staffed solely by Egyptian professors (*Middle East Report* 1961, 150). By 1956, *The New York Times* reported that Libya hosted 'large contingents of Egyptian teachers, advisers, and government administrators [whose] penetration into almost every field of Libyan life has become a matter of Western alarm. For these Egyptians are also helping carry on Premier Nasser's anti-Western campaign. There are almost 500 Egyptian teachers in Libyan secondary schools' (*The New York Times,* 24 May 1956). Within schools, seconded Egyptians taught a distinct, pro-Nasserite version of history:

The presence of Egyptian teachers explains why so many classrooms show the influence of Egyptian propaganda. Pupils do crayon drawings of Egyptian troops winning victories over Israel or Britain. In Benghazi, Libya, a complete course in Egyptian history is given to secondary school students. A display in a high school art exhibit showed pictures of the leading rulers of Egypt; on one side were the 'bad' rulers, on the other the 'good' rulers. The bad rulers began with the Pharaoh Cheops, who enslaved his people to build the pyramids, and ended with Farouk. The good rulers began with the idealistic Pharaoh Ikhnaton and ended with, of course, Gamal Abdel Nasser. (Wynn 1959, 137)

Teachers' work in Libya was aided by the fact that the textbooks used were printed and imported from Egypt, and hence were heavy on ideas of pan-Arabism and anti-Westernism. A seventh-grade reading book contained 'the elements that make the Arab student feel that a new spirit exists in him, and create in his character the pride in language, Arab nationalism and the Arab Nation'. A chapter under the title 'I am an Arab' states: 'I am an Arab. Yes, I say it with all pride and happiness. I am not alone. Every Arab is my brother in language, religion, feeling and nationhood . . . Yes, I am an Arab from Libya' (Obeidi 1999, 37). The broader effects of the Egyptian presence in Libya were arguably predictable: 'the people, particularly the schoolchildren, are always ready to applaud Nasser' (TNA – FO 407/236, 1957). Seconded Egyptians' political activism was widely known to the Libyan regime, which enjoyed Egypt's sponsorship but did not hesitate, in extreme cases, to take action against Egyptians. British diplomatic reports detail how, in July 1965, Libyan secret police were planted in secondary school classrooms to detect Egyptian teachers who were disseminating Nasserite ideas. Eighty Egyptians were sent back to Cairo, and were replaced by Tunisian teachers (TNA – FO 371/97338, 1952). According to British reports:

The planting of secret police in class-rooms in secondary schools may seem grotesque, but it is to be remembered that many of the twenty-one and twenty-two year old pupils are very grown up in appearance. Outwitted in the schools, the Egyptians have apparently turned to the mosques. Many Egyptian, Azhar-trained, sheikhs are now in Libya and use the pulpit (*minbar*) as a political forum. (TNA – FO 371/97338, 1952)

Expulsions of politically active Egyptian teachers occurred regularly across the Arab world – from Kuwait in the mid-1960s (Asmar 1990, 158), to Lebanon, where Egyptians were charged of 'inciting the Lebanese to revolt and paying money to foment revolution' (*The New York Times*, 5 July 1958). Saudi Arabia also expelled Egyptian teachers multiple times in the 1960s due to their political activism (Lackner 1978, 100; cf. 'Egypt's Campaign', *Monroe Collection*). Yet, Arab regimes' inability to find adequate numbers of replacement teachers elsewhere meant that such expulsions were only temporary. In Libya, King Idris had stated 'very emphatically' how he aimed to terminate the contracts of all Egyptians, and replace them by having 'all students do a period of schoolteaching before they were able to obtain employment, e.g. in government offices' as a type of 'national service', a plan that never materialised (TNA – FO 371/97338, 1952). 'Time and again, they have been expelled by various Arab governments for political agitation . . . in the end they are taken back. Arabs must become literate, and to do so they must accept Egyptian teachers' (Wynn 1959, 137).

A notable exception is Syria, with which Egypt formed the short-lived *al-Jumhūriya al-'Arabiyya al-Mutaḥḥida* (United Arab Republic – UAR, 1958–1962) at a time when Nasser's 'influence in the Arab world was at its height' (James 2006, 47; Podeh 1999). A year before the creation of the UAR, on 25 March 1957, the two states' Ministers of Education signed an agreement to unify their school curricula (TNA – FO 371/128222/1015, 1957).[1] Egypt proceeded to nominate the Egyptian Minister of Education, Kamal al-Din Husayn, as UAR Education Minister and the head of a United Teachers Council. Nasser began the process of transferring Egyptian professionals and army personnel to Syria, and vice versa (Podeh 1999). By mid-June 1958, 16,000–20,000 Egyptian soldiers had been relocated to Syria. The Syrian army, on the other hand, was reduced to 55,000 men (*al-Hayat*, 13 June 1958). In Damascus, seconded Egyptian teachers were expected to join the Syro-Egyptian Club, which had been established under the auspices of the Egyptian Embassy. According to diplomatic archives, 300 Egyptians served in the Education and Agriculture Ministries, while 130 were employed in the Public Works Ministry. During March–August 1960 alone, Americans estimated that 325 teachers, 29 doctors, 35 judges, and 150 engineers arrived in Damascus from Egypt (TNA – FO 371/134385, 1958).[2] The report argued that every Syrian ministry included a top Egyptian official who ran its affairs. In addition to seconded professionals, some 10,000–20,000 further Egyptians were working independently in Syria (Hofstadter 1973, 87).

Seconded Egyptians' reported desire to spread Nasserite ideals created an array of problems in Syria. Syrians equated Egyptian presence with Ottoman, French, and British colonialism, and seconded professionals' activities with Egyptian *tasallut* (domination). A common Syrian perception was that Egypt aimed to lower domestic unemployment by exporting Egyptians en masse to Syria (*al-Ahram*, 10 November 1961). Nasser's management of the UAR was deemed to be one of 'Egyptianization instead of unification'.[3] As Mahmud Riad, Nasser's adviser on Syrian affairs, noted: 'the term Egyptian *haymana* [hegemony] was often used when an Egyptian ... was found in a Syrian working place', while Riad himself was often characterised as a 'high commissioner' and a 'viceroy'. Mustafa al-Barudi, the Syrian Minister of Propaganda, complained that 'the smallest member of the (Egyptian) retinue thought that he had inherited our country. [Egyptians] spread "like octopuses" everywhere' (*Middle East Report* 1961, 619).[4]

The 1961 disintegration of the UAR signalled the return of Egyptians from Syria. In fact, the repatriation of Egyptians started within a day of the coup d'état that put an end to the union: Kamal Rif'at, the Minister of Labor, and Tharwat Ukashah, the Minister of Education, were reported to be on their way back to Egypt, accompanied by 85 Egyptians. The exodus via Lebanon started on 1 October. By 4 October, 7,000 Egyptian civilians had reportedly been repatriated (*al-Ahram*, 30 September 1961; *Middle East Report* 1961: 620). 'Who were the Egyptians in Syria?' Heikal asked. 'They were not in Damascus [and] they were not in Aleppo. They were engineers who went to supplement the Syrian engineers. They were doctors in the villages'. Attempting to ward off criticism of Egyptian secondees' conduct in Syria, Heikal argued that it was 'the voluntary, pioneering work of Egyptian technicians in Syria [that] gave rise to the charge that Egypt was unloading her unemployed on Syria' (*al-Ahram*, 10 November 1961). Nasser similarly commented: 'we are at a loss. If we send people to Syria, it is said that they have come to rule. If we do not send them, it is said that Egypt does not care' (TNA – FO 371/134385, 1958).

The abundant presence of trained local staff in Syria created pro-blems for Egypt's secondment policy that were not encountered else-where: already by 1956, the British alarmingly reported that 'the Egyptians have a definite policy which can be fairly easily defined [as] virulent and hostile propaganda' across the countries of the Arabian Gulf (TNA – BW 114/3–1956). While there exists, of course, a degree of exaggeration in the British reporting of the era, similar observations are found across other primary sources of the period. In Bahrain, Egyptians and other Arabs 'played a major role in the development of the political and cultural consciousness of [Arab] nationalism in Bahraini society', spreading Nasserite ideas and advocating for a constitution and representative institutions (Chalcraft 2010, 8). In Dubai, Egyptian intelligence officers were reported to have infil-trated groups of incoming teachers in order to incite students and spread Nasserite ideas (Davidson 2008, 41). Donald Hawley, a British diplomat stationed in Dubai in the late 1950s, describes in his memoirs how pictures of Nasser decorated school walls. He details how celebrations supporting Egyptian policies were held at a school event in 1961, while school sports days were usually employed for Nasserite speeches (Hawley 2007, 116). He also recalls young boys shouting out to him, 'Down with colonization and long live Gamal!' (Hawley 2007, 116). According to interviewees' recollections of events in Dubai:

[M]any young boys were encouraged by senior students and expatriate staff to demonstrate in the streets while carrying banners and photos of Jamal Abdel Nasser. Most worryingly, Sheikh Rashid's guards had to be called in to disperse the students, as it seemed that they were heading towards the only school in Dubai that was not participating in the agitation. (Davidson 2008, 41)

By 1957, Kuwait was 'heavily infiltrated with Egyptian influence', as *The New York Times* reported: 400 Egyptians were reported to be working within the Kuwaiti government, while only 97 out of the

1,100 teachers in the country were Kuwaiti citizens. Teachers were also reported to be inciting the nationalist movement against the Sabah regime, which was not able to expel them because of strong popular sympathy for Egypt, particularly in the aftermath of the 1956 War. The Suez Crisis led to a series of long strikes across Kuwait in October and November 1956, while some 4,000 Kuwaiti youths had officially volunteered to fight in Egypt, despite Sheikh Abdullah's strong disapproval. A countrywide boycott of British and French goods was organised by the Ministry of Education, and enforced by groups of seconded teachers. Abdul Aziz Husayn, the Ministry's Director, had been educated in Cairo, and 'naturally lean[ed] towards Egyptian educational methods and the employment of Egyptian teachers in Kuwaiti schools'. Until 1950, the Director of Education in Kuwait was, in fact, Egyptian (TNA – FO 464/12, 1956). According to British reports, the boycott's enforcement was organised by

'young women patrols (mostly Egyptian teachers) who started going round in twos and threes visiting shops and preaching to the shopkeepers the sin of selling to the foreigner. Their methods are "highly abusive and large and small merchants are warned by the patrols that they are being watched and that any slackness on their part, or if one English woman was seen in their shops, a report would straightaway be sent to the "Cultural Club", whence orders would at once go out to have their shop windows broken. These young women patrols have been seen at work', the report concludes, 'but it would appear that all are Egyptians'. (TNA – FO 371/120558, 1956)

Overall, 'the education system and the social clubs [were] completely Egyptian influenced', while Egyptians pressured for sharing of the oil profits across all Arabs: 'Egyptians have said that Kuwait's oil is Arab oil and that in the interests of the Arab people all Arab resources should be shared among all the Arabs' (*The New York Times*, 15 March 1957). A particularly striking display of Egyptian teachers' influence in Kuwait, that mirrors the Egyptian regime's wish for external legitimation, was the Sports Gala of Kuwaiti Secondary Schools in Shuwaikh, held in May 1957 and featuring 2,100 student participants from 26 schools across the country. According to an eye-witness report of the event:

The tune which welcomed spectators just before the gala began was that of the favourite song of 'Voice of the Arabs'. It was entitled, 'Woe to the Colonisers'.

The historical tableaux which appeared in the programme included: a representation of the battle of Port Said, which took the form of a float bearing a boat with sailors and an effigy of a descending parachutist. The sailors in the boat were shooting down the parachutist. Written in large letters on the side of the float was: 'Get out of my Canal'.

A physical training display which was the last event in the programme, consisted of exercises performed to the tune of a song specially composed for the occasion by an Egyptian inspector of education. Each verse of this song recalled one of the Arab states: Egypt was represented as the champion of Arab freedom and the repeller of the aggressors; Yemen as the protector of Aden who was called upon to liberate her; Syria was described as the home of true nationalism, while Iraqis were the subject of sarcastic praise for their skill in picking dates with their finger-tips'.

These points together with the lengthy displays in which hundreds of small boys took part with air-rifles, made this gala nearer in character to a military rally than to a sporting event. (TNA – FO 371/126899, 1957)

Similarly, Egyptian teachers were welcomed in Qatar, which did not develop a formal educational system until the mid-1950s, because Sheikh Ali Abdullah al-Thani 'did not accept the idea of modern education until 1956' (Misnad 1985, 35). The Iraq, on the other hand, was less amenable to seconded Egyptians' political activism: in early 1957, the Iraqi government claimed that 'teachers were a potent factor in the spread of Nasser propaganda and that they helped incite youths to demonstrations that resulted in eleven deaths [in November 1956], mostly in Mosul. [Teachers were found to] have agitated against the regime by encouraging students to howl on streets for severance of relations with Britain and France'. As a result, *The New York Times* reported how twenty-five Egyptian teachers were expelled, albeit in an operation that was 'carried out with restraint', and which spared university professors, 'who are still needed' (*The New York Times*, 17 May 1957). The animosity between Egypt and Iraq subsided in the immediate aftermath of the 1958 Iraqi Revolution: 'co-operation with the UAR is being steadily pursued in the educational field', the British reported, 'both in matters of syllabus and in the recruitment of Egyptian teachers, and Egyptian experts have been accepted in the Codification Department of the Ministry of Justice, in the Oil Affairs Department of the Ministry of Economics, and in the Government Oil Refineries Administration' (TNA – FO 481/12–1958).

Beyond the Arabian Gulf, it was in the context of the 1962–70 Civil War in North Yemen that Nasser's secondment policy was most extensively employed for the support of pro-Egyptian regimes abroad. While Nasser's increasing engagement in the conflict and the travails of more than 60,000 Egyptian soldiers in Yemen is well known (Dawisha 1975, Ferris 2013), little research has been conducted in seconded Egyptians' involvement in Yemen throughout this period. Nasser, eager to promote a nationalist uprising in Yemen since the mid-1950s, was initially supposed to send teachers and other professionals to Yemen at the request of Crown Prince Muhammad al-Badr, the oldest son of Imam Ahmed bin Yahya, in 1959. This request was formally cancelled by the Imam himself, who was aware of Egyptians' political activism in Yemen: earlier, on 20 March 1958, a 'crowd of roughly five hundred led by Egyptian teachers, marched with flares to the [Yemeni] Palace'; a few days later, 'all Egyptian teachers' in Sana'a marched 'together with 2,000 demonstrators' towards the Saudi Arabia Delegation in Sana'a, where they 'broke into the courtyard and smashed all the windows'. The Yemeni Imam apologised to King Saud in a cable, noting 'we are Arab brothers and must accept sorrow with good heart' (TNA – CO 1015/1267–1959).

Cairo continued dispatching Egyptian teachers and other professionals across Yemen with the Imam's tacit permission (see Figure 3.3), as their presence was deemed necessary for the country's process of modernisation, despite the fact that they were known to engage in political activism: 'to the pervading influence of Cairo radio among the common people and intellectuals', a 1958 British report notes, 'should be added the disproportionate influence of the Egyptian teachers in Sana'a and Ta'izz' (TNA – CO 1015/1267–1959). In 1959, seconded Egyptians began arriving with their families in Hodeida, where the Imam 'welcomed', them by declaring that Yemen was 'waiting for UAR experts to start building the first Yemeni spinning and textile factory' (*BBC radio broadcast*, 19 January 1959). As O' Ballance explains:

Partly because there was no alternative, Egyptians working in the country as military instructors, school teachers and doctors, all subtly and insidiously aided the spread of Nasser's views. Under the Crown Prince's urging, Imam Ahmed had allowed some Egyptian school teachers into the Yemen to start a few secular schools and to give advanced education to sons of richer families, and their number had been increased during the Imam's absence in Italy. All this had a profound effect on young, restless, impressionable minds in the Yemen [resulting in the August 1962] demonstrations in some of

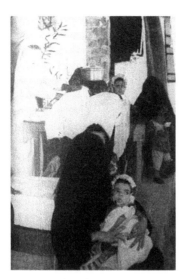

Figure 3.3 Egyptian nurses employed in Yemen
(*Arab Observer*, 5 October 1964)

the secular schools against alleged approval by the Imam of the American bases in Saudi Arabia. (O' Ballance 1971, 63)

In particular, the arrival of Sayed Abdul Ghani Mabrouk, Mahmoud Mohamed Mahmoud, and Hindawi Yaseen Hindi – three teachers Egypt seconded to the Ta'izz School in Yemen in January 1959 – led the British to report that 'the school in Ta'izz [was] now controlled by the Egyptians'. British reports argued that:

All three are believed to have been especially selected by the Egyptian government. Their teaching of course follows the usual line of the unity of the Arabs and the infallibility of Nasser. The leader is Abdel Ghani Mabrouk, an athletic type and a boxer who has the admiration of the students. He played a leading role in the Accession and Port Said celebrations in November and December. We also learn that he was active earlier in his career in Libya, where he is alleged to have been imprisoned for political activities and indecency. (TNA – CO 1015/1267–1959)

A few months later a number of different pamphlets, originating from Egypt, were intercepted by the British in Ta'izz (see Figure 3.4). One read:

Oh sons of Yemen, the army and the people! Your brothers in the United Arab Republic and the Republic of Iraq know everything about you. All of them wish to rid themselves of the cheating gang which adopt guile and lies ... All the Arabs are with us if, in the first place, we can prove that we are with each other. We must march to the battle lines and those free rebels who toppled Farouk and Faisal would not abandon us. (TNA – CO 1015/1267–1959)

Another intercepted pamphlet that was being distributed in Yemen read:

Do not clap for Gamal. Oh sons of Yemen whose hearts are shaken whenever Gamal is mentioned and whose tongues constantly speak of him. Gamal Abdel Nasser does not need your applause nor does he require your admiration. ... Your biggest compliment to Gamal would be when you united together and organise yourselves, eliminating the monarchy and declaring the birth of the new Yemeni People's Republic, as your brothers have done in Iraq ... The nation is above all and under no rule but that of the people. (TNA – CO 1015/1267–1959)

Once Iman bin Yahya died in September 1962, Abdullah al-Sallal challenged the legitimacy of Mohamad al-Badr by announcing the creatio of the Yemen Arab Republic. Effectively, the royalists, headed by al-Badr, now the new Imam, and backed by Saudi Arabia, were pitied against the republicans, headed by al-Sallal and supported by Egypt. Confidential archival documents report how al-Sallal,

appealed to Egypt primarily for support against potential foreign interven-tion, from Saudi Arabia or the British in Aden, and for Egyptian technical and administrative help. Consequently, Egypt moved into Yemen, not only with tanks, jets and soldiers, but also with almost 300 primary and secondary school teachers, administrative advisors, doctors for the new hospitals (Rahmy 1983, 143).[5]

By 1964, the *Arab Observer*, a mouthpiece for the Egyptian regime, was reporting that Egypt had helped establish fourteen hospitals staffed by thirty Egyptian doctors, a psychiatric hospital in Sana'a, a veterinary administration, and two agricultural institutes. According to Abdel Rahman al-Attar, an Egyptian engineer serving as the Director of the Technical Aid Office for Yemen,

The UAR took great care to send to Yemen the best teams and experts in spite of their being badly needed in the UAR ... Experts from the UAR Ministry of Scientific Research and the Ministry of Agriculture were sent to Yemen ...

Figure 3.4 Egyptian pamphlets intercepted in Yemen
(The National Archives, CO 1015/1267–1959)

Economists and finance experts were also seconded to Yemen and the result was the emergence of a State Budget covering the expenses and revenues for a whole year; the first of its kind in the history of Yemen. (quoted in *Arab Observer*, 5 October 1964)

Egyptians' presence in Yemen was instrumental in developing the country's infrastructure. According to *The New York Times* correspondent's account:

I was impressed also by the extent of the Egyptians' 'hearts and minds' campaign among the Yemenis [such as] installing water pumps, school-teaching and providing all kinds of professional services and advice – agricultural, engineering and medical. These were all ways of introducing the Yemenis to modern life, ways in which the Egyptians could do things for the Yemeni people which their traditional leaders could not. The Egyptians had also brought 100 Egyptian ulema into the country, in the hopes of persuading the Yemenis that there were really no important differences between the Sunnis and the Shia in general, and the Shaffei and Zeidi sects in particular.

They may even have tried to persuade the Zeidis that they did not really need an Imam. (Schmidt 1968, 208)

Yet, to a certain extent Egypt repeated the same critical mistake that had caused friction in Syria, by adopting an air of superiority against the Yemenis. Heikal wrote how Yemen is 'a backward and medieval country. While some Arabs live in the twentieth century . . . others find themselves still existing in the conditions of the thirteenth century' *al-Ahram* (19 October 1957). This did not go unnoticed in Yemen: 'The republic needed Egyptian help and protection, but the condescension of Egyptian teachers, experts and officials infuriated the quick, intelligent Yemenis' (Schmidt 1968, 55). 'You would not believe what goes on in Sana'a', President Nasser complained. 'Half of the Ministers never go to their offices, and the other half don't know what to do when they get there' (Dawisha 1975, 55).

Figure 3.5 Egyptian military in Sana'a (Schmidt 1968, 154)
Egyptian instructor at the San'a military academy showing a Yemeni how to use a bayonet affixed to a Mosin-Nagant rifle.

Figure 3.6 Infrastructure in Yemen built by Egyptians
(*Arab Observer*, 5 October 1964)

Conclusion

Egypt is the biggest Arab country and the greatest source of human talent in the Arab world. It was Egyptians who brought about the renaissance in many Arab countries. The universities were set up by Egyptian professors and the newspapers were set up by Egyptian journalists. The institutes of art, cinema, and theatre were set up by Egyptian artists. The cities and houses were built by Egyptian architects, the hospitals were established by Egyptian doctors, and even the laws and constitutions there were mostly drawn up by Egyptian law professors … The Arab oil-producing countries are indebted to Egyptians in everything they have achieved. It was Egyptians who taught them at school and at university, who planned and supervised the construction of their cities, who set up radio and television stations, and who drafted their constitutions and their laws … The Algerian national anthem itself was composed by the Egyptian composer, Mohamed Fawzi.

Alaa Al-Aswany (2011, 127)

Labour emigration features in the workings of non-democratic powers both domestically, as the previous chapter has demonstrated, but also internationally, as a strategy of external legitimation. In the context of Egypt under Nasser, this chapter has highlighted how high-skilled professionals were employed by the regime in supporting like-minded political movements abroad, in tandem with the priorities of Nasserism: anti-colonial ideals, anti-Western rhetoric, and pro-Egyptian, pan-Arabist agenda. It outlined the long history of Egypt's educational system, which endowed the state with the capacity to cater to its Arab neighbours' educational and developmental needs through the dispatch of trained professionals. This fledgling policy was organised, systematised, and politicised under the Free Officers regime, which was eager to establish its rule. The Egyptian state developed a well-defined policy of incentivising regional emigration of professionals, as the organised dispatch abroad of thousands of teachers, doctors, and other professionals allowed the regime to project its prevailing political vision across host states in Africa and the Middle East. The second part of the chapter examined the type of political activism that Egyptians engaged in across the Arab world, again highlighting how high-skilled, short-term migration was able to enhance the Egyptian regime's regional political aims.

Chapters 2 and 3 focused on the politics of Egyptian labour emigration under the reign of Nasser, between the 1952 Free Officers Revolution and his death in 1970. They identified how policy-making on matters of labour emigration was not driven solely by economic considerations, but reflected the regime's multiple political priorities, both domestically and internationally. Yet, by the mid-1960s and, in particular, after the 1967 Arab–Israeli War, things had started to change. Domestically, even if a restrictive emigration policy contributed to the regime's goals of state developmentalism during the 1950s, this was no longer the case for a state near the brink of bankruptcy in the late 1960s: as numerous elites and experts highlighted to the Egyptian president, a permissive emigration policy would be economically beneficial for the state, if combined with a reorientation of the economy towards the free market. Yet, despite some isolated experiments with population mobility agreements, Nasser was never politically comfortable with espousing labour emigration, as it would contradict the Free Officers' claims on a wealthy, strong, Non-Aligned Egypt. It would also arguably complicate his efforts at containing any opposition actors within state borders and dealing with them accordingly. Similarly, the subsidisation of high-skilled, short-term regional emigration entailed a significant economic burden for the Egyptian state. Yet the policy reflected the regional political ambitions of the Free Officers. The Egyptian regime under Nasser employed emigration policy as a tool towards expanding its political power, both domestically and internationally, irrespective of the economic cost – but, by the time of Nasser's death, the situation was completely different. It was up to his successor, Anwar Sadat, an untested, largely unknown military officer, to revise how Egypt's emigration policy would support the ruling regime in the post-1970 era.

4 | 'Our Most Precious Asset'

The Domestic Politics of Migration Liberalisation

Anwar Sadat was following the line of Nasser,
but with an eraser at hand.

Hamdeen Sabahi (*al-Akhbar English*, 23 May 2012)

Chapters 2 and 3 demonstrated the twin labour emigration policy of the Egyptian regime between 1952 and 1970, the year of Nasser's death. Chapters 4 and 5 explore how emigration policy reflected the political aims of the ruling regime following Nasser's death. In sharp contrast to the restrictive measures of the Nasserite period, Sadat adopted a permissive labour emigration policy almost immediately upon coming to power, in 1971, which has been in place ever since. This chapter explores this shift and the political rationale behind it with regard to ensuring the ruling regime's durability. It begins with a brief discussion of Anwar Sadat, particularly the prevalent perception of him as a weaker political leader than Nasser. This paves the way for an understanding of how Sadat embarked on a transformation of state emigration policy in order to achieve three goals: firstly, a permissive emigration policy allowed Sadat to differentiate himself from his predecessor, complementing a process of *de-Nasserisation* that was embodied in the *Corrective Revolution* of 15 May 1971 and served as an instrument of internal legitimation. At the same time, it facilitated the regime's low-intensity repression tactics, encouraging political dissenters to move abroad and fostering the (re-)emergence and gradual empowerment of the Muslim Brotherhood. Finally, a permissive emigration policy facilitated the regime's co-optation of business elites that benefitted from, and espoused, economic liberalisation and unrestricted population mobility.

The emergence of a new emigration policy for Egypt occurred following Nasser's unexpected death on 28 September 1970. This signalled a complex political process, for Nasser had not prepared anyone to succeed him. The precarious position of Sadat at this critical juncture is key to understanding the shift in Egypt's emigration policy within a broader framework of the regime's internal restructuring. Despite the fact that Sadat held the official title of vice-president, he had only been assigned to the position less than a year earlier, in December 1969. This appointment had been the fortuitous result of the president's insecure 'insistence on rotating the vice presidency among nonthreatening candidates'. On top of that, his personality was no match for Nasser's larger-than-life image: Sadat 'was perceived as weak and unpopular within and outside the ranks [for] unlike most Free Officers, he had never seen war' (Kandil 2012, 99; cf. Waterbury 1983, 307). During the 1948 Arab–Israeli War, for example, when his fellow military officers were fighting in Palestine, Sadat was a prison runaway in Egypt. Furthermore, 'his career under the revolution had been among the less spectacular', and he was a far cry from Nasser's energy and charisma. Nasser 'had a seemingly unassailable place in the national esteem, as the son of Egypt who had thrown off the foreign yoke' (Lippman 1989, 25); in sharp contrast, 'as a personality, Sadat inspired neither awe nor envy' (Cooper 1982, 66). Others considered him a 'a political opportunist, a "trimmer"' (Hopwood 1991, 105), or an 'unknown quantity [without] the deep respect enjoyed by his predecessor' (Brand 2014, 69). The possibility of Sadat succeeding Nasser was seen as a *nukta* (a joke) (Shukri 1981, 37). For Henry Kissinger, the new Egyptian president initially appeared to be nothing more than a 'political clown' (Kissinger 1979, 1276).

Even Nasser would refer to Sadat as *Bikbāshi Aywa*, or Colonel Yesman (Dawisha 1985, 6; Beattie 2000, 43). A common joke pertained to how Sadat got the *zabīb*, the dark prayer bump on one's forehead that served as a symbol of Muslim piety, and which would become key in his later image as *al-Ra'īs al-Mu'min* (the Pious President). It had come not from repeated contact with the prayer mat, but from Nasser poking him in the forehead whenever Sadat tried to speak his mind in cabinet meetings. Heikal argued that 'part of the trouble was Sadat's own character'. He explained:

[Sadat] had never had the education – or, indeed, the time – to give serious consideration to the problems that were going to confront him. He had no real understanding of Egyptian history ... He enjoyed the trappings of supreme power without appreciating the responsibilities [that] go with it. Nor did he understand the true nature of Egypt's relations with the rest of the

Arab world ... The subtleties of leadership, the inevitable give-and-take demanded of it, completely eluded him. (Heikal 1983, 62)

Despite his constitutional right to the presidency and the 17 October 1970 national plebiscite, granting Sadat a margin of 90 per cent, his actual battle for political power was just beginning. Given the factionalism that existed within Egyptian politics, Sadat's tenure was far from secure (Ansari 1986, 154). Political figures of the Nasserite years vied for power, including Zakariya Muhi al-Din, Sha'rawi Jum'a, and Samy Sharaf. Most importantly, 'Ali Sabri, now Vice-President, was a key figure of the political Left with ties to the Egyptian intelligence. Sabri controlled the Arab Socialist Union (ASU), the sole legal political organisation of the time. Under Nasser, these political figures had been identified as *marākiz quwwa* (centres of power), given their hold over key parts of the Egyptian state apparatus: repressive, political, and economic (Amin 1989, 83). Sadat, a politically inexperienced man of rightist leanings, was now competing with political stalwarts of the Nasserite years. Perhaps most troublingly of all, he faced the impossible task of living up to his predecessor. For all of Nasser's shortcomings, his appeal remained extremely strong across Egyptian society – Nasser's funeral had drawn millions to the streets of Cairo and Alexandria (Lippman 1989, 1) – and Sabri's group aimed to 'control domestic and foreign policies in the name of Nasserism' (Ansari 1986, 158). Sadat's initial promises that he would continue Nasser's visions and policies were met with distrust, if not disdain. As his daughter, Camelia Sadat, cautiously wrote in her memoirs: 'I believe Father had doubts that the Egyptian people would accept him as their leader, since Nasser had been so charismatic' (Sadat 1985, 99). Overall, "the ghost of Nasser" haunted Sadat's early time in power.[1]

In a clear effort to differentiate himself from his predecessor, Sadat embarked on a 'dramatic' reform and strengthening of the laws on desequestration and property confiscation, on 20 December 1970. This was a first step towards marking his own path through a decision that was anathema to the Nasserites and the Egyptian Left (Beattie 2000, 49). But it was Sadat's proposal to create the Federal Arab Republic, a union of Syria, Egypt, and Libya, that provoked a *bras-de-fer* with Sabri: through Sabri's intervention, Sadat's proposal was duly defeated at the ASU Executive Committee, which had been 'virtually taken over' by these 'centres of power' since 1967 (Lippman 1989, 30). The president's response to this challenge on his authority was immediate: he dismissed Sabri from the ASU's Supreme Executive Committee and purged from the party three other ASU members: Abu al-Nur, Labib Shuqayr, and Dia' al-Din Dawud. He publicly declared that an attempt at a coup d'état had occurred, and duly arrested Sha'rawi Guma'a (an ASU Supreme Executive Committee member), General Muhammad Fawzi Hakhu (Minister of War), Sami Sharaf (Minister of State), Muhammad Fa'iq (Minister of Information), Sa'd Zayid (Minister of Housing), and Hilmi al-Sa'd, who was the Minister of Electricity (Dekmejian 1971, 309). By December 1971, as part of the Corrective Revolution, 'ninety-one Nasserist politicians and senior officers, who were arrested in May, had been sentenced to various prison terms', including Sabri himself (Stacher 2012, 53).

Yet, despite what *The New York Times* reported as a 'masterly lesson of how to proceed from quasi-importance toward supreme power', the socialist ideas that permeated, and supported, the leftist opposition to Sadat remained strong both across the regime and across Egyptian society (*The New York Times*, 18 July 1971). Even in the aftermath of the Corrective Revolution, Nasser's presence remained palpable (Brand 2014, 70). Sadat had to continue the political fight for domestic survival that pitted him against the old Nasserite ideology in pursuit of a constituency of his own. That said, his early attempt at reversing Nasser's sequestration laws had born fruit: 'his property de-sequestrations were heartening to a broad range of civilian political and economic interests in urban and rural areas alike' (Beattie 2000, 92). But Sadat needed to think more ambitiously, and act on a larger scale; thus, on 27 May 1971, Sadat appointed a new committee to draft Egypt's new *Permanent* Constitution – so named in order to differentiate it from Nasser's various "provisional" constitutional declarations. One of the most striking statements of the new document, which was drafted, submitted to a popular referendum, and quickly put in effect before the end of 1971, was Article 52's declaration that 'citizens shall now have the right to permanent or temporary migration' (Arab Republic of Egypt 1971).

Exorcising Nasser's Ghost:
Labour Emigration and Regime Legitimation under Sadat

The first day Anwar Sadat got into Nasser's limousine as Egypt's new president, he waited until the car reached a crossroads, and then asked

the chauffer: 'Where did *al-Ra'īs* [the president] turn here?' The driver
replied, 'He turned left'. 'Signal left, and then turn right', ordered Sadat.

Popular Egyptian joke

From the moment he rose to power, Sadat was driven by an emphasis
on individual freedom, economic liberalisation, and a careful move
away from Nasserism. His early promises to continue on the ideological path of Nasser – espousing Arab socialism, state developmentalism,
and a Non-Aligned foreign policy– were gradually set aside, as the new
president sought to make his own mark on Egyptian politics. 'His tactic
was to embrace the legitimacy of the 1952 Revolution and its goals –
independence, prosperity, egalitarianism', Lippman wrote, 'while dis-
mantling its works – state socialism, futile confrontation, police state
government – as aberrations or deviations to be corrected' (Lippman
1989, 29). Sadat rightly perceived that, in the post-1967 era, the ideals
of Nasserism had lost much of their stamina; in any case, he did not
seek to be – indeed, could not afford to be – compared to Nasser. This
section explains how the liberalisation of emigration policy uniquely
complemented the descriptive and material legitimation strategies of
the Egyptian regime under Sadat, particularly from the prism of de-
Nasserisation.

By 1971, Sadat had proclaimed the need to view freedom of movement as a personal right that contradicted Nasserite values, effectively
using Egypt's permissive emigration policy as a strategy towards
descriptive legitimation. While some initial limitations on emigration
were put on specific professions, the regime proceeded with the full
lifting of all restrictions in the aftermath of the Corrective Revolution.
In doing so, the president consistently employed a language of liberalisation, which marked the difference between himself and his predecessor. 'In the Nasser years', Lippman argued, 'individuals had not
been permitted to possess foreign currency. Now, worker remittances
became a crucial component of Egypt's foreign exchange earnings'
(Lippman 1989, 107). Employing state-owned newspapers and
the *October* magazine (which was effectively a mouthpiece of the
Sadat entourage), the president tried to generate a discourse on civil
and political liberties, as well as 'individual freedom and initiative ...
while alluding to Nasser's errors over economic policy' (Vatikiotis
1991, 427).

If one keeps in mind the earlier emphasis placed on Egyptians' rejection of migration, the distance between Nasser and Sadat on this issue becomes painstakingly clear. The abolition of any restrictions on Egyptians' emigration was tied to a sustained language of liberalisation that purposefully set itself against the Nasserite ideals. For one, the Sadat regime invited back Nasserite-era political dissenters in late 1971, under the rubric of its liberalised emigration policy (*Akhbar el-Yom*, 22 October 1971). *Al-Ahram* printed an emotionally charged letter by an Egyptian called Ibrahim Saeda, who had 'committed an offence against [his] homeland and repented'. The former dissident was now very happy to return to Egypt (*al-Ahram*, 22 October 1971). State newspapers printed cables from such returnees to President Sadat. One reads:

On my own behalf and in the name of hundreds of other Egyptians who were deprived of their nationality for strange reasons and stranger accusations, I thank you. We have been living in countries to which we do not belong and without a nationality to boast of until we heard of your historic decision, which restored to us our nationality and our dear homeland. We thank your Excellency. (*al-Ahram*, 22 October 1971)

Certain changes in emigration policy were employed in order to solidify the image of Sadat as independent of Nasser. For instance, the regime had state media note that Sadat personally ordered authorities to begin issuing passports within 24 hours – a far cry from the bureaucratic labyrinth that existed in the pre-1970 era (Rousillon 1985, 2). Egyptians' passport validity was later further extended from two to seven years (Lesch 1986, 5), while embassies abroad were able to renew them without having to go through the Interior Ministry (Talani 2010, 65). Even the policy of organised secondment, a key aspect of the pre-1970 era, was gradually replaced by individual secondment (Roy 1991, 555). Such measures enjoyed tremendous popular support. At the same time, Sadat decided to grant a general amnesty to all young Egyptians who had emigrated abroad during the previous decade in order to escape mandatory conscription under Nasser (and who had found themselves unable to return to Egypt, where they would be imprisoned upon re-entry). Sadat even dispatched military delegations abroad to invite Egyptians who had escaped the draft to return. This reversal of Nasserite policy, effectively pardoning a tactic that had been increasingly employed by middle-class Egyptian families under Nasser, only served to increase Sadat's popularity (Ali E. Hillal Dessouki, *personal interview*). By the mid-1970s, the Minister of War also exempted from conscription any Egyptian men aged 25–30 whose families had emigrated (Dessouki 1982, 59).

Very importantly, in the post-1971 period, the Egyptian state ceased collecting statistical data on emigration flows. The detailed state report, entitled *Population Movements across the Frontiers*, published annually since 1968, abruptly suspended its publication in 1973, just as Egyptian emigration was beginning to gain momentum (cf. Amin and Awni 1986, 2). As a result, no public state data exists as to the exact number of Egyptian emigrants in the post-1970 era, with estimates varying enormously. This statistical lacuna has traditionally been attributed to the inability of Egyptian state officials to keep count of outmigration and to the difficulty of measuring such frequently clandestine or irregular movements: one cannot be sure, the argument goes, that Egyptians travelling abroad are doing so in pursuit of employment or for other purposes, or if they intend to return. In fact, this was a political, top-down decision: the Egyptian regime instructed state officials to retreat from administering any effective control over emigration, including keeping count of emigration-related statistics, under the aegis of full liberalisation (Kareem Amin, *personal interview*). This key point has been corroborated by a number of other interviewees; namely, that the post-1970 absence of reliable statistics is not due to the Egyptian bureaucracy's institutional deficiencies, or the difficulty of measuring emigration, but was a distinctly political decision. As LaTowsky argues:

Paradoxically given the scale of this labor movement, the historical responsibility of the Egyptian bureaucracy for the centralized planning and allocation of domestic factors of production (including labor), and a developed tradition of demographic enumeration dating from the last century, accurate and comprehensive figures for this number of Egyptians working and/or residing abroad are non-existent. Nor can such statistics be found in the public records of almost all labor importers, including Saudi Arabia and Libya, where Egyptians are most predominant. The notable exception is Kuwait, whose annual labor statistics are valuable resources ... Such deliberate omissions are born out of political calculation. Few governments involved in this massive transfer of labor desire the accountability and public review implied by such information. (LaTowsky 1984, 12)

The regime's decision to stop collecting statistical data on Egyptian emigration served regional and domestic political purposes. In terms of regional politics, the absence of statistical records facilitated Sadat's goal of convincing Arab states to admit as much Egyptian labour as possible. As will be described in more detail in Chapter 5, the Gulf states were particularly apprehensive due to the political repercussions of Arab immigration, and the absence of sending-state statistics was aimed at appeasing their fears. But in terms of domestic politics, Sadat was clearly aiming to 'establish his own print'; or, to draw yet another differentiation between himself and Nasser (Bahgat Korany, *personal interview*), and to complement the regime's descriptive legitimation strategies. Thus, this decision served the broader regime strategy towards post-1971 de-Nasserisation. The difference was striking, particularly if one bears in mind the precision with which the Nasserite state measured emigration and immigration, and duly made statistics publicly available throughout the 1954–70 period. According to Awad, this decision similarly aimed to illustrate that Egypt was now a state where citizens were free from Nasserite-era restrictive accounting and paperwork (*personal interview*).

What is important in terms of this study's argumentation is that Sadat did not hesitate to assume all responsibility for this massive policy shift, most likely in an attempt to profit from the fact that these reforms moved away from 'the harsher aspects of Nasser's rule [, and were] immensely popular' (Carroll 1982, 63). The inclusion of a provision on emigration policy in the new constitution is a clear indication of this tactic. The 1971 constitution was a document meant to serve as a testament to Sadat's personality and to reflect his own values, which did not necessarily coincide with his predecessor's. As previously mentioned, the very designation "permanent" aimed to differentiate the document from the constitutions that Nasser had put forth in his time (Ansari 1986, 171). In terms of migration, Sadat explained his rationale quite clearly: in the past, he wrote, Egyptians had been 'turned into puppets. They became *duma* [dummies] in the hands of their rulers, who did with them as they pleased. People were not allowed to travel' (Sadat 1978a, 289). Under his rule, however, a citizen's repertoire of actions was shaped around the ideal of personal freedom: this statement did not replicate the Free Officers' Revolution values espoused by Nasser, but those of the Corrective Revolution. Sadat often repeated similar assertions: 'First, I want to make it clear that if we do not hold to the complete freedom of the individual in the shadow of competition, we cannot realize any progress. He who wants to travel, let him travel' (quoted in Cooper 1982, 97). This strategy tied a permissive emigration policy to the descriptive legitimation of the ruling regime, which highlighted aspects of personal freedom. 'All young people want to go abroad', 'Ali Hamdi al-Jammal summed up in his 'People's Talk' column for al-Ahram. 'This is their right, which no one can deny' (al-Ahram, 6 July 1974). Under Nasser 'censorship was in force. Travel was restricted. Economic activity was calcified by restraints', Lipmann argued, espousing the Sadat-era rhetoric. In turn, 'Sadat peeled this structure away layer by layer. In 11 years as president, from 1970 to 1981, Sadat lifted from Egypt the fear of war and death that had hung over every family for a generation' (Lippman 1989, 6). As Sadat wrote in his memoirs, '[f]reedom is the most beautiful, holy and precious fruit of our culture; an individual should never be made to feel that he is at the mercy of any force or coercion or that his will is subjected to that of others' (Sadat 1978a, 78).

The lack of reliable data on emigration flows – which, as discussed, served the regime's de-Nasserisation goals – also conveniently allowed the Sadat regime to grossly inflate estimates of Egyptians abroad (Lesch 1986), given that the state was no longer releasing statistical records of migrants. In 1978, for instance, while the International Labour Organization estimated 403,908 Egyptian emigrants to be working in Arab countries, al-Ahram put the number at 1,390,000 (Oweiss 1980, 203). In 1982, the Ministry of Labour put the number of Egyptians abroad at 3 million, while the Central Bureau of Statistics estimated them at 1,600,000 (al-Siyassa al-Dawliya, No. 73, July 1983). The inflation of statistics served to normalise the phenomenon of mass emigration, thereby contributing to the regime's goal of descriptive legitimation. One key example of this is the president's response to protesting university students in mid-1971: in a long session he held with the protesters' representatives, he instructed them to pursue the opportunity of seeking employment abroad (thereby encouraging political opponents to emigrate, as seen earlier in this chapter). Without any statistical data to verify his claims, Sadat went on to argue that 'there had never been as many young people migrating as there have been this year' (quoted in MENA, 10 October 1971).

But beyond descriptive legitimation, the shift to a permissive emigration policy was aimed at enhancing the regime's material legitimation tactics. It is important to note that the popularity of labour emigration was partly based on the vast differences in wages between Egypt and Arab host states (See Table 4.1). It was often observed that 'during the 1970s an unskilled rural Egyptian would earn *thirty times* more money working at a Saudi construction site than he could on an Egyptian farm' (Cammett et al. 2015, 390). As *The Washington Post* reported:

It is in the villages that the deepest changes seem to be taking place as Egypt's poorer come into heretofore-unimaginable wealth and opportunities. In the past decade, the standard farm wage has soared from half a pound – less than a dollar – for a dawn-to-dusk workday to five pounds for an eight-hour one, complete with a meal, cigarettes and tea breaks. Tenant farmers suddenly have become landowners, and illiterate peasants, or their sons, have become plumbers, carpenters and masons, earning $9 to $12 a day. This is four or five times the wage of the village teacher or civil servant. (*Washington Post*, 29 January 1985)

A similarly striking phenomenon occurred with skilled professionals' wages. In 1980, Messiha calculated that, during the four or five years that seconded Egyptian teachers spend in Kuwait or Saudi Arabia, they receive an amount of money that vastly exceeds their prospective earnings in Egypt for the entirety of their professional life (Messiha 1980, 61–63). According to *The New York Times*:

Table 4.1 *Wages in Egyptian pounds, local and foreign*

Activity Sector	Average Local Wage	Average Foreign Wage	Ratio of Foreign / Local
Agriculture	141	596	4.2
Mining	465	1,454	3.1
Construction	388	484	1.2
Transportation and Storage	472	1,502	3.2
Finance	356	2,684	7.5
Services	528	1,364	2.6

Source: Zaki 1980, 598

Table 4.2 *Estimated number of Egyptian regional migrants, 1975–1983*

Year	Number of Migrants	Employed Manpower in Egypt	Migrants to Manpower Ratio
1975	520,000	9,606,000	5.4 %
1976	750,000	9,946,000	7.8 %
1978	1,400,000	10,216,000	13.7 %
1980	1,600,000	11,057,000	14.4 %
1981	2,300,000	11,600,000	19.8 %
1983	2,900,000	12,110,000	23.9 %

Source: Feiler 1986, 11

Schoolteachers, notoriously underpaid in Egypt, can earn five times as much in hard currency abroad. An office manager can quadruple his salary to about $10,000 a year by going to Kuwait. One prominent Egyptian surgeon who goes to Saudi Arabia to operate every year said that he made more than $8,500 in two weeks during his latest trip, four times what he would have earned in his busiest comparable period in Cairo. (*The New York Times*, 8 July 1979)

Mohie El-Din's 1980 survey research revealed that a university professor's maximum salary was LE 150/month, while earnings over thirty years would be LE 48.600; the same professor in Kuwait would earn LE 1,750 per month plus free housing, or LE 84.000 in four years – in other words, more money in four years in Kuwait than thirty years in Egypt (Mohie El-Din 1980). In 1985, the *Washington Post* calculated that an Egyptian teacher with a master's degree could save up to $12,000 a year in Saudi Arabia, when the wage in rural Egypt would be $600 to $720 a year (*Washington Post*, 29 January 1985).

The regime was well aware of these wage discrepancies. Dr Abdel Meguid al-Abd, deputy minister of labour in the 1970s, stated that

if I pay an auto mechanic 18 pounds a month, he has to take another job to support his family and when he is offered a job outside Egypt that pay [*sic*] 10 times that, he takes it. We have to meet the challenge of getting away from the snob appeal of university education. We must stress the importance of attitude training. (Lippman, 1989, 74)

Table 4.3 *Income of migrants before and after emigration (in LE and at official rates)*

Occupation	Country of Destination	Average Income		
		Before Emigration	After Emigration	Ratio
Construction	Saudi Arabia	33.44	378.22	11.31
Workers	Libya	35.83	289.55	8.08
	Other Gulf States	33.33	260.42	7.81
	Average	34.00	336.19	9.98
University	Saudi Arabia	210.58	1,485.71	7.06
Staff	Libya	239.29	992.86	4.15
	Kuwait	160.00	1,056.25	6.60
	Average	200.42	1,235.89	6.17
Teachers	Saudi Arabia	56.25	492.55	8.76
	Libya	51.97	481.88	9.27
	Kuwait & Gulf States	45.39	508.93	11.21
	Average	52.83	494.11	9.35

Source: Hansen and Radwan 1982, 91

Arguably there existed a wish to undermine the Nasserite social contract, which stipulated that a quality education would lead to employment within the public sector or comfortable living conditions; labour emigration highlighted that in a direct, articulate manner. With regard to al-Abd's interview, Lippman further argues that the Egyptian regime

has struggled valiantly to break the psychological reliance on the government and the public sector, and Egyptians say they detect signs that people are more willing now to take initiatives, to go outside the established decision-making networks, to take economic risks in the pursuit of gain. But the universities continue to churn out thousands of unemployable graduates every year and Egypt cannot risk the political liability that would be posed by armies of unemployed, overeducated young people, so jobs continue to be made for them. (Lippman, 1989, 74–75)

While wage differentials are key to understanding a main "push" factor for Egyptian labour emigration, one should also keep in mind the fact that the regime took additional measures to increase the material appeal of moving abroad: for instance, it ensured that economic remittances or imported goods would not be subject to any taxation (a controversial issue with significant consequences, which will be discussed in Chapter 6). At the same time, the regime under Sadat incentivised home ownership, at the expense of rentals and rent control policies put in place under Nasser. This meant that new entrants into the housing market were faced with significant economic barriers to purchase, as they now needed to possess a significant amount of initial capital. By early 1976, urban housing was effectively only available on an ownership basis at prices that were unaffordable to Egyptians living on state salaries: according to journalist Mustafa Amin, 'a five room flat was offered for a total of 26,000 Egyptian pounds, with 5,000 pounds to be paid in advance and 3,500 in instalments every 6 months ... Well, this is hardly the solution for a 30-year-old engineer with a monthly salary of about 60 pounds' (quoted in Lippman 1989, 150). Renting property was also extremely difficult, as the regime's policies made mortgage credit inaccessible. Beyond demanding high prices for apartments alone, landlords also began asking for exorbitant amounts of "key money" in advance, and other forms of side-payments (Singerman 1995, 111–13; cf. Waterbury 1983, 185). New housing development was limited – partially as a result of an absence of construction workers, the majority of whom had emigrated (Wheaton 1979, 8–9).

Thus, labour emigration became the only solution for large segments of the Egyptian middle class and the younger generation, for whom owning a new flat always constituted a social prerequisite to marriage (Ghannam 2013, 99). The traditional social expectation that the prospective couple must save a certain amount of money so as to move into a new home immediately after their wedding was now achievable primarily through work abroad (Singerman 1995, 123). In fact, at the time Fergany identified that saving for marriage was Egyptians' primary motive for emigration, with the need for housing second (Fergany 1988, 107). Political sociologists working on Egypt have identified a side effect of this, where young return migrants tend to be highly sought-after as bridegrooms, a phenomenon that only serves to perpetuate the popularity of migration as a venue for future social inclusion: a prospective groom's status as a return migrant from the conservative Gulf countries is typically highlighted in social interactions, contributing to his valorisation as a financially successful and, at the same time, presumably pious Egyptian. Egyptians who have secured a position of work abroad also enjoy a dominant role under these social conditions; in that case, an engagement takes place, following which the fiancé departs for abroad, where he saves money for a few years, before he returns to his new home, and family, in Egypt. A death of an Egyptian in Saudi Arabia – the land of the Two Holy Mosques – is considered a *mūta kwaysa* (good death) or *ḥusn el-khātimah* (good ending) (Ghannam 2013, 29).

Pressures to migrate were accentuated through what sociologists term a "demonstration effect" of conspicuous consumption by the families of Egyptian emigrants and return migrants (Singerman 1995, 152). As the 1978 Five-Year Plan highlighted, 'growing numbers of Egyptians work abroad for very high wages, if compared with domestic salaries. These individuals return to Egypt possessed of high purchasing powers, which they individually direct not to savings and investment, but to flagrant and luxurious consumption' (Ministry of Planning 1978, 33). This created an additional pressure upon the Egyptian social body, and further normalised the solution of migration.

It was only necessary to be in the customs hall at Cairo Airport when a planeload of migrant workers came in from the Gulf to see what was happening: huge mounds of stereo equipment, clothing, electric appliances, toys, watches and cigarettes were being brought into Egypt ... The money [migrants] brought or sent back was converted into possessions – automobiles, apartments, land, appliances – that hardly anyone had been able to afford for a generation. (Lippman 1989, 108)

One side effect of this phenomenon, which further attests to the popularity of labour emigration, was a grave housing shortage across urban centres, as 'the growing demand for luxury and middle-class housing by the transnational community and Egyptians who worked in oil-producing countries inflated the price of land, especially in the city center, and increased the cost of construction materials' (Ghannam 2002, 29). Put differently, the popularity of emigration in Egypt, at least partly due to the country's housing crisis, exacerbated such shortages that, in turn, served to encourage further waves of emigration. Another example of this "demonstration effect" is the introduction of television sets in the 1970s, which 'became very widespread during this period' (Amin 2011, 95, see also Figure 4.1). According to *al-Ahram*, a colour television set cost

Figure 4.1 Televisions in Egypt (*al-Ahram*, 21 December 1975)
  'We don't have a colour television set yet …
But hopefully by Easter-time, God willing!'

LE 400, when 77.6 per cent of Egyptian families spent less than LE 250 on a year's worth of household expenses, and 21.5 per cent spent between LE 250 and LE 1000 annually (25 August 1974). 'It was not merely that television entered all homes', Amin argued, 'but the programs it presented [exhibited] to all the new style of life that everyone might lead. Some new consumer goods came within reach of almost everyone, such as tape recorders, transistor radios, and sunglasses, in addition to the services of hairdressers ' (Amin 2011, 95–96).

Arguably, Egypt's permissive labour emigration policy served the regime's material legitimation strategies by endowing key social groups with access to wealth. It is widely reported that migration created a 'frenzy of consumer spending. Demand had been pent up for more than a decade. Egypt was an austere country in the 1960s and early 1970s; Egyptians did without for so long that they were like children on Christmas when the restrictions were lifted' (Lippman 1989, 109).

[M]igration leads to social polarisation within the society, since not all those wanting to migrate can find an opportunity to work in one of the oil countries. The lucky ones manage to solve their material and sometimes their human (social?) problems, while others continue to suffer. This sometimes occurs within the same family. The truth of the matter is that migration to work abroad leads to a re-distribution of income in the country of origin against the poorer sections of the population. For these sections carry a heavier social burden in terms of the cost of educating and training those who migrated and who belong, to a great extent, to the richer sections of society, while the material benefits of migration go to a greater extent to those very sections which are richer. (Fergany 1983, 106)

While these statements are difficult to prove without access to reliable statistical data, they are included here given the frequency with which they occurred in the academic and public debates of post-1970 Egypt. While there are dissenting voices (Amin and Awni 1986, 145), it cannot be denied that the view that Egyptian migration engendered 'uncaptured remittances that go to consumption [and] can create socially visible evidence of accentuated income inequalities' has been widespread, both in urban and in rural areas (Choucri 1988, 5). The International Labour Organisation's research identified that, in 1980:

Preliminary results from a two-village survey in Upper Egypt point to the possibility that remittances may in fact aggravate intra-group and intra-village distribution. The survey shows that migrants do not come from the poorest households but from those with both previous experience and savings, and remittances, therefore accrue to families which are already relatively well-off (in this case, the households of construction workers). Furthermore, of the two villages, located very near each other, one had a higher incidence of emigration, while the other had almost none. (International Labour Organisation, quoted in Amin and Awni 1986, 110–11)

A key analyst of Egyptian migration economics noted that:

Egyptian labour emigration to the oil countries, with its various levels of skill, has led to the widening of the income gaps in Egyptian society ... We may even allege that the process of labour migration and the intensification of income inequality have led to the emergence of a kind of obvious 'dualism' in the 'mechanism' of Egyptian economic life ... With the passage of time, this gap separating the two sectors in incomes, prices and the quality of the goods and services circulated and consumed tends to widen, thus strengthening the schizophrenia which characterises Egypt's economic life. (Abdel-Fadil 1980, 25, 27)

At the same time, in another move aimed at tying labour emigration to material legitimation of the ruling regime, the state relinquished control on import duties: starting in October 1974, select electrical appliances were able to be imported duty free. Additionally, 'instructions had been issued to competent airport officials not to open baggage of ordinary passengers for inspection except in cases of suspicion and within 10% of the total number of arriving and departing passengers' (al-Akhbar, 27 October 1974). Car imports were also facilitated, with any Egyptian residing abroad for more than three years now able to import any car to Egypt (MENA, 27 October 1974). By 1975, Cairo airport authorities reduced customs staff once a new system was put in place for outgoing passengers to pass without inspection of their bags, except in cases of doubt. From the late 1970s onwards, the image of Egyptians returning to Cairo or Alexandria airports loaded with consumer goods – from television sets and record players to smaller appliances and clothes – became commonplace.

The Egyptian regime was heavily involved in this process: state-owned media presented an attractive image of labour emigration, from sympathetic coverage of expatriates' lives, such as those of film star Omar Sharif and the space scientist Faruk al-Baz (Ayubi 1983, 442), to enthusiastic exaggerations. According to al-Akhbar's coverage of Egyptians in the United States: 'Some of them get higher salaries than Dr Henry Kissinger while still in their forties. Some lead the same lavish life as Hollywood stars. They own villas with fragrant gardens and as many as three cars each. One of them travels by private helicopter from his country home to his place of work inside New York!' (al-Akhbar, 30 June 1975). In the immediate aftermath of the 1973 War, the press ran frequent articles

detailing the wealth awaiting Egyptian emigrants: in a lengthy article entitled 'The rich hive invaded by foreign bees', *al-Ahram* reporter 'Ali Hamdi al-Jamal describes the 'the wealth that flows into the
Arab Gulf states is enormous and will remain so for years to come'
(*al-Ahram*, 8 June 1974).

Beyond advertising or sympathetic media coverage, the Egyptian
state would grant the right of re-employment in a migrant's previous public-sector post, should they be unable to find employment
abroad, as mentioned earlier. This was done in order 'to encourage
the Egyptian citizen to knock on the door of emigration without
apprehension or failure', according to the Minister of Migration
and Manpower, 'since his motherland will not deny him
a dignified return that would protect his full rights' (*al-Ahram*,
9 February 1979). Low-paid state employees – such as schoolteachers or bureaucrats – would patiently wait for *dawruhum* (their
turn) for the opportunity to spend some time in an Arab country,
based on unwritten, informal rules of rotation within each agency
or ministry (Waterbury 1983, 240). This discursive shift towards
promoting emigration not only targeted adults, it was even aimed at
schoolchildren: Egyptian school curricula were now required to
teach that 'people emigrate, just like the birds' (*Al-Ahram al-
Iqtisadi*, No. 745, 1983; see also Figure 6.4). The 1977 preparatory
school certificate exam asked students to write an essay on 'the joys
of a person who could obtain work in an "Arab" country, thus
managing to accumulate money and return home to start a new life'
(*al-Ahram*, 18 May 1977).

Nasserite-era concerns on the brain drain of educated Egyptians
were bypassed by explicit support for brain gain and material
development:

But when we started exporting such surplus manpower, some of us were
dismayed by the prospect of a possible exhaustive brain drain! It was
only natural that we should have exported only good elements, for
nobody abroad would tolerate rotten fruit or ignorant Egyptians! ...
But the presence of those intellectuals abroad is still beneficial to Egypt.
They provide income for Egypt, which is tantamount to a new Suez Canal
or wells of black gold! (*al-Akhbar*, 9 April 1975)

The extent to which a permissive emigration policy constituted
a popular measure (and thereby contributed to the regime's

legitimation strategies) cannot be overestimated. Despite a lack of reliable statistics, Fergany argued that, with about 2.8 million Egyptians involved in labour emigration between 1974 and 1984, more than one-fifth of the Egyptian labour force had been employed abroad (Fergany 1988). As Sell highlighted:

There is hardly an urban family in 1980 [that] does not have members working abroad. And in rural Egypt, it is no longer extraordinary for village labour to move directly to the international market, thereby skipping the intermediate urban market. Looking at Egypt in 1980, the international migration process appears to have not only been accepted, but more importantly internalised by many Egyptian families. (Sell 1988, 93)

Population Mobility and Low-Intensity Repression under Sadat

[It is now time to] open the universe ... open the door for fresh air and remove all barriers and walls that we built around us to suffocate ourselves by our own hands.

Anwar Sadat (1981, 12)

Beyond questions of de-Nasserisation and regime legitimation, a permissive emigration policy facilitated the Egyptian regime's low-intensity repression tactics, mainly through opposition management. This was achieved in two ways: firstly, the new state policy provided the legal means for the emigration of various *ancien régime* political elites, which opted to pursue employment opportunities abroad rather than risk harassment in Egypt (and, even worse, incarceration or death), a process that clearly supported the restructuring of the Egyptian regime under Sadat. Secondly, a permissive labour emigration policy led to the empowerment of the Muslim Brotherhood, a key opposition movement that Sadat aimed to employ against his Nasserist opponents.

The weakening of voices against Sadat within the Egyptian Left was a key aim of the Corrective Revolution. However, the latter's coercive elements were further facilitated by the fact many political dissenters had taken advantage of the deregulation of migration and the absence of strict border controls in order to flee the country. During Sadat's first years in power, 'the regime got rid of dissidents who went abroad, and thus ensured the country's domestic political stability', argued Saad Eddin Ibrahim (*personal interview*).[2] At the same time, the president carefully intensified his criticism of Nasserite-era politics, stressing how personal liberties were now ensured under the Corrective Revolution. 'I am saying this for the first time today: from 5 June 1967, Nasser was indeed a shattered man', Sadat declared in 1976, accusing the Nasserite regime of 'excessive measures, arrests, detention, dismissals and destitution' (quoted in *MECS* 1, 1976, 286).

As a result, Egyptian Communists became scattered across the Arab world and beyond: the Egyptian Communist Party, for instance, was re-established in Beirut in August 1975, while Egyptian Marxists in Paris began publishing the *al-Yasar al-'Arabi* from 1977 onwards. Many Nasserites had already left Egypt, such as 'Abd al-Majid Farid, the head of Nasser's Presidential Office, who became an adviser to Algeria's Boumedienne until 1978, and Himkat Abu-Zayd, Nasser's Minister for Social Affairs, who relocated to Libya (*Akhbar el-Yom*, 27 May 1978). Egyptian intellectuals, journalists, and politicians organised in the Socialists' Vanguard [*Tali'at al-Ishtirakiyyin*] in 1979, and engaged in limited anti-Sadat propaganda. In Damascus, in March 1980, *al-Jabha al-Wataniyya al-Masriyya* (Egyptian National Front) was established by General Sa'd el-Din al-Shadhili, the Egyptian Chief of Staff who had been dismissed during the 1973 War. After serving as Ambassador to Great Britain and Portugal, he resigned in protest against the Israeli Peace Treaty. While al-Shadhili vowed to make the Front 'a heavy burden to the regime', he did not succeed and was tried in absentia in June 1981 (*MECS* 4, 1979, 342). Overall, the dispersal of opposition groups also hindered anti-mobilisation, implying that they posed little threat to the regime.

Beyond providing an exit strategy for his opponents, Sadat employed the new, permissive emigration policy in order to strengthen the power of the Egyptian Muslim Brotherhood. Egypt's top-down Islamisation process from 1970 onwards has been extensively researched, as well as how the regime aimed to use this to consolidate authoritarianism (Esposito 1998; Kepel 1985; Wickham 2005). Yet, the connection between the liberalisation of migration and the *Ikhwan* has yet to be fully explored: arguably, the latter were aided by the regime's new labour emigration policy, both politically and economically.[3] The literature has already established that the Sadat regime employed Islam, Islamic discourses, religious institutions, and various religiously driven actors as a way of supporting its stay in power (Albrecht 2013, 17; Haddad 1987). 'In Egypt', Belaid noted, 'the state was aware of the importance of Islam as a means of political control and sought to use religious institutions to consolidate its legitimacy and channel its ideology and policies throughout the country' (Belaid 1988, 159). The relationship between the regime and the Muslim Brotherhood continued under Mubarak, albeit vacillating in intensity (Al-Awadi 2005; Wickham 2005). The assassination of Sadat on 6 October 1981 by members of the Egyptian Islamic Jihad, and the Mubarak regime's crackdown on the Muslim Brotherhood in the 1990s, do not take away from the fact that both Sadat and Mubarak had, at various points throughout the 1971–2011 period, undeniably benefitted from a co-optation of political Islam. The *Ikhwan*, an important controlled political opposition group with an exclusionary vision of politics and a penchant for the use of violence (Albrecht 2013; Lust-Okar 2010), served as an element of low-intensity repression. Achcar's argument accurately described the 1971–2011 period:

The Egyptian bourgeoisie is ... very obliging toward the fundamentalist movement. The fundamentalists constitute in its eyes an ideal 'fifth column' inside the mass movement – a particularly effective 'antibody' to the left. That is why the Egyptian bourgeoisie is not worried about the fundamentalist movement's trying to outbid the Left on the Left's two favourite issues: the national question and the social question; any gains made by Islamic reaction on these two issues mean equivalent losses for the Left. (Achcar 2004, 56)

For the movement's empowerment to occur, it was vital that Egyptian migration policy and population movement controls did not inhibit the free movement of Islamists out of Egypt and across the Arab world. In June 1971, Sadat arranged for the release from jail of several hundred members of the *Ikhwan* in the name of personal freedom and de-Nasserisation (Vassiliev 1997, 384–85; see Figure 4.2). This included Muslim Brotherhood notables such as Zeynab al-Ghazali, 'Umar al-Telmesani (who became the organisation's Supreme Guide in 1973), Shukri Mustafa (the future head of the *Takfir wa-l Hijra* group) and others – a process that continued until March 1975 (Wickham 2013, 30; Beattie 2000, 114). At the same time, in March 1974, the regime decided to abolish the Nasserite-era lists of individuals forbidden from travelling abroad – the so-called *black lists* discussed in Chapter 2 (*al-Ahram*, 27 March 1974). These lists, according to *al-Gomhuria* (28 March 1974) included about 1,000 entries. Their abolition

Figure 4.2 Sadat demolishing *al-Torah* (*Akhbar el-Yom*, 10 May 1975)
The *al-Torah* prison, to be torn down in 1975. Sadat wields the axe and releases `Justice', 'Democracy', and 'Freedom'

facilitated the empowerment of the *Ikhwan*, who were now able to relocate abroad, work, and establish networks across the Arab world and the West. Following their release from Egyptian prisons, Islamists were granted the right to travel, seek refuge, and pursue employment in Saudi Arabia, as the regime allowed them to 'compensate themselves financially for the time they served in prison' (Kandil 2015, 133).

Cross-border mobility was important for the Muslim Brotherhood as, according to Kepel:

Most of the [Society of Muslims] group's resources came from money sent back from Saudi Arabia, Kuwait, or elsewhere by members whom Shukri had sent into emigration by turns. There were thus two *hijras* for Society members: the internal withdrawal from *jahiliyya* society to their life in the furnished flats of the Society of Muslims, and physical emigration outside the country like other young Egyptians, except that the income they earned was redistributed to support the rest of the members back in Egypt. (Kepel 1985, 5)

Importantly, under the aegis of a permissive migration policy, the regime encouraged exiled members of the organisation, who had sought refuge particularly in Saudi Arabia and other Gulf states, to return to Egypt (Kassem 2004, 141). Sadat made clear that the state was now willing to receive all 'her sons' who had been forced to reside abroad, and to shift Egyptian state policy in order to reinstate citizenship to them. Besides the return of draft evaders, as discussed in the section 'Exorcising Nasser's Ghost', the regime invited back Muslim Brothers who had escaped to the Arabian Gulf or had been stripped of their citizenship by Nasser (*al-Gomhuria*, 9 March 1974). Sadat introduced a policy of amnesty for those who had fled to Arab countries to escape the Nasserite regime, many of whom were members of the *Ikhwan*. This move, which constituted one of Sadat's 'first liberalisation measures' (Baker 1978, 151), was presented in the official press as a move away from Nasserite-era movement restrictions and a shift towards freedom within the directives of the Corrective Revolution. This enabled, for instance, return to Cairo of Salih 'Abd Allah Sirriyya, who the Iraqis had sentenced to death in absentia in 1972, and who later organised the attack against Sadat in the Heliopolis Military Academy in April 1974 (Kepel 1985, 94–95). In January 1976, 'Abd al-Hakim 'Abidin, the former Secretary-General of the Muslim Brotherhood, was allowed entry to Egypt after 22 years in Saudi Arabia. On 9 February 1977, Sa'id Ramadan was similarly given amnesty by Sadat (*Saudi News Agency*, 9 February 1977, as quoted in *MECS* 1, 1976).

This process formed part of the Egyptian regime's strategy to make the *Ikhwan* 'allies against the Nasserite ideology then current' (Sayyid-Marsot 2007, 163; Kandil 2015, 130). The Muslim Brothers, enjoying a form of *carte blanche*, were specifically employed in order to 'confront the Marxists, Liberals and Nasserists among the university youths' (Shukri 1981, iii; McDermott 1988, 188). Not incidentally, the *Ikhwan* 'criticised the socialist economy of Nasser because it failed to introduce a society of equality and justice and denied people their liberty ... Under Sadat they aimed for the abolition of the left-wing parties, the banning of communism as an atheist creed, and the purging of the government and bureaucracy' (Hopwood 1991, 117). The international aspect of Sadat's relationship with the *Ikhwan* will come into focus when discussing the regime's relations with Saudi Arabia in Chapter 5. In terms of this chapter's argumentation, one needs to bear in mind the importance of mobility in Sadat's attempt to defeat remaining ideas of Nasserism domestically. In fact, in this secret meeting with Ramadan, 'Sadat argued that he and they were confronted by the same enemies, atheism and Communism, not to mention surviving Nasserist ideas. He said that, if they were prepared to come out in the open and give him their support, he was ready to make a pact with them' (Heikal 1983, 116). Not incidentally, in 1983, the Interior Minister invited Umar al-Tilmisani, the General Guide of the *Ikhwan*, to take part in the government's efforts to promote Islamic education in the media (*MECS* 8, 1983, 368), while members of the Brotherhood began participating in elections as part of the New Wafd Party from 1984 onwards.

Of course, this is not to say that Sadat did not gain in popularity from such measures, which served to distance him even further from Nasser and complemented ongoing legitimation strategies. The re-introduction of the *Ikhwan*, for Vatikiotis, coincided with 'a wider Arab revulsion against and hostility to the [Nasserite] regime in Egypt and Nasser's leadership. There was an outpouring of highly critical and soul-searching writing occasioned by the debacle of June 1967' (Vatikiotis 1991, 411). At the same time, the new president adopted the name Mohammad Anwar Sadat, and presented himself as the *al-Ra'īs al-Mu'min*; rarely would his speeches not begin, or end, with a reference to the Qur'an, while state media began duly reporting the mosques where Sadat would perform his Friday prayers. 'Islam was central to Anwar Sadat's self-image and claim to political authority' (Wickham 2005, 95). Esposito argued that 'in cultivating a public image as a pious Muslim ruler, the President [promoted] a more liberal attitude towards Islamic groups, in particular the Muslim Brotherhood and Islamic university student organisations. This was done to counter the influence of pro-Nasser secular leftists' (Esposito 1998, 236–37). According to Camelia Sadat's memoirs:

Father became a hero to many when he ordered the release of those – mostly Muslim Brotherhood members – who had been made political prisoners during the Nasser regime. The personal dimension of the imprisonments became obvious to us, because one of my mother's relatives was among those who were released ... The popular response to the freeing of the political prisoners seemed to me a sure sign that Egyptians were coming to recognize Father as a leader in his own right. (Sadat 1985, 99)

Beyond questions of freedom of movement, a second key issue involves the economic linkages between state emigration policy and the Islamists' empowerment in Egypt. This is evident, firstly, in the proliferation of mosques across Egypt (cf. Atia 2013).

A major source of financing for the new private mosques was the voluntary donations of private Egyptians collected through the system of *zakat* (the Islamic religious tithe); private mosques also received financial support from institutional and individual patrons in the Gulf. The proliferation of new mosques was encouraged by legislation making any building containing a mosque a religious site and therefore tax exempt. With a domestic construction boom under way, builders had a clear incentive to establish new 'mosques', which often consisted of little more than a tiny prayer room (*zawiya*) located on the ground floor or in the basement. (Wickham 2005, 98)

That ties back to specific goals of the regime's economic policy: 'Giving impetus to the construction of new mosques is Sadat's policy of granting exception from taxation to anyone who builds a mosque on his property', argued Haddad. 'This has led to mushrooming of "tax shelter" mosques on sidewalks, staircases, and basements of large apartment buildings' (Haddad 1987, 250). Many of the executives working in Egypt's Islamic banks, on the other hand, such as the Faisal Bank, had ties to the Muslim Brotherhood (Birks and Sinclair 1979, 243). It has been estimated, for instance, that about 1 million Egyptians invested in the Islamic investment companies between 1974 and 1984 (Springborg 1989, 47).

A decade later, following the Mubarak regime's privatisation programme that was introduced under the auspices of the 1991 International Monetary Fund agreement, a second wave of Muslim Brothers returned. This 'new breed of Brotherhood businessmen', as Kandil termed them, 'invested in construction, luxury housing, car dealerships, electronics, Islamic schools, media, and tourism (mostly pilgrimage – a multimillion-dollar business)' (Kandil 2015, 78). At the same time, according to Wickham,

While the Brotherhood was reconstituting itself as a national political organization and Islamic groups were gaining ground on university campuses, a new wave of Islamic institution building began to reshape the landscape of Egyptian cities and towns. Economic liberalisation facilitated this trend by expanding the private wealth available for investment in communal projects. Fuelled by the regional oil boom, Egypt's GDP grew by an average of 9 percent per year in the decade between 1974 and 1984, more than doubling the per capita income from \$334 to \$700 by 1984. A major new source of capital was the remittances of Egyptian migrants working in Libya and the Gulf, who increased in number from about 10,000 in 1968 to 1.2 million in 1985. Much of this remittance income, officially valued at more than \$3 billion annually in the early 1980s, found outlets beyond state control. Some of it was captured by the Islamic banks and investment companies that were established under the new investment laws ... Under Mubarak, the parallel Islamic sector continued to grow in absolute size and complexity, although its exact parameters are difficult to pin down. For example, there are no systematic data on the number of Islamic institutions in Mubarak's Egypt, let alone how they are disaggregated by size, function, or geographic location. (Wickham 2005, 96–97)

The Promise of Prosperity: Emigration Policy as Co-Optation

> Every Egyptian citizen has the right to get married, own a villa, drive a car, possess a television set and a stove, and eat three meals a day.
>
> Anwar Sadat (1981)[4]

Beyond the aforementioned factors aimed at enhancing regime durability via a permissive labour emigration policy – internal legitimation and low-intensity repression – the liberalisation of Egypt's emigration policy also fostered patterns of co-optation of key business elites. This occurred, initially, by countering political opposition to economic liberalisation via the highly contentious question of unrestricted emigration. The regime had aimed to disempower any opposition voices of the Egyptian Left that remained in the domestic political scene. At the same time, the regime tied labour emigration into a wide-ranging programme of economic liberalisation, termed the open-door policy, or *al-Infitah*, with distinct benefits for well-connected domestic business elites. A full analysis of the complex phenomenon of *al-Infitah* is beyond the scope of this study (Moore 1986; Richards 1984); suffice it to say that it presented a direct opposite to *al-Inghilaq*, the closed system that existed under the Nasserite period (Ansari 1986, 171). Increasingly from 1971 onwards, and more visibly following the 1973 Arab–Israeli War, the Egyptian regime aimed to 'open the door' to private investment, reduce the centrality of the public sector, and build up private enterprise, as well as attract foreign capital. Within this shift lay, implicitly or explicitly, a promise of socio-economic prosperity and wealth. A notable journalist of the time, 'Ali Amin, wrote in his popular weekly column:

The thousands of millions of pounds that will enter the Arab area over the next few years, if properly exploited and not squandered on luxuries and imaginary projects, can give a house to every Arab family, cultivate hundreds of thousands of kindergartens for Arab children, and build tens of thousands of factories, schools, hospitals, universities, and research laboratories ... Within years, the Arabs will live in a paradise as yet unknown to the peoples of America, Europe, or Asia. Envy, hatred, rancour and egoism will disappear from our land. (*al-Akhbar*, 24 February 1975)

As seen in Chapter 2, one of the main characteristics of the Nasserite era had been the centrality of the state in organising economic behaviour, a phenomenon that, by the 1970s, led to the public sector's domination of the domestic labour market. A permissive labour emigration policy aimed to undermine this, and to co-opt the Egyptian business elites into processes of economic liberalisation that were compatible with *al-Infitah*. Initially, labour emigration policy was employed in order to weaken long-standing Nasserite political opposition to economic liberalisation. The Egyptian regime and other forces of 'the right pushed for a very open approach to liberalisation',

ا نجـــاه واحـــد !
ـ لا الى اليمين . . ولا الى اليســــار . . الى مصر . . !

Figure 4.3 'One Way!' (*Akhbar el-Yom*, 3 February 1973).
'One Way! Neither to the right ... nor to the left ... toward Egypt..!'

identifying the 'large surplus of labour' that Egypt possesses (Cooper 1982, 95). These popular measures put political figures within the Egyptian Left – or whatever remained of it, following Sadat's 1971 purges – on the defensive, given the immense popularity of emigration. This is not something that Sadat attempted only on this policy issue: the new president pursued a similar agenda in splitting the Egyptian press corps and, thereby, weakening it greatly in 1973, when he engaged in a selective purge of leftist journalists (Beattie 2000, 121–22). In terms of emigration policy, leftist groups pushed unsuccessfully for a rationalised approach to the liberalisation of migration, rather than its complete deregulation. A handful of political figures were mostly active in the pages of *al-Tali'a* and *Rose al-Yūsuf*. Marxists and Nasserite parliamentarians included Ahmad Taha, Khalid Muhi al-Din, Abu Said Yussef, and Dr Mahmud al-Qadi, a long-time parliamentarian better known as "Dr No". They argued that, were emigration to be fully liberalised, then the country's most productive labour groups would abandon the public sector and the domestic economy in order to pursue employment abroad (see People's Assembly; Legislative Council, *The Law for Arab and Foreign Investment and Free Zones*). As Cooper notes;

The left responded, arguing that if labour and the wage rates were freed, foreign projects would attract the most productive labour, sapping the public sector and the domestic economy. Permitting skilled labour to migrate abroad, when such labour was in short supply at home and when the state had expended considerable resources in training it, seemed like an expensive way to help some countries industrialize. The left was not convinced that the

118   *'Our Most Precious Asset'*

savings, which this labour would repatriate, would find their way into productive uses. Moreover, freeing the wage rate would undermine the equity principles that had been established by the Arab Socialist regime. (Cooper 1982, 95)

Leftist politicians also highlighted that allowing skilled labourers to emigrate abroad, after the state had spent considerable resources in training them, was a rather ill-conceived way of aiding in Arab states' industrialisation. Nor would migrants' savings be employed in productive ways back home: 'we are rich in manpower but we suffer a great dearth of technicians, and cannot afford to export them abroad', Ahmad 'Izz al-Din Hilal, the Petroleum Minister argued. 'While all nations, big and small, import technicians by luring them with a variety of attractions, we alone open our doors to let them out' (quoted in *al-Ahram*, 25 February 1976). Dr Husayn Fawzi al-Najjar examined Egypt's liberalised emigration policy, and highlighted the lack of a framework of 'protection of Egyptian workers abroad against exploitation by their employees' (*al-Ahram*, 16 July 1976). These debates had persisted since the regime had begun seriously contemplating such a shift, during Nasser's last months in power: 'Should the state encourage emigration or restrict it? Should a citizen who wants to emigrate be regarded by the state as less loyal to his country? Should the state detach itself from, and ignore, the citizen who has decided to emigrate?' (al-Akhbar, 3 March 1969).

Other voices of dissent within the bureaucracy pointed to the fact that, in its decision not to introduce a more coherent response to the management of emigration, particularly in the fields of secondment and corporate labour migration, the regime missed an important opportunity to develop, and regulate, forms of migration that would be of long-term economic benefit for the Egyptian state (Said 1990). Instead, the regime developed a novel emigration policy that was ostensibly justified as serving political and civil liberties, rather than addressing economic necessities. Despite a strong degree of state control over printed media, these views did come through quite clearly in various opinion pieces: 'Are we in desperate need to *open the door* of emigration? Should we have it open to all or restrict it? How to encourage emigration? Whom to allow and whom to prevent?'(*al-Gomhoriya*, 24 June 1971). Writer Dr Yusef Idris for instance, wondered on the gap between a liberalised emigration policy and the state's attempt to attract wealthy Egyptians back to Egypt:

For if we have an exportable surplus manpower, why should we have to import it after being exported and at a much higher price than the price obtaining on the local market? ... Under the working conditions now prevailing in our country, a worker, whether he be man or woman, has come to be the cheapest article on the market. Therefore, unless we immediately and radically change our ways or working relations, our human capital will constantly dwindle, Egyptian stupidity will continue chasing off Egyptian intelligence beyond our borders, and will further aggravate our poverty problems. (*al-Ahram*, 31 November 1974)

It is worth noting that the deregulation of emigration and Sadat's enthusiastic support for intra-Arab migration also became embedded in a context of providing help to Egypt's Arab neighbours, a traditional pan-Arab theme. Egyptian Nasserites found this argument harder to dispute. Albert Salama, the Minister of Immigration and Egyptians Abroad, for instance, claimed that Egyptians in the Arab world 'are stimulated to work there by feelings of national loyalty and duty to participate in the building and modernizing of Arab and African states', echoing sentiments that were prevalent in Nasser's programme of secondment. 'Of course improving their standards of living is another reason', he also added (quoted in *Cairo Today*, May 1984). Naturally, the extent to which such statements are accurate is debatable. Yet, there is no denying that such processes would be supported by at least some Nasserite political figures:

Today we are a nation of thirty-seven million people. If we were not concerned with training centres to create skilled labour in the past, today we are concerned and our need for this kind of labour will compel us to train manpower in these specialties. We must not believe that the lack of labour hinders the battle for development. This is not true: freedom and competition create abundance. The carpenter who goes abroad transfers a hundred pounds a month in hard currency to Egypt, i.e. in excess of a thousand pounds a year in hard currency. We do not achieve such income from the export of the yield of ten feddans of cotton, on which we spend much for fertiliser and seed. (quoted in Cooper 1982, 97)

Having prepared the way for economic liberalisation, the regime's new labour emigration policy also served to materially benefit business elites, within the broader agenda of *al-Infitah*. One aspect of this included deregulation, as the regime ordered that public sector employees be encouraged to pursue employment abroad: following the liberalisation of emigration policy, 'all ministers were instructed to relax their conditions of secondment or unpaid vacations for seekers of jobs abroad. This was increasingly done, albeit with frequent intervention by top officials' (Said 1990, 20). A 1971 law further specified that the first son, and the brother in case the father passed away, of an Egyptian emigrant would not be drafted in the Egyptian army, bypassing yet another obstacle to emigration (*al-Ahram*, 26 December 1971). The Legislative Committee of the People's Assembly voted for dual nationality in March 1975 (*al-Akhbar*, 9 March 1975). The state negotiated well-publicised agreements with other states to send workers abroad, to Sweden (*al-Ahram*, 22 October 1971), 5,000 Egyptians to Bulgaria (*Akhbar el-Yom*, 7 January 1971), 15,000 building workers to Czechoslovakia (*al-Gomhuria*, 5 February 1972), emigrants to Greece (*al-Akhbar*, 26 April 1975), and so on. Intra-Arab migration was facilitated by the abolition of visas for work in Libya or Syria (*al-Ahram*, 15 December 1971), and later Iraq and Jordan. At the same time, it bears mentioning that post-1970 Egypt never adopted any provision to combat illegal emigration. There was no legal punishment for Egyptian citizens that attempted to emigrate illegally. This has been interpreted as tacit encouragement of Egyptians' emigration, both legal and otherwise. But was this a conscious move towards co-optation for purposes of political survival? Given the secrecy around the regime workings, we have only select pieces of evidence that corroborate this view – for instance, Sadat announced a decision to provide visas for travel abroad within as little as twenty-four hours in his discussion with student protesters in 1971 (*MENA*, 10 October 1971).

While a full discussion on the socio-political effects of *al-Infitah* would be beyond the scope of this study, it is necessary to underline that labour emigration became an important component to the regime's strategy of co-opting strategic actors within the Egyptian economic elites into the process of liberalisation. Gradually during the 1970s, 'a "new bourgeoisie" [arose] from the interpenetration of three social groups: the old landed aristocracy, in some cases returning from abroad, the upper strata of the technical bureaucracy, and various nouveaux riches comprador elements', as Richards points out. 'This new class ... both benefited from the (partial) economic liberalization and encouraged the regime to continue to liberalize' (Richards 1984, 325). *The New York Times*' coverage of Egypt carried the headline 'New Millionaires Flourish in Egypt's Liberalised Economy', identifying 500 new Egyptian millionaires, quoting the Secretary-General of the Socialist Union (*The New York Times*, 10 February 1976). By 1981, one estimate put them at 17,000 (Heikal 1983, 87). As Weinbaum describes:

The distributive effects of the economic liberalisation were instrumental in promoting class divisions and tensions ... While the lowest 20 per cent of the population held 6.6 per cent of national income in 1970 and had improved their share to 7.0 per cent in 1965, they dropped to 5.1 per cent by the late 1970s. By comparison, the income of the highest 5 per cent dipped slightly to 17.4 per cent from 17.5 per cent between 1960 and 1965 but increased markedly to 22 per cent after several years of Sadat's policies. (Weinbaum 1985, 217)

Al-Infitah became linked to the creation of a new creed of millionaires, or 'fat cats' as the 1970s debate termed them (Waterbury 1983, 259). Indeed, permissive migration was vital to the co-optation of these new economic elites, given that 'the money they brought or sent back was converted into possessions – automobiles, apartments, land, appliances – that hardly anyone had been able to afford for a generation. Virtually overnight, the migrant workers, educated or not, became a new privileged class, a privileged class based entirely on money' (Lippman 1989, 108).

The money was there. It was concentrated in the hands of the 'new class', of the parasites who, via the mechanisms of *Infitah*, thrived on the backs of the poor, of the upper reaches of a bourgeoisie which, in aggregate, absorbed such a disproportionate and growing share of the nation's wealth. Nobody really knew how much was there. The ostentation of the 'new class' only furnished a highly visible and offensive, but not very scientific measure of it. There were now said to be more millionaires in Egypt than before the Revolution. For the critics of *Infitah*, that was a bitter reproach, for its supporters it seemed almost a boast. Just how many millionaires was controversial; sometimes it was 500, sometimes 5,000. (Hirst and Beeson 1981, 230)

As Heikal put it:

Before the revolution of 1952 most of the commercial and industrial life of the country (including of course the Suez Canal) had been in foreign hands or under foreign control. The revolution had changed all that, expropriating most foreign businesses and greatly enlarging the public sector. Now new groups were emerging – it would not be accurate to refer to them as classes –

which benefitted from the new conditions. These groups included the families of people in responsible positions, those who had been working outside Egypt in the oil-producing countries and had accumulated wealth there, and those who were able to acquire influence in the banks and other foreign enterprises that were springing up almost daily. (Heikal 1983, 85–86)

In 1977, the year of Egypt's worst economic crisis, the Italian Chamber of Haute Couture named Sadat one of the year's ten best-dressed men. One of the slogans of the 1977 Bread Riots, playing on how the Egyptian words for "fashion" and "room" rhyme, went: '[The president] dressed in the latest fashion while we slept ten in a room'. In his memoirs, former Foreign Minister Kamel recounts an anecdote on how Sadat, 'known for his fondness of dress and uniform on every conceivable occasion', reacted to the news of a fire during the January 1977 Riots. Arriving in Cairo from Aswan only to hear that the fire had been extinguished, he cried: 'What a pity! It would have been a splendid opportunity to wear my uniform of commander-in-chief of the fire brigade!' (Kamel 1986, 119). Two years before, in the celebrations for the reopening of the Suez Canal, an exuberant Sadat appeared in a navy uniform (Figure 4.4) decorated with multiple medals, despite never having served in the Egyptian navy. Tales of the Sadat family economic excesses – from private helicopters to numerous palaces – are not hard to locate (Kays 1984, 114; see Heikal 1983, 169–200 for a particularly damning account). Sadat's wife, for instance, did not 'emulate the traditional, cloistered behaviour of Nasser's wife', and instead adopted the title of al-sayyida al-ūlā (First Lady), a novel introduction of Westernization into Egyptian political life (Beattie 2000, 111). As Hirst and Beeson critique:

Certainly few heads of state lavished such attention on their own person as [Sadat] did, from cuff links to the polished English cane which was one of his special affectations. Whether he was formal and dark-suited, casual and open-necked, there was always something of the mannequin, the fashion magazine, about his all-too-perfect appearance. Rarely did he wear the same outfit twice, and his vast assortment of 'costumes', by Balmain or Cardin, bore the most prestigious names. It was after the October 'victory', in his capacity as Supreme Commander of the Armed Forces, that Sadat crossed the sartorial borderline between an excessive, if perhaps harmless, passion for ceremonial display into a self-aggrandising narcissism. His dress uniforms were foreign creations too. (Hirst and Beeson 1981, 211)

Figure 4.4 Anwar Sadat, at the June 1975 re-opening of the Suez Canal (*al-Ahram Archives*)

The new, co-opted millionaires developed close ties with the regime, and the deregulation of Egypt's emigration laws was instrumental in this process. One example is the use of migration to flee persecution for issues of corruption. A number of newly wealthy Egyptians fled the country, usually to North America, to avoid persecution. These include one of the officials of the El Habiby Timber Company in Mansoura, accused of losing $4 million; a senior government official who obtained LE 8 million from the General Workers Union; Dr Mohamad Magdy, the director of El Salam International Hospital; and Mahmoud Ismail, the owner of the Alex Shopping Complex, who borrowed LE 17 million from Bank Misr, L.E. 17 million from Bank al-Qahira, and LE 2.4 million from the International Arab Bank, and then fled the country (Ibrahim 2001, 125, 140). As Central Intelligence Agency (CIA) declassified documents highlighted:

ثورة ١٥ مايو
الثـــــــورة التّى حطّمت الأغـــلال ! ٠٠

Figure 4.5 'The 15 May Revolution' (*Akhbar el-Yom*, 10 May 1975)
'The Revolution that smashed the shackles'

Sadat has substantial assets in coping with [many] formidable challenges [such as t]he support of bourgeois elements of Egyptian society: These elements are still numerous despite suppression under Nasser, and have lauded Sadat's policies of opening Egypt's doors to foreign investments and goods and of providing wider scope for cultural interchange with the West. Egypt's bourgeoisie has long had a cultural affinity with the West and resented Nasser's socialism and closed society. (Interagency Intelligence Memorandum, 1976, 17).

Sadat further stressed the point that the liberalisation of emigration differentiated him from Nasser by having the abolition of exit visas, an undisputable feature of the Nasserite era, take effect on 15 May 1974, the third-year anniversary of his Corrective Revolution. The Minister of Interior announced the decision to replace all exit visas with a standard form, prepared by the Passport Administration. The form was distributed across all state organisations, to be stamped when authorising the emigration of an employee, who would then merely have to present it at the point of departure. In case the symbolism was not adequately clear, the state-owned media agency repeated the point that:

The decision to abolish exit visas was taken in accordance with President Anwar el-Sadat's directives. It was also inspired by the principles of the Corrective Movement of May 15, which underlined the citizen's freedom and the removal of all restrictions on the exercise of his liberties [see also

Figure 4.5]. Exit visas have been required for Egyptians and foreigners for the past 25 years. (*MENA*, 15 May 1974)

Overall, Sadat was quite direct in his intentions to use these reforms as both driven from a sense of initial insecurity vis-à-vis his predecessor, a lack of popular faith in his abilities, and his attempt to solidify his place. For Vatikiotis, with Nasser's ghost still lingering in Egypt, it was 'Sadat's desire to escape from [Nasserism] which led him on to the dangerous road to liberalization' (Vatikiotis 1991, 427). As Sadat stated in a 1975 interview:

It was said, after the death of President Abdel Nasser, that there would be no successor. The American delegation which came to offer the condolences of the American people, on the occasion of his death, submitted a report, affirming that I would not remain in power for more than a few weeks. I have consistently worked for the people, and every year of the past five years I have important decisions. In 1971 – I endeavoured to give Egypt a permanent constitution, [and] I liquidated concentration camps. (Sadat 1975, 7)

Under the Chairmanship of Vice-President Hosni Mubarak, the Commission for Rewriting the History of the Revolution was established in 1975, which broadly accommodated Sadat's revisionist history of Egypt: 'the fifties were years of achievements; the sixties were years of successive defeats; the seventies witnessed the beginning of decisive resolutions and complete victories' (quoted in *MECS* 1, 1976, 286). In all this marginalisation of Nasserite opposition, the Corrective Revolution and the new-found personal liberties of the individual were at the forefront: 'From May 15 onward, we began carrying out the battle of liberation and the battle of construction simultaneously – the battle of building the Egyptian through freedom, democracy and security; and the battle of building the Egyptian's honour, security, and dignity' (*MECS* 1, 1976, 286).

Overall, it is clear the new, non-regulated emigration policy elucidated Sadat's broader emphasis on liberalisation and freedom (points that he increasingly contrasted with the Nasserite period), and aimed to legitimise the new regime. 'The retreat from Nasserism, in style and substance, was not an abstract political exercise', wrote Lippman. 'It was intended to consolidate Sadat's own power' (Lippman 1989, 31). In an attempt to establish his rule in the tumultuous Egyptian politics of the post-1970 era, Sadat did not hesitate to buttress the regime's new ideological tenets with a broader shift in Egypt's emigration policy. A closer examination of the de-Nasserisation process elucidates a main reason behind Sadat's decision to fully deregulate Egyptian emigration policy – namely, the intention to support ideas of complete "freedom", and to further distance himself from Nasser's restrictive emigration policy. The liberalisation of emigration was crucial in sustaining the process of deep economic liberalisation that the Egyptian state underwent under Sadat and Mubarak, and in co-opting the labour force into its workings. The upward socio-economic mobility afforded by emigration, coupled with the social pressures of return migrants' 'demonstration effect' contributed to the popularising of a new social model based upon individualism, quick profits, and consumption – not incidentally, ideas that were fostered by the entire *al-Infitah* process.

Conclusion

> It was clear to me in 1970 that what we called the socialist experiment and which we carried out in the 1960s was a 100 percent failure ... It was a summit operation carried out in the name of the peasants and workers, but it served only the summit and never resulted in a social revolution ... There is no doubt that anyone who writes the history of this period will say that the 1960s were nothing but years of defeat and pain ...
>
> Anwar Sadat (quoted in *al-Ahram*, 27 June 1977)

Chapter 4 demonstrated the ways in which the liberalisation of Egypt's migration policy, ensconced in the 1971 Constitution and applied over the following few years, served to solidify Sadat's domestic political standing in the aftermath of Nasser's death. Firstly, as a policy that directly contradicted Nasserite customs, it served as a forceful instrument of de-Nasserisation, through which Sadat marked his place as the successor, rather than the weak replacement, of his predecessor. Secondly, it complemented the regime's repressive strategies, marked by the empowerment of the Egyptian Muslim Brotherhood and the exodus of many leftists from Egypt, both results of Sadat's shift in Egyptian migration policy. Finally, as a controversial yet extremely popular policy, it placed his domestic competitors on the defensive, as they now had to debate the issue on Sadat's terms. In effect, the deregulation of migration served to herald a deeper and wider socio-economic shift towards liberalisation under the policy of *al-Infitah*, which was supported by an increasing number of Egyptians who had benefitted economically from free movement within, and out of, Egypt.

It should be noted that these three strategies were never as distinct as this analysis presents them. More often than not, issues of de-Nasserisation blended in with Sadat's fostering of religious discourse, for instance. This was the case when Sadat professed that 'the Nasser era [was] a period of materialism and unbelief and he professed himself to be a sincere, believing Muslim' (Hopwood 1991, 116). Other times, the move away from Nasserite self-sufficiency was underlined by the co-optation not of business elites, but of societal groups that had been economically empowered by emigration and were now 'not shy about showing off their wealth' (McDermott 1988, 78, 82). Overall, this chapter has aimed to underline how the diverse linkages between labour emigration and these three elements were aimed to contribute to regime durability. Chapter 5 takes the discussion to the international level, and examines how the liberalisation of emigration following Nasser's death served as an instrument of external regime legitimation.

5 | 'The Rich Hive Invaded by Foreign Bees'

Migration and External Regime Legitimation under Sadat and Mubarak

> One must never consider Egypt as an independent entity; it must be seen within the framework of the Arab world, for there is no hope for her to pull through alone.
>
> Boutros Boutros-Ghali (quoted in Waterbury 1983, 414)

Chapter 4 examined the interaction between Egypt's permissive emigration policy and the domestic determinants of regime durability – namely, regime legitimation, low-intensity repression, and elite co-optation. At the same time, Egypt's permissive labour emigration policy functioned as a strategy of external legitimation. In the pre-1970 era, Egyptian emigration facilitated cross-regime relations abroad with Egyptians supporting the political and socio-economic development of nascent regimes across North Africa, the Levant, and the Gulf region according to Nasserite ideals. Under Sadat, Egypt lacked the capacity to continue doing so. The centre of economic power moved away from Egypt towards the oil-rich countries of the Gulf in the aftermath of the 1967 War, as the balance of power shifted away from Egypt and in favour of the conservative Arab monarchies. Sadat realised that Egypt needed to develop closer ties with the Gulf states, most notably Saudi Arabia. In this, the role of Egypt's emigration policy was crucial: irrespective of their tremendous natural resources' wealth, the Gulf states were sparsely populated and in dire need of high-skilled immigrant labour. The political opportunity was obvious to the new president, as the Gulf monarchies would gain much-needed Egyptian migrant labour, while the Egyptian regime would secure the international support that he sought in order to maintain his power.

This chapter examines, firstly, the shift in regional balance of power that occurred in the aftermath of the 1967 War and underscored Egypt's need to pursue a closer relationship with the Gulf states.

Secondly, it identifies in detail how the ruling regime under Sadat employed Egypt's permissive labour emigration policy in order to pursue a rapprochement with its Arab partners, in three ways: one, the liberalisation of emigration marked a significant policy shift that allowed Sadat to distance himself from his predecessor two, it concretely demonstrated the regime's desire to benefit economically by contributing to neighbouring states' labour needs; finally, it strengthened personalistic ties between Egyptian and Arab elites through increased levels of diplomatic activity. The final section focuses on a time of major crisis for the Egyptian regime's regional relations, namely the aftermath of the harmonisation of bilateral relations with Israel, and evaluates the importance of Egyptian migration in repairing cross-regime relations.

A Changing Regional Order:
Egypt and Oil in the post-1970 Era

> The Arab world is now in what may be termed the Saudi epoch in modern Arab history.
>
> Muhammad Hasanayn Heikal (*al-Anwar*, 20–23 May 1977)

Chapter 3 analysed the extent to which the short-term migration of Egyptian professional staff featured in the workings of the Arab Cold War and constituted an instrument of competition between Egypt and conservative Arab regimes in the 1950s and 1960s. By 1967, the time was ripe for a reappraisal of Egypt's regional policy for a number of reasons. In popular discourse, the 1967 Arab–Israeli War is remembered as *al-Naksa* (defeat), as 'the regime's stunning military defeat by Israel in the 1967 War opened a Pandora's box of accumulated frustrations and disappointments' (Wickham 2005, 31). The post-1967 economic, military, and moral bankruptcy of the Nasserite system increased pressures for emigration that Sadat then capitalized upon, as discussed in Chapters 2 and 3. In face of a number of economic problems, a weakened Egypt began seeking financial support from the Gulf states, a pattern that intensified following Nasser's death. The economic divergence between Egypt and the oil-rich Arab states was striking, particularly after the '1970s oil boom [when] the differential between the rich and the poor Arab states reached a peak' (Ayubi, 1995, 159). The 'unprecedented' increase in oil revenues for

Saudi Arabia, in particular, (its GDP more than doubled, from 40.5 billion Saudi riyals in 1972 to 99.3 billion riyals in 1973) signified that it, together with other oil-exporting Arab countries, had 'entered the age of affluence' (Al-Rasheed 2010, 133). In contrast, Egypt's position in the regional system clearly diminished on multiple fronts:

The [Arab oil countries'] grants after the 1967 War were the only significant financial source for Egypt, and this aid prevented it from going completely bankrupt. Arab aid enabled Egypt to go to war in October 1973, and after the war to maintain a higher level of investment ... Also its balance of payments deficit in 1974–6 was largely covered by [Arab oil countries] aid – which was substantial until 1976, relative to other aid sources – and Iranian and American aid. Arab aid enabled Egypt to import large quantities of food and raw materials, even when global prices were skyrocketing, and although the Egyptian government had not significantly increased its export revenues, aid prevented a reduction in the GDP following the import of capital products and the increase of industrial products, particularly because of the low level of Egypt's savings accounts. According to World Bank data, (civil) Arab grants alone covered 111, 78, 40 and 41 percent of the current account deficit in the years 1973–6, respectively. (Feiler 2003, 40)

In light of the new balance of power within the Middle East, Sadat moved steadily towards fostering a closer relationship with Egypt's Arab neighbours. In particular, he sought to court the Gulf regimes and, chief among them, Saudi Arabia (Hinnebusch 1985, 65; Waterbury 1983, 361). Gaining the material support of the oil-rich Arab states was paramount for the economic survival of the Egyptian state and, for the purposes of this analysis, for the durability of the Egyptian regime. This was recognised by American observers at the time – as CIA declassified documents argued, 'Sadat's domestic position depends to a considerable extent on his international and intra-Arab stature' (Interagency Intelligence Memorandum, 1976, 15). Egypt's emigration policy became a key instrument in Sadat's strategy of external legitimation.

Labour Mobility and Sadat's Quest for Regional Rapprochement

Her son responded with another miracle: 'The Egyptians are the only Arabs who enjoy the affection of the Saudis.' 'It's because they have a good sense of humor.' The cousin denied this immediately. 'Not at all. It's because they don't get involved in politics, and all they're interested in is making a bit of money.'

Sonallah Ibrahim, Zaat (2001, 149)

This section examines how labour emigration complemented Sadat's regional aim for a rapprochement with the oil-producing Arab states. The ruling regime initially faced difficulties in convincing Arab states to recruit Egyptian labour. On the one hand, it was clear that Egypt was able to satisfy the labour needs of its neighbours: by 1970, Egypt's population had grown from 21 million in 1952 to more than 33 million. Egyptians were relatively well educated, as a result of Nasser's 1962 decision to make all levels of education free, and they faced 'increasingly bleak' job prospects that made them more likely to seek emigration (Beattie 2000, 13). At the same time, oil-exporting Arab countries had clearly stated their need for foreign workers well before the 1973 oil embargo dramatically increased their monetary resources and labour needs. By 1972, the GCC countries held 26 per cent of all Arab GNP, but only 7 per cent of the total Arab population – a decade later, they contained 8 per cent of the population but 52 per cent of all Arab GNP (Ayubi 1995, 159). Already in 1970, the Saudi Five-Year Plan reported that '[t]he employment of non-Saudi personnel is considered a partial answer to the Kingdom's needs of manpower necessary for development processes because of the number of Saudis working in both the private and public sectors who possess academic qualifications and adequate training required for fast development will continue to be relatively low' (quoted in Barsalou 1985, 136).

On the other hand, however, the memories of Egyptians' activism during the Nasser years remained fresh across Arab monarchies, who were wary of recruiting additional Egyptians that could potentially increase political instability. Elites across the Gulf states have traditionally been worried about the political effects of immigration within state borders, particularly given the fact that expatriate labour outnumbers nationals (see Table 5.1). As the Qatari Minister of Labour, Abd al-Rahman al-Dirham, stated:

The question of foreign labour is of great concern. Our social customs are threatened by foreigners. The problem is not just in Qatar but also in other Gulf countries. We prefer it if we can get suitable people from Arab countries who can live in the Gulf area without changing it' (*MEED*, August 1982, 40).

Table 5.1 *Population of the GCC states, 2004*

	Nationals	%	Expatriates	%	Total
Bahrain	438,209	62.0	268,951	38.0	707,160
Kuwait	943,000	35.6	1,707,000	64.4	2,650,000
Oman	2,325,812	80.1	577,293	19.9	2,903,105
Qatar	223,209	30.0	520,820	70.0	744,029
Saudi Arabia	16,528,302	72.9	6,144,236	27.1	22,673,538
United Arab Emirates	722,000	19.0	3,278,000	81.0	4,000,000
Gulf Cooperation Council	21,184,323	62.9	12,486,349	37.1	33,577,832

Source: Kapiszewski 2006, 4

Nasser's Egypt shared part of the blame for these host states' concerns, given the Gulf regimes' turbulent experience with Arab Cold War-era politics. Only a few years back, they had to grapple not only with intense migrant activism within their borders, encouraged by Nasser's development of a permissive emigration policy, but also with the political attitudes of their citizens, many of whom had been educated in Egypt: for Gulf elites and their children, pursuing a secondary or higher education in Egypt was the main route to attain a quality degree qualification within the region at the time (Szyliowicz 1973). Yet, many were reported to return to their countries of origin infused with the political ideas prominent in 1950s and 1960s Cairo, including elements of Nasserism (Qubain 1966). Belgrave describes how at one point under the Nasserite era:

[Bahrain's] Government sent a number of boys to Egypt for advanced education. The experiment was short-lived and unsuccessful. Few of the boys did any work, some left their hostel and returned to Bahrein, others took part in political disturbances and demonstrations, causing uneasiness to the Government and their parents. Within a year we withdrew all the boys from Cairo. Afterwards, the only boys who went to Egypt were sent privately by their parents. This brief excursion into Egypt had subsequent consequences; some of the young men who went to Cairo became the most bitter opponents of their own Government. (Belgrave 1960, 145)

Egypt's permissive labour emigration policy under Sadat aimed to appease Arab host states' concerns by demonstrating that Egypt was committed to a new role as a regional provider of de-politicised migrant labour. Sadat would repeatedly signal that the era of dispatching Egyptian professionals abroad to serve as political agitators was gone. This was linked to the process of de-Nasserisation discussed in Chapter 4, and was made obvious in the state's newly implemented permissive emigration policy. Prominent journalist 'Ali Amin underlined that 'Egypt will [now] never think of interfering with the internal affairs of any Arab state. Neither will it impose an opinion, a certain person, policy, or form of government on them, be it Beirut, Amman, Damascus, Tripoli, Kuwait, or the Arabian Gulf' (*al-Ahram*, 7 April 1974). While, in the past, 'Arab states' suspicion of Nasser's political motives was reflected in a reluctance to encourage the emigration of Egyptians', Arabs were now urged to abandon such scepticism (Choucri 1977, 6). As Anis Mansur, the later editor-in-chief of the regime mouthpiece *October*, explained:

[An] Egyptian was looked upon as the man with the 'ugly face' throughout the Arab world. For twenty years, every Egyptian had seemed to turn into a spy or saboteur. Every Egyptian teacher was thought to have come to overthrow the standing rule and to distribute subversive literature. Every Egyptian doctor was considered a spy acting for Egyptian Intelligence Service to set one class against another ... Now he is not interested in other peoples' affairs. 'Give and take' is his motto. [Under Nasser] every Egyptian was treated as a *persona non grata* and he had to isolate himself to affirm that he had nothing to do with what happened in Egypt. [Under Sadat] this abominable picture changed and will continue to change to the better, for Egypt came to be governed by a ruler not by a leader ... Egyptians abroad form a 'working army' for the sake of Egypt and all Arabism. (*al-Akhbar*, 13 March 1974)

What explains this shift in discourse on labour emigration, and the abandonment of a decades-long tradition of political activism outside Egyptian borders? For one, these statements, which were commonplace in Sadat-era Egypt, buttressed the new president's internal legitimation strategy of distinguishing him from Nasser in the eyes of Egyptians. At the same time, they contributed to Sadat's external legitimation tactics by signaling a shift in Egyptian foreign policy in the eyes of Arab elites. Former Minister of Migration and Manpower Nahed

Ashry confirmed this strategy: 'Presidents Sadat and Mubarak did not wish [for] Egyptian workers' involvement in politics abroad' (*personal interview*). In a similar tone, *al-Akhbar*'s Mostafa Amin, in a column entitled '"Ugly Egyptian" Image Removed', argued that the Egyptian regional migrant was formerly considered as 'a hooligan holding a knife in his mouth and a heavy club in his hand. Unfortunately, the Egyptians helped maintain that ugly picture by their behaviour, and this explains to a great extent the pleasure that the world showed upon our 5 June 1967 defeat. Today the situation is totally different' (*al-Akhbar*, 23 May 1976). The use of regional migration as a signal that Egypt is ready to aid, rather than antagonise, its Arab neighbours is evident in Sadat's introduction of the term 'temporary migration'. Law 111|1983, still valid today, explains the difference between 'temporary' and 'permanent' Egyptian migrants, first highlighted in the 1971 Constitution: a 'permanent' emigrant is one who 'stays abroad permanently by obtaining the nationality of a foreign country and/or a permanent residence permit, stays abroad for a period of at least ten years, or obtains an immigration permit from one of the countries of destination. A 'temporary' emigrant, on the other hand, is 'someone (not a student or seconded worker) who works abroad for twelve consecutive months'. However, in practice, this differentiation has been based upon migrants' country of destination: Egyptians living in Arab countries are invariably considered temporary emigrants, or temporary workers abroad, even when they have lived there for decades. All those emigrating to Australia, Europe, North America, or elsewhere, on the other hand, are considered permanent emigrants, even if they just arrived in their host countries (Zohry and Harrell-Bond 2003, 34).

The literature has typically accounted for this by citing foreign workers' inability to settle permanently in the countries of the Arab Gulf, and the relative ease of doing so in the West. Ashry argued that 'Egyptians in the Arab world are not migrants. They are temporary workers, who will return home' (*personal interview*). Former Minister of Health and president of Cairo University Ibrahim Gamil Badran suggested that the Egyptian state's formal emigration policy 'targeted the sons of Egypt abroad, not Egyptians in the Gulf. Egyptians do not emigrate to Arab countries' (*personal interview*). Yet, this post hoc explanation is not entirely convincing, given that it does not problematise why this distinction first emanated from the Egyptian state itself. Also, it is somewhat inaccurate, given that not all regional emigration is de facto temporary: Syria, Jordan, and Libya, which constitute traditional destinations of Egyptian migrants in the Arab world, have, at times, granted citizenship to emigrants, particularly to Arabs (Dib 1978). In the Arabian Gulf, the United Arab Emirates and Kuwait would, until the 1980s, grant citizenship to Arabs after ten and fifteen years of residence, respectively. Iraq would also proceed to naturalise Egyptian migrants throughout the 1980s, as seen earlier. But even when naturalisation is not an option, it is not unusual for Egyptian migrants to remain there for more than two or three decades, or even to stay abroad until their death. If the 'transformation of temporary immigrants into settlers cannot be ruled out' in the Gulf, then Egypt's decision to bifurcate its policy merits deeper analysis (Kapiszewski 2001, 193).

As I have shown elsewhere (Tsourapas 2015b, 2208), by emphasising the "temporary" aspect of regional migration, Egyptian elites wished to increase the flow of migration towards oil-exporting countries of the Arab world.[1] The invention of Egyptian migrants' non-permanence was aimed at mollifying Arab countries' misapprehensions about opening their borders to potentially millions of Egyptian immigrants. This is best understood through, firstly, the politicised nature of Egyptian regional migrants in the pre-1970 period, and, secondly, the regional political climate of the 1970–71 period. In terms of the former, Sadat did not hesitate to signal the transience and depoliticisation of Egyptian regional migration as another distinctive feature that differentiated Egypt under his rule from the Nasserite era. Post-1970 migration was depoliticised, driven by economic rather than ideological reasons, and, above all, "temporary". This coincided perfectly with host states' wishes. 'The intent of Saudi Arabia's policies are as straightforward as those of Kuwait', writes Sell. 'The Saudis wish to keep migrants temporary and have them return home when their labour is no longer wanted' (Sell, 1988, 95).

While one cannot definitively demonstrate that Egyptians abroad abstained from political activism in the post-1970 era, there exists scant evidence of any mobilisation attempts. Egyptian regional migrants confirmed the regime's promises by generally developing a reputation of political pacifism, to the delight of their host states. 'Statistics show', Haddad argued in the late 1980s, 'that both Saudi Arabia and Kuwait reduced the recruitment of Palestinian labourers' after 1970, opting instead to employ 'large numbers' of Egyptians who would not 'function as a fifth column and eventually endanger the host countries' (Haddad 1987, 248). Roy similarly argues that, under Sadat, the Egyptian state effectively ceased to promote migrants' political activism abroad: 'It must be stressed that, for the most part … Egyptians go abroad for purely economic reasons. They may not like the conditions or the social values of the countries hosting them, but they are totally disciplined [not] to jeopardise the opportunity to earn money by indulging in political activities' (Roy 1991, 574). Policies examined in Chapter 4, such as the decision to abolish exit visas on the third anniversary of Sadat's Corrective Revolution, had a similar rationale.

Importantly, as seen earlier, the regime's granting of freedom of movement to the members of the Egyptian Muslim Brotherhood was an attempt by Sadat to ideologically distance itself from Nasser, and to have the group act as a counterweight to the rise of communism or Nasserism. The regime's coalition with the *Ikhwan* was struck with regional, rather than solely domestic, goals in mind, aiming at a rapprochement with its Arab conservative neighbours, particularly Saudi Arabia. Not surprisingly, the decision to release the *Ikhwan* from Egyptian prisons was timed so as to coincide with the June 1971 'triumphal reception' that Sadat had prepared for King Faisal's visit to Cairo. The Egyptian president intended to employ the release of the *Ikhwan* in an attempt 'to please his Saudi guests' (Vassiliev 1997, 384–85). The difficulty in collecting any data relevant to this sensitive matter in either Egypt or Saudi Arabia prevents a more detailed discussion on the matter. Yet, while we cannot know the extent of the two leaders' discussions or agreements, Mohamed Hassanein Heikal's memoirs recount a key detail of the actual encounter:

King Feisal in the summer of 1971 arranged for some prominent members of the Brotherhood to be given a safe conduct for their return to Egypt so they could have discussions with Sadat. The meeting was held at the Janaklis rest house, in conditions of strict secrecy, the representatives of the Brotherhood being led by Said Ramadan, who had lived in

Saudi Arabia for some years and was at this time living in Geneva in charge of a Saudi-sponsored organisation called the General Islamic Movement. (Heikal 1983, 116)

By ending the great *Miḥna* (ordeal) of the *Ikhwan*, Sadat took another step to distance himself from his predecessor's policies, an effort that conservative Arab regimes appreciated (Kandil 2015, 128–37). Sadat's gesture was duly rewarded by the Saudi monarch: King Faisal responded with a monetary reward to Egypt of LE 30 million, and by lifting any travel restrictions on Saudi citizens arriving in Egypt (*al-Ahram*, 2 July 1971). At the same time, he adopted policies, such as the expansion of religious education in higher education, which further fostered the return of the *Ikhwan* to Saudi Arabia (Al-Rasheed 2010, 138). It is interesting to note, given Faisal's notorious antipathy for communism, that Sadat had imprisoned a number of Egyptian leftists during the Corrective Revolution, only a month before the Saudi king's visit to Egypt. A year later, in July 1972, Sadat would deport some 15,000 Soviet military and civilian advisers out of Egypt. Ibrahim concurred that:

Sadat's move to liberalize emigration in 1971 is tied to the connection between the Egyptian regime and the Saudis. Sadat released the Islamists from the prisons, promoted contacts with Saudi Arabia, where many of the prisoners emigrated to in the early 1970s, encouraged their printing activities, and allowed them to take over the universities – out of where most graduates ended up in Saudi Arabia. (*personal interview*, 21 October 2013)

While the subjugation of a key state policy, such as migration, to Sadat's regional goals might initially appear unconvincing, or too risky a gamble, the personality of the new president has been established as prone to such spectacular, unexpected, and improvised moves, particularly when it came to his foreign policy objectives. In administering state relations with Arab elites, in particular, Sadat was a 'one-person thinker', as Hegazy recalled (*personal interview*). In August 1974, for instance, while showing the Saudi king around the rebuilding of a city around the Suez Canal following the 1973 War, Sadat unexpectedly declared that 'the people had decided to name one of the districts after King Faisal', in recognition of Saudi help for Egypt. This was politely, but vehemently, rejected by the Saudi king himself, who suggested the name 'The Peace District' rather than 'King Faisal's District', adding, 'I am only an Arab citizen' (*al-Ahram*, 7 August 1974). According to Heikal's more florid account, the Saudi king retorted, 'Please, Mr President do not do that. Today we are friends, but tomorrow, who knows, we may be no longer. In which case naming a town after me would only be an embarrassment for you' (Heikal 1983, 85).

Overall, the deregulation of Egyptian population controls allowed the regime to move away from Nasserite-era regional antagonism and strengthened its ties with the Muslim Brotherhood – both of which signalled a wish for rapprochement with Saudi Arabia. By the early 1980s, Hosni Mubarak would emphatically declare that '[t]he days when a citizen [of Egypt] residing abroad was viewed with suspicion, as if he had not fulfilled his national duties, are over ... we must all guarantee, in actions and not in words, that an Egyptian working abroad is a good citizen, who has not renounced his identity' (quoted in *al-Akhbar*, 15 August 1983). Beyond its utility in distancing Sadat from Nasser, the choice of emigration as an instrument for signalling Sadat's wish for rapprochement was not incidental, for it caught the attention of labour-poor, oil-rich Arab states. In essence, Sadat ensured that Egypt would provide continuing trained and untrained labour for Arab states' rising labour needs.

To drive this point home, the Egyptian regime employed the October 1973 War. Sadat would refer to an upcoming military confrontation with Israel since 1970, but it was not until October 1973 that hostilities between Arabs and Israelis broke out. Through a surprise offensive, the Egyptians reoccupied the eastern coast of the Suez Canal, while the members of the Organisation of Arab Petroleum Exporting Countries (OAPEC) proclaimed an oil embargo against select Western countries. Saudi Arabia, in particular, imposed a complete embargo on exports to the Netherlands and the United States. 'The campaigns showed once more the military superiority of the Israelis', wrote Hourani, 'but neither in the eyes of the Arabs nor in those of the world did the war seem to be a defeat' (Hourani 2013, 418). In fact, Sadat welcomed the result of the 1973 (or October) War as a much-needed corrective to the devastating 1967 defeat and valuable proof of intra-Arab solidarity. In doing so, Sadat was able to solidify his standing as president of Egypt, highlight the human sacrifices of Egypt in the Arab–Israeli Wars and link them to the need for Arab economic aid. Having achieved an initial rapprochement with other Arab leaders in the 1970–73 period, Sadat now signalled that

Egypt, a populous state, should continue providing labour for oil-rich states' developmental needs in peacetime, much as it provided military support during wartime. Even as the centre of Arab power was moving towards the oil-rich monarchies, Sadat's migration diplomacy was meant to ensure that Egypt would continue to enjoy an important, albeit no longer central, role in intra-Arab politics. Sadat's Foreign Minister wrote in his memoirs:

The shock of the 1967 War and the defeat – psychological and moral as well as military – suffered by the Arabs, sparked a spirit of Arab resurrection, especially since this was coincident with the emergence of the area's vast potentialities in oil and manpower, making it a strategic and economic power to be reckoned with. The end of the 1973 War saw the Arab world transformed. It had become a mighty giant that had awakened from its torpor and realized its own strength as soon as it had regained its self-confidence and self-esteem. (Kamel 1986, 29)

As a result of the 1973 War, according to the Egyptian regime's rationale, 'Saudi Arabia and all the Gulf emirates were awash in surplus earnings from oil exports. Sadat was not at all reticent in claiming his share' (Waterbury 1983, 416). Securing increased financial aid from Saudi Arabia was a chief goal of Sadat (*al-Akhbar*, 21 March 1974), and promoting Egyptian migration became an intrinsic part of this strategy. This was justified in two ways: first, Egyptian efforts during the Arab–Israeli Wars carried a moral implication that Arab states contribute to its economic well-being; second, the heightened need for migrant workers in the oil-producing Arab countries, combined with Egypt's labour surplus, suggested a mutually beneficial, honourable solution that allowed Sadat to save face – bypassing a main problem that had dissuaded Nasser from espousing labour emigration. The conflation of these two elements occurred through a strategy that linked Egypt's "extra-ordinary" sacrifices during the various conflicts with Israel to continued Arab aid, albeit in an indirect form, through the absorption of its excess labour force.

Egyptian labour, in its perceived importance for the Arab–Israeli Wars and its potential utility to labour-poor Arab countries, gradually dominated the Egyptian elite's discourse in the post-1973 period. 'Egypt is the Arabs' fortress', prominent journalist Musa Sabry wrote, referring to the Arab–Israeli Wars of 1948, 1956, 1967, and 1973. 'She has sacrificed 100,000 martyrs over 4 wars' (*al-Akhbar*, 21 March 1974). Implied here was an economic quid pro quo:

Table 5.2 *Destination of Egyptian migrants on government contracts, 1973*

Country	Number	Percentage of Total
Libya	13,355	38.58
Saudi Arabia	10,591	30.60
Kuwait	4,365	12.61
Algeria	2,085	6.02
United Arab Emirates	1,014	2.93
North Yemen	783	2.26
Oman	622	1.80
Lebanon	473	1.37
Qatar	464	1.34
Bahrain	287	0.83
Sudan	269	0.78
Iraq	161	0.47
Syria	59	0.17
Jordan	34	0.10
Morocco	25	0.07
Tunisia	19	0.05
South Yemen	5	0.01
Palestine	3	0.01
Total	34,614	100.0

Source: CAPMAS, 1973

according to Sadat's rationale, Egypt's sacrifice in labour necessitated not only closer cooperation between the Arab states, but also concrete aid. 'We believe that Egypt should call for an immediate Arab meeting, and that the Arab countries should be frankly told that Egypt has shouldered the burden of the Arab cause for 30 years and, as a result, has suffered hunger, become impoverished and made sacrifices' (*Akhbar el-Yom*, 22 January 1977). Sadat, according to journalist and confidant Anis Mansur, 'considered his preoccupation with Egyptian affairs too onerous for him to add any Arab problems to them, and [felt] that to manage the affairs of the 37 million Egyptians is too heavy to be made heavier by the misery of 70 million more Arabs. Egyptians abroad', Mansur claimed, 'form a "working army" for the sake of Egypt and of all Arabs' (*al-Akhbar*, 12 March 1974). According to Sadat himself:

In order to repel aggression, the Egyptian people lost more than LE 10,000 million, this besides the lives of the fallen soldiers, which cannot be evaluated in terms of money. The Egyptians did not pay this price just for their own defence, but in defence of the whole Arab nation ... the burden of military expenses adversely affected the level of development in Egypt, which dropped from 6.7 per cent during the period from 1956 to 1965 to less than 5 per cent annually. (Sadat 1974, 6)

The strategy of highlighting Egypt's importance in the fight against Israel was not new, tracing its roots to the late Nasserite era and, particularly, the 1967 Khartoum Conference negotiations, when the conservative monarchies agreed to support the Egyptian state financially 'until the elimination of Israeli aggression' without any written conditions (Gilbar 1997, 105). The Saudis had then declared that 'Egypt is not standing on its own, the Saudi government, which never hesitated to assist its big sister in the various stages of its conflict with the enemy ... feels today, as always, that it is supporting Egypt' (Feiler 2003, 7). After 1973, Egypt discursively equated the importance of the oil embargo, imposed by the OAPEC countries in shaping the war outcome, with the Egyptians who had lost their lives fighting against Israel. 'Who won the [1973] War?' *Akhbar el-Yom* asked. 'Faisal, or Sadat?' (*Akhbar el-Yom*, 22 March 1974).

Sadat would similarly argue that 'other Arabs, despite their opposition, for the moment could do very little about Israel without Egypt's leadership and support; nor could they deny Egypt a role in the Arab world, by virtue of its sheer size, the dynamism of its experience and the momentum of its human resources' (Feiler 2003, 125). The president vehemently supported that 'everything [the Arabs] possess was given them by the blood of our sons in Sinai' (*Al-Siyasi*, 3 May 1981). Whereas Egypt under Nasser had attempted to profit from Arab oil via the use of migration as soft power, Sadat adopted a different strategy altogether. As Sadat declared:

'The October battle would not have been possible had I not worked for two years to make the Arab nation one family again. The decision for the crossing was Egyptian-Arab; the solidarity was Egyptian-Arab; the surgeforward was Egyptian-Arab. Thus from being disunited, we became united; instead of acting against each other, we developed an understanding.' Arab unity was real, for Sadat, and it was no longer dependent on 'empty slogans'. (quoted in Brand 2014, 81)

Egypt's contribution to the 1973 War became enmeshed with the responsibility, or duty, of oil-exporting Arab states to accept Egyptian

Figure 5.1 'The Peak | The Summit' (*al-Ahram*, 27 November 1973)
'Arab Kings and Presidents Began their Conference Yesterday'

migrants in such a way that the Egyptian regime would not "lose face": 'We do not want gratuities', Hegazy declared; 'we do not state our needs and ask for aid. Egypt has huge trained manpower potential ... Egyptian manpower is the most precious capital we possess' (*al-Ahram*, 27 October 1974). It is in this light that Egypt's decision to have the 'export of labor become an officially recognized policy objective' should be understood (Dessouki 1982, 59). According to Sadat, 'Egypt is the heart and mind of the Arab world ... And the biggest asset in Egypt is the human being, the Egyptian man, who is a doctor, engineer, labourer, teacher, with 13 universities here and with the pride and heritage of seven thousand years' (quoted in Lippman 1989, 262). In other words, if Egyptians contribute to the Arabs' well-being during wartime, it is only logical they should continue to do so in times of peace. As Saddam Hussein graciously acknowledged, Egyptian wartime sacrifices needed to be repaid through cross-regime coordination on migration:

> There is not a single Arab citizen or a single Arab country that is not indebted to the Egyptian people, and the Egyptian soldiers, for their sacrifices at all times … It is nationally incumbent on every true Arab to hasten to repay part of that debt so that giant and generous Egypt should continue to stand on its feet in full grandeur. We in Iraq are prepared to contribute to that duty, and that honour. Our doors are flung open to Egyptian farmers, workers, and intellectuals. They will be assured here of the same treatment as their Iraqi brothers, without the least discrimination. (quoted in *al-Ahram*, 21 February 1975)

This was not mere rhetoric: in fact, Iraq had put forth an official request for 'large numbers of Egyptian farmers to migrate to Iraq with their families, where they will be given title to agricultural land with the aim of increasing the country's wheat and maize crops', only a month earlier, in January 1975 (*al-Ahram*, 20 January 1975). By March 1975, an agreement between Manpower Minister Saleh Ghareeb and his Iraqi counterpart was reached on Egyptians being remunerated ID 130/monthly and enjoying all the privileges granted to Iraqi citizens (*al-Ahram*, 1 March 1975). It was decided that the first 500 Egyptian *fallāḥīn* families would move to the *al-Khalsa* Settlement, some 36 miles south of Bahdad (*October*, 4 July 1982). There, they would be assigned 20 feddans of land (later reduced to 8 feddans, or approximately 8.5 acres of land), a three-room house, a shed, and cattle free of charge (*al-Ahram*, 8 March 1975). Importantly, the land deeds would be indefinitely leased to the Egyptian farmers' families (*el-Solh*, 1984). Applications for the scheme reached 4,000 people by mid-June 1975 (*al-Ahram*, 13 June 1975). The process was later lauded by the Iraqi Minister of Information, Tariq ʿAziz, as 'a confirmation of the necessity of Arab cooperation in the fields of development and production' (quoted in *MENA*, 11 August 1976). A second village was built in the *al-Wahdah* area of *Karrada*, a Shia-majority district of Baghdad, while in 1983 authorities agreed to build three new villages (*al-Ahram*, 17 December 1983).

At the same time, the Egyptian regime made sure to drive home the point that Egyptians 'have a small cultivable area of land, [and] a big population that is increasing maybe by the biggest rate in the world (Sadat, quoted in *Time*, 18 March 1974). 'The supply of Egyptian manpower was essential for the Gulf countries, and the president realized the country's potential in bringing them closer to Egypt', recalled Hegazy (*personal interview*, 27 April 2014). Indeed, one of the goals of the Higher Council of Manpower and Training, newly formed through Presidential Decree No. 795, was the 'fulfilment of the needs of Arab and other friendly countries' (Messiha 1980, 12). At the same time, Egypt introduced training regulations that ensured that the state 'provides the specialized manpower required and regulates the supply of workers whose services are sought by the sister Arab states' (*al-Ahram*, 30 April 1974). In 1974, the regime announced that:

Evening classes will be arranged for government employees. Within the framework of planning to meet the requirements of Arab, African and foreign countries of skilled workers in building, electricity, factories and services, practical technical training centres will be set up in order to meet increased demand of Egyptian workers who receive high wages abroad. In view of the need of Egyptian teachers in the Arab and African countries, the ministry of higher education will set up special institutes to train those who wish to work as teachers abroad from among holders of university degrees and government employees. (*MENA*, 3 July 1974)

By 1979, Egypt put forward a plan for the creation of specialised offices in 'every faculty' of Egyptian universities that would supply students with accurate information on vacant employment posts across the Arab world (*al-Ahram*, 8 February 1974). Prime Minister Mamduh Salim had already officially declared that 'Egypt's policy is to encourage export of its manpower to the Arab world ... so that Egyptians can participate in the development plans of sister Arab states' (*al-Akhbar*, 15 August 1975). The Undersecretary of the Ministry of Immigration supported such statements: 'we must supply the Arab countries with the manpower to develop ... This is our duty. They need our manpower and we have good relations. They are our brothers' (*Cairo Today*, May 1984; see also Figure 5.2). These measures, and the discourse accompanying it, make little sense unless examined within the Sadat regime's regional foreign policy goals.

Overall, the Egyptian regime signalled a wish to work closely with other Arab regimes by promoting Egyptian emigration as a solution to oil-rich countries' labour shortages. Sadat would publicly declare that sustained emigration is part of the responsibility of Egypt towards 'our Arab brothers and Third World friends who are in need of Egyptian expertise' (*al-Gomhoriya*, 29 August 1974). In 1975, Egypt announced

Figure 5.2 'After the battle for Sinai, Golan and Oil ... Success' (*al-Ahram*, 14 November 1973)

Arabs embracing: 'I think after we have reached this peak we should have a summit conference!'

that its formal policy 'to export its surplus workers to other Arab countries and elsewhere' (*The Middle East*, October 1975). In terms of Saudi Arabia, in particular, Kerr described this systematic dispatch of Egyptian migrants as an 'unspoken bilateral relationship' (Kerr and Yasin 1982, 6). More broadly, by the end of the 1970s, as concerns over domestic labour shortages were invariably bypassed for Arab states' developmental needs and any political economy cost was set aside in favour of Egypt's bilateral relations, Egypt's role as a regional supplier of labour had 'become a tradition, an accepted part of Middle Eastern economy and society' (Birks and Sinclair 1980, 43).

Finally, a third element that identifies the extent to which Egyptians' emigration was employed as a strategy by the Sadat regime to consolidate its ties with Arab regimes is the preference that migration issues be coordinated on a top-level, rather than through any institutional, or bureaucratic, process: Egyptian strategy on migration, according to Hegazy, 'always focused on bilateral agreements at the top level. The [League of Arab States] spoke about the use of Arab labour, but did not have any power, and no policy on this issue' (*personal interview*).[2] This allowed the Egyptian regime to employ migration matters in order to benefit from closer, stronger ties to other Arab regimes. One example of this is the amendment of Law No. 97|1969, which under Nasser prohibited former government officials and ministers from working in the Arab world for five years after the termination of their work in Egypt. The new version, No. 38|1973, vested the president himself with the power to make exceptions as he deemed fit. The reason cited for this amendment was the need of Arab countries for Egyptian expertise.

This shift gave more political power to the Egyptian president, but also heightened levels of cross-regime relations that developed as a result of emigration management processes. When the Sadat regime abolished exit visas, it replaced them with two types of bilateral agreements (see Table 5.3): first, those that would allow Egyptians entry to foreign countries such as Libya or Syria with any official document of identification; second, those agreements that set ceilings on the numbers of immigrants that host states in the Arab world were willing to receive, and regulated labour conditions abroad. At the time, the latter were an odd occurrence, as Middle East 'labour movement has been spontaneous' (Birks and Sinclair 1980, 84). It is safe to assume that these frequently overlapping accords aimed less at regulating regional emigration than at consolidating intra-regime ties of collaboration. These agreements 'only described very general principles of cooperation' (Collyer 2004, 11), eschewing mention of medical care or end-of-contract bonuses (Farrag 1998, 52); even then, they were rarely followed, nor were the ceilings they set on the number of immigrants imposed. The 1971 protocol with Libya, for instance, was frequently violated. In fact, former Minister of Manpower and Migration (2006–11) Aisha Abdel Hady admitted she was unaware of many of these treaties' content, which is typically not made public (*personal interview*). Nor, in some cases, was she even aware of their existence. Overall, the utility of such agreements becomes increasingly suspicious given the readiness with which most Egyptian officials admit that regional migration

Table 5.3 *Emigration-related accords between Egypt and Arab states, 1971–2011*

Year	Countries
1971	Egypt – Libya
1972	Egypt – Algeria
1974	Egypt – Jordan
1974	Egypt – Qatar
1975	Egypt – Iraq
1981	Egypt – Jordan
1985	Egypt – Jordan
1985	Egypt – Iraq
1987	Egypt – Jordan
1993	Egypt – Iraq
1993	Egypt – Lebanon
1993	Egypt – United Arab Emirates
1994	Egypt – United Arab Emirates
1994	Egypt – Libya
1997	Egypt – Yemen
1998	Egypt – Lebanon
2001	Egypt – Tunisia
2003	Egypt – Sudan
2007	Egypt – Jordan
2007	Egypt – Saudi Arabia
2009	Egypt – Libya

Source: Tsourapas 2015b, 2210

processes are so complex that they cannot be effectively regulated through intra-state accords (Lesch 1986).

'Migration helped restore the relationship between Egypt and the Arab countries', Hegazy recently recalled (*personal interview*). The 1972 dispatch of 6,000 Egyptian workers to Algeria, for instance, was agreed under the aegis of increased bilateral coordination between the two countries (*Akhbar el-Yom*, 7 January 1972). In the 1980s, Algeria's decision to replace French teachers in the natural sciences, mathematics, chemistry, and physics with Egyptians was also dependent on the cordial relationship between the two regimes (*MECS* 11, 1987). A similar 1973 agreement to dispatch Egyptian agricultural experts to Iraq was signed under similar

Figure 5.3 Sadat embracing Faisal (*al-Gomhuria*, 8 March 1974)
'Every smile here . . . is followed by a tear there!'

rhetoric (*MENA*, 20 February 1973). In an October 1971 visit to Kuwait, Sadat received representatives of the '36,000 strong' Egyptian community, underlining the 'fraternal ties binding Egypt and Kuwait' (*October* 11, 1971). By doing so, Sadat began a process of labour migration coordination through the heads of state – for instance, Oman's Sultan Qaboos did not hesitate to directly replace all Bahrainis working in the country with Egyptians, following his 1971 coup d'état (Graz 1992). This was to the benefit of the Gulf states:

Post-Nasser Egypt, with its large population, relative development, and low national income, posed a major source of labor, the use of which could allow the Gulf states to accomplish two aims at the same time: to create a foreign work force, and to assist the Sadat regime in defusing political unrest through emigration of labor, in the interest of forestalling any reappearance of Nasserism in Egypt. (LaTowsky 1984, 12)

This process did not necessarily have the state's or the migrants' best interests at heart. Tying issues of migration with the cross-regime ties between Arab leaders instigated a tradition by which migrant communities became victims of the Egyptian regime's relations with host states' authoritarian regimes. When bilateral relations flourished, migratory movements between countries increased. The example of Libya is key: the liberalisation of Egyptian emigration restrictions had initially facilitated the close economic and political coordination between Egypt and the new Libyan regime in the 1969–73 period (Moench 1988, 176). The arrival of Colonel Gaddafi to power in September 1969 brought with it enhanced political coordination with Egypt and resulted in thousands of Egyptian workers filling government posts and construction sites in that country between 1969 and 1973. Reminiscent of the rhetoric around Egyptian migration to the Gulf, migration to Libya in the mid-1970s was put forth by the government and official media sources as 'a national obligation of Egypt towards the people of Libya'. The free movement between the two states supported a key belief in Gaddafi's mind regarding the 'unification of all Arabic-speaking people. Only in total Arab union ... can there be Arab strength' (Cooley 1982, 101). In fact, *The New York Times* reported how Egyptians abroad would pose as Libyan officials in negotiations over the purchase of the Mirage fighter plane from France, in an Egyptian effort to bypass the French-imposed arms embargo (*The New York Times*, 24 January 1970). Egyptian pilots, based in

Libya, were even dispatched to France for training purposes for the new Mirage fighter plane, again, posing as Libyans (Cooley 1982, 101). The French–Libyan arms deal, concluded in 1972, was one of the many instances of Libyan purchases of arms for Egypt from both Western and Soviet sources. When bilateral relations deteriorated, however, as in Libya and Iraq (examined in Chapter 6), Egyptian migrants suffered imprisonment, expulsions, torture, and even death (Tsourapas 2015a).

This also resulted in a hesitation on behalf of the Egyptian state to proactively protect its citizens' rights within the Arab world. A permissive Egyptian emigration policy appeared to be closely aligned to the interests of the oil-producing states, which preferred individual migrants that were free of home control, and which could be monitored easily through their lab or patronage system – or *al-Kafala* (Kapiszewski 2001b). In Lebanon, the Egyptian embassy has been accused of 'not asking about the status of the [Egyptian] citizens or paying attention to their complaints' (*al-Masry al-Yawm*, 31 March 2008). Egyptians in Kuwait had to gather the necessary funds amongst themselves in order to build a consulate and, then, donate it to the Egyptian government (*Middle East Times*, 14 December 1986). Despite a long tradition of dispatching labour attachés in its embassies abroad – as of 1960, Egypt had labour offices in Washington, London, Paris, Bonn, Prague, Accra, Kuwait, and New Delhi (Dessouki 1982) – these either closed down or, when they reopened under Sadat, were significantly understaffed. More broadly, it contributed to a relegation of Egyptians to the needs of Arab host states. In doing this, the Egyptian regime again appeared to prioritise short-term political benefits for the regime (in the form of closer relations with its Arab counterparts) than long-term state ones. As Fergany wrote,

Attempts to organize the pan-Arab labor market have fizzled out into ineffective declarations of intent that have been impeded in reality by perceived narrow national interests, particularly of countries of employment, acting the mind set of buyers in a buyers-market ... Labor movement in the Arab region has been captive to the ups and downs of Arab politics, sometimes with devastating consequences to the welfare of embroiled migrants. (Fergany 1983, 37)

Inter–Arab Relations in the Aftermath of the Camp David Accords

The Arab world without Egypt is an incomplete world.

King Husain of Jordan (*MENA*, 30 January 1982)

Arab capital plus Western technology plus Egypt's labour, markets and population explosion equals economic growth.

Sayyid Marei (*Akhbar el-Yom*, 19 April 1975)

This section will examine how a permissive labour emigration policy impacted upon one of the most important regional crises that Egypt faced: the aftermath of the Egypt–Israel peace treaty that 'shattered the alliance between Egypt, Saudi Arabia and Syria which had dominated (and to some extent stabilised) Arab regional politics since October 1973' (Ayubi 1991, 327). As a result of the 1977 Camp David Accords, where Egypt became the first Arab state to recognise the state of Israel, the League of Arab States organised an economic and diplomatic embargo that threatened the Sadat regime with loss of revenue, political isolation, and eventual collapse. Treating this boycott, and Egypt's political isolation imposed by the League, as a moment of crisis, this section examines how close cross-regime relations via migration allowed Egypt to survive this critical point, lending support to the argument that links authoritarian power to labour emigration policy.

Sadat's shifting of Egyptian regional foreign policy 'culminated in the late seventies in a remarkable revolution in Egypt's international alignments which sacrificed its place in the Arab world for a separate peace with Israel' (Hinnebusch 1985, 65). 'If the 1967 war signified the withdrawal of Egypt from its struggle with Saudi Arabia', Gilbar writes, 'the 1973 war signified the start of Egypt's virtual withdrawal from the conflict with Israel' (Gilbar 1997, 110). The story of this highly controversial shift has been recounted innumerable times – either applauding Sadat's strategic vision of peace in the Middle East (Israeli 1985), identifying the geostrategic and economic necessity of this rapprochement (Boutros-Ghali 1997), or criticising the president's diplomatic manoeuvres (Kamel 1986; Shukri 1981). An evaluation of this decision is beyond the scope of this study; however, it is indisputable that Egypt, in the aftermath of Sadat's initiative, faced one of its most important crises in its relations with the Arab world.

'No one would have expected that the president of the largest Arab state ... would declare his readiness to go to the land of the enemy', Sadat argued (Brand 2014, 83) – indeed, this was met with shock from Egypt's Arab counterparts. The immediate effect of the Egypt–Israeli rapprochement was the convening of the November 1978 Arab League Summit, held in Baghdad in the absence of Egypt. Arab leaders, 'enraged by his peace treaty with Israel' (Carroll 1982, 91), agreed on a full economic and political boycott against Egypt (Tripp 2007, 211). Diplomatic relations with Cairo were suspended; major joint economic projects with a significant labour component were cancelled, such as the Arab Military Industrial Organisation; and all transport links to Egypt were severed. The League of Arab States' headquarters were moved from Cairo to Tunis, while Egyptian membership of the League, and of other regional organisations, including the Islamic Conference Organisation, was suspended (Feiler 2003). The hostile climate between Egypt and its Arab counterparts, culminating in the decade-long boycott, was a major crisis for the Egyptian regime. 'After the peace treaty with Israel, Egypt became isolated from most other Arab states', Hopwood describes. 'Arab airlines stopped flying to Cairo, embassies were closed and the Arab League expelled Egypt and moved its headquarters from Cairo [to Tunis]' (Hopwood 1991:120). Handoussa and Shafiq argue that

Egypt ... was isolated both politically and economically ... Generous US economic aid could hardly compensate for the abrupt cessation of all Arab aid, trade, and capital flows ... Arab aid and private capital immediately dried up, Arab markets were effectively closed to Egyptian-based enterprises, tourist flows from Arab countries dwindled, and large Arab investments pulled out of numerous major joint venture projects in tourism, manufacturing, the free zones, and defence. (Handoussa and Shafik 1993, 25)

Indeed, at least initially, Sadat voiced his discontent, stressing the very issue of cross-regime relations in matters of migration in long verbal attacks against his Arab counterparts:

They came out with attacks and took decisions full of invective against Egypt, which represented a deviation from all true values. Their main decision was to starve the Egyptian people, those dwarfs who have been fed, protected and educated by Egypt and are still being educated by Egypt. You heard me say that Egypt was not only sending professors and teachers to one of these dwarfs' emirates but also schoolbooks, pencils, and chalk. [Now] all of this manifests itself in attacks against Egypt and attempts to starve the Egyptian people so as to keep them in the same position as prior to the October war: a defeated and wounded people, and this at a time when their own coffers are bulging with gold and dinars amassed at the expense of our people's sacrifices of blood and resources ... Without Egypt, the Arabs are zero. Egypt is the heart and mind of the Arab world and for the next generations to come they will never catch up with Egypt and it is not oil that builds Egypt, no. The fortune of Egypt is not like Saudi Arabia and the others. (quoted in Lippman 1989, 261–62)

The durability of the Egyptian regime at this moment of crisis was enhanced, partly, due to the pre-existing cross-regime interaction on issues of migration. The *Economist Intelligence Unit* reported how Sadat appeared 'to be treating the matter [of boycott] as a gigantic bluff on the part of the other Arab countries', partly due to the strong labour linkages between them (Handoussa and Shafik 1993, 25). Assuming that a mass deportation of the millions of Egyptian migrants across the Arab world would be logistically impossible might have been a gamble on the part of President Sadat, who was particularly prone to such risks. The CIA documents tell a slightly different story, one again dependent on Egyptian emigrants: as early as 1977, the CIA proposed that, in case of a complete rupture with the Arab world, 'Egypt could launch a "peace bond" drive among expatiate Egyptians. Egyptians abroad are already financing imports of luxury goods worth at least $400 million annually. A well-managed bond drive might conceivably siphon off some of this cash for essential imports' (National Intelligence Daily Cable, 1977). That plan never needed to materialise, however – by 1978, the CIA itself had estimated that 'Egyptians comprise at least 10 percent of the labour force in many [Arab] countries, and an expulsion of the Egyptians would cause a shortage of workers and disrupt the Arab countries' development programs' (*CIA Weekly Summary*, 27 October 1978). Indeed, the 1979 *Middle East Economic Digest* highlights how the Arab states did not consider banning, or limiting, Egyptian immigrants from their countries as part of the economic boycott – which was initially one of the biggest fears of the Egyptian regime (*MEED*, 12 October 1979). Kuwait's Minister of Interior stressed that 'we have not taken any measures against [Egyptians]. On the contrary, they are welcome. We have not prevented any from entering, nor have asked any of them to leave' (*al-Ahram*, 8 April 1979). The Saudi Minister of Interior issued a similar statement (*MENA*,

29 April 1979), while North Yemen asked for 1,340 additional teachers to complement the work of some 2,700 Egyptians already present (*MENA*, 3 June 1979). According to *The New York Times*, Egyptians' post-1979 presence throughout the Arab world typified 'the most conspicuous inconsistency of the cold war' between Egypt and the other Arab states (*The New York Times*, 8 July 1979).

Indeed, Arab states' reliance on Egyptian migrants in the 1970–79 period made it logistically impossible to remove them: by 1979, official statistics put the number of regional Egyptian migrants at 1,365,000, with unofficial numbers indicating almost twice that number (Amin and Awni 1986, 25). No doubt realising the detrimental effect a mass expulsion of Egyptian migrants would have on their economies, elites in Saudi Arabia and elsewhere gradually began arguing that 'there is no boycott against the Egyptian people' (Oweiss 1980, 170). As Ayubi wrote in 1983, Egyptian teachers 'are particularly needed by practically all countries of Arabia and the Gulf to foster and support their ambitious educational programmes' (Ayubi 1983, 439).

It is important to note that the recruitment of Egyptians was particularly crucial because Gulf states were unwilling to recruit non-Egyptian Arab working staff, such as Palestinians.[3] Significantly, Kuwait, Qatar, and the United Arab Emirates took active steps during the 1980s to prevent the growth of Palestinian migrant communities within their borders in order to stop 'the influx of disturbing or radical political thought' (including, for instance, purchasing specific software to screen for illegal Palestinian immigration to Kuwait). Egyptian immigrants were unaffected (See 'Gulf Limits on Palestinians', *Foreign Report*, 21 July 1983). In the early 1980s, Yemeni migrants were also targeted for deportation in Saudi Arabia, given Yemenis' involvement in the takeover of the Grand Mosque in Mecca. Egyptians were unharmed, despite proof of at least six Egyptian *takfirs* (religious fanatics) being involved. Egyptian communities developed a reputation of pacifism abroad: 'we didn't like the idea of having a *kafeel* like Egyptian migrants', explains one Yemeni returnee from Saudi Arabia in 1993; 'they will say you are their slave' (quoted in Van Hear 1998, 91).

While instances of Egyptian involvement in political protests continued to occur, these were generally sporadic. In the post-1979 era, 'the Palestine Liberation Organisation had hoped that the Egyptian migrants might be radicalised into a counterforce opposing the Sadat peace policy, but that has not happened' (*The New York Times*, 8 July 1979). Only isolated instances of violence were reported – for instance, when *The New York Times* reported on an Egyptian beaten up in Jordan and told 'by the assailants to have the Israelis find him a job' (*The New York Times*, 8 July 1979). Saudi Arabia's 1980–85 Five-Year Plan, aimed at reducing the number of migrant workers, did not significantly affect the Egyptian community (*al-Gomhuria*, 14 August, 1983). 'As an educated and politically conscious group, the Palestinians are particularly closely observed', writes Lackner about Saudi Arabia; on the other hand, 'the main priority for Egyptians ... is to make as much money as possible as fast as possible, to send it back home, and to survive' (Lackner 1978, 193). Kuwaiti expulsions of about 4,000 migrants in 1985, for instance, exclusively targeted Shia Muslims of Iranian or Lebanese descent (*The New York Times*, 6 October 1985). In Iraq, Egyptians 'were not thought to be a potential source of political disturbance' (Feiler 2003, 101). In fact, 'the oil countries prefer to deport first the Asian foreign labourers, then the Palestinians and Syrians, and only in the end the Egyptians' (*MECS* 11, 1987). As *The New York Times* bluntly stated:

In theory, it would be possible to replace the Egyptian expatriate work force with Palestinians, who constitute the region's other major pool of skilled labour. However, Palestinians are often discriminated against as political risks ... Saudi Arabia tends to view Palestinians as potential fifth columnists and prefers Egyptians who may be less motivated but are more 'harmless and submissive', as one Saudi employer put it. (*The New York Times*, 8 July 1979)

The Egyptian regime shrewdly capitalised on this by dispatching more trained professionals across the region (Table 5.4), and a major socio-economic crisis was averted.

At the same time, coordination on matters of migration allowed low-level linkages to be built between Egypt and Arab states, gradually spilling over into limited military and security collaboration. This constituted what Heikal termed a cross-regime "silent dialogue". Egypt was able to open a special labour office in Riyadh in 1978 to look after the rising number of workers in Saudi Arabia (*MECS*, 3, 1978). By 1981, a new building was being planned for the Egyptian embassy in Riyadh (*al-Ahram*, 21 June 1981). Furthermore, taking advantage of a loophole in the Baghdad Summit agreement, Kuwait and other Gulf states did not boycott the Egyptian national airline

Table 5.4 *Egyptian teachers officially seconded to Arab countries,*
1983–1989

Year	1983	1984	1985	1986	1987	1988	1989
Algeria	505	358	394	642	562	2	301
Bahrain	206	535	239	107	128	77	140
Kuwait	491	428	350	344	170	247	111
Oman	1,257	1,034	2,028	2,063	1,623	1,208	972
Qatar	33	101	46	52	29	57	98
Saudi Arabia	6,283	3,665	1,165	1,288	5,794	1,811	1,337
Somalia	42	41	61	8	39	45	51
Sudan	436	626	413	528	396	278	295
United Arab Emirates	273	319	285	344	164	302	174
Yemen	976	1,156	1,708	666	788	916	1,430
Others	28	42	54	45	21	0	0
Total	10,530	8,305	6,743	6,087	9,714	4,943	4,909

Source: Arab Republic of Egypt, Ministry of Education and Technical Education,
2014

completely, but only its flights to and from Israel (Sela 1998, 210).
In March 1979, *Saudi Arabian Airlines* introduced ten weekly flights
between Cairo and Jeddah, Medinah, Riyadh, and Dammam to accommodate migrants' transport needs. *Egyptair* quietly resumed flights to
Amman in April 1979, and by mid-year to Morocco, Saudi Arabia, and
other Gulf states. Flights to and from Baghdad had resumed by the
summer to accommodate Egyptian migrants' summer return. *Iraqi*
EgyptAir had resumed its flights to Cairo by May 1982.

How cross-regime interaction on issues of population mobility supported the Egyptian regime is evident in its relations with Iraq's
Saddam Hussein: despite his strong early insistence that Egypt be
isolated, Hussein acceded to the dispatch of Egyptian military experts
to Iraq in 1980, including sixty flying instructors (*Newsweek*,
26 July 1982), given the country's massive military needs in face of
the confrontation with Iran.[4] By late 1981, the ban on former Egyptian
servicemen from enlisting in the Iraqi army had been lifted (*Reuters*,
31 July 1981), while Egyptians enjoyed visa-free entry in order to serve
as a labour substitute for drafted Iraqis during the Iran–Iraq War

(*MEED*, 31 July 1981). From 7,400 Egyptians in 1977, around 1.5 million migrants had entered Iraq by 1982. The same year, the Iraqi government began enlisting non-Iraqi Arabs into the military. Initial Iraqi reticence at publicly supporting Egypt was overcome after Operation Beit al-Muqaddas, which allowed Iranians to recapture the strategic city of Khoramshahr.

Egyptian migrants in Iraq, Hussein attested, 'despite their large numbers ... have no political problems at all', while journalists, lawyers, medical staff, and 'others' would be welcome to migrate to Iraq (*MENA*, 24 May 1982). It was agreed that Egyptian migrants would pay no taxes while they were serving as a substitute for drafted Iraqis (Ahmed 2003, 313) in *al-Jaysh al-Sha'bi* (the Iraqi Popular Army). At the same time, the Iraqi government reportedly issued a decree that made any insult to Egyptians because of Sadat's peace treaty with Israel punishable by a six-month imprisonment (Badry 2010, 254). In 1983, Iraqi Vice-President Taha Yasin Ramadan al-Jizrawi announced that Iraq had a set policy favouring Egyptian migrants over other nationalities (*al-Musawwar*, 10 June 1983). By 1984, *al-Ahram* estimated there were 2 million Egyptians working in Iraq (*al-Ahram*, 23 November 1984), while a cap was introduced on the numbers of foreign Asian workers within Iraq that also favoured Egyptians (Feiler 2003, 101). In August 1985, noting the demographic superiority of Iran, the Revolutionary Command Council announced that Iraqi citizenship would be granted to Arab migrants, and they would be allocated housing land in any province outside Baghdad after three years (*al-Thawra*, 20 August and 22 September 1985, quoted in *MECS 10* 1986). Despite the fact that a formal re-establishment of diplomatic relations did not occur immediately, Hussein supported that 'the basic ties [between Iraq and Egypt] are in our hearts and consciences. Relations ... are not defined by official formulas' (*DR*, 19 March 1985). By 1988, Mahmud 'Abbas, the Director of Immigration Affairs at the Egyptian Ministry of Foreign Affairs, would put the estimate of workers at 1.6 million (*Egyptian Gazette*, 11 March 1987).

The involvement of the Americans in this is unclear (although interviewees in Cairo have hinted at their importance in this process of rapprochement), but declassified CIA documents reveal that Washington was indeed aware of the importance of migration management in restoring intra-Arab ties, and that it was repeatedly asked to intervene in favour of Egypt. A 1983 report marked *Egypt: Regional Issues and Relationships – An Intelligence Assessment* highlighted that 'expatriate Egyptian workers, most of whom are in Iraq and the Arabian Peninsula countries, are an important economic and human link between Egypt and other states' (p. 15). It also recognised that 'the Mubarak government is relying heavily on the United States to help it attain its regional objectives' (p. 10). A later report underlined that

active economic contacts have helped blunt the effects of the 1979 sanctions against Egypt ... In addition to Jordan, Egypt has signed economic and techni-cal agreement with Iraq. Trade officials travel frequently between the two countries, and bilateral cooperation has become substantial in such areas as labor, youth, and cultural affairs ... Approximately 2.2 million skilled Egyptian expatriate workers – a major source of foreign earnings – are employed in the Arab states. (Egypt and the Arab States: Reintegration Prospects, 1986, 6)

The report ends with a detailed breakdown of the numbers of 'Egyptian workers in the Arab states' and their estimated remittances.

Gradually, Egypt was able to introduce low-policy matters linked to labour migration in its negotiations to reverse its isolation. By November 1985, the Transport Ministers of Egypt, Jordan, and Iraq would meet in Cairo to plan for joint projects that would enhance sea and land transportation links between the three countries (*DR*, 26 November and 3 December 1985). These were preceded by an agreement on regulat-ing Egyptian migration to Jordan, in March 1985, that complemented two separate agreements, in 1981 and 1987 (*al-Ahram*, 25 March 1985). In this process of reconciliation, the improvement of transport linkages was a key issue (particularly the Nuweiba–Aqaba route). Egypt responded by completing a new road (in 1986) across Central Sinai that cut the distance between the Suez Canal and Nuwayba by 150 km, thereby increasing the volume of people crossing borders (*MECS* 10, 1986, 110). Despite the Jordanian economic recession, and the boycott against Egypt, the number of Egyptian migrants in Jordan increased to more than 125,000 by mid-1990 (Lesch 1986, 5). Jordan became the first Arab country to formally re-establish diplomatic relations with Egypt in 1984. By the end of the decade, Egypt had reversed its economic and diplomatic isolation: in May 1989, Egypt resumed its membership in the League of Arab States, while the headquarters of the regional organisation returned to Cairo in 1990.

Table 5.5 *Egyptian workers and families in key Arab countries*

	1970	1975	1976	1980	1982	1985
Saudi Arabia	n.a.	95–120,000	100–140,000	150–250,000	800,000	1.4 million
Iraq	n.a.	7,000	32,500	223–342,000	1.25 million	1.25 million
Libya	60,752	200–230,000	250,000	250–340,000	300,000	100,000
Kuwait	17,714	40–60,000	139,000	60–105,000	200,000	220,000
Jordan	n.a	5,300	4,500	56–70,000	125,000	160,000
United Arab Emirates	11,100	13–15,000	12,500	28–50,000	150,000	110,000
Qatar	600	3–5,000	12,200	6–20,000	25,000	30,500
Oman	n.a	4,600	5,000	5–6,300	11,500	8,700
Bahrain	n.a.	1–3,000	2–3,000	1,350–5,000	6,000	n.a.
North Yemen	n.a.	2,000	n.a.	4,000	6,000	n.a.

Source: Kerr and Yasin (1982, 34)

Conclusion

This chapter has examined how Egypt's permissive emigration policy under Sadat and Mubarak fostered the external legitimation strategies of the ruling regime, particularly under the Sadat period. It detailed how the shift in the regional balance of power, occurring in the aftermath of the 1967 War and Nasser's death, led Sadat to pursue a closer relationship with the conservative regimes of the GCC states. In developing a process of rapprochement, labour emigration fostered this, in three ways: firstly, the liberalisation of emigration marked a significant policy shift that allowed Sadat to distance himself from his predecessor; secondly, it concretely demonstrated the regime's desire to benefit economically by contributing to neighbouring states' labour needs; finally, it strengthened cross-regime ties between Egyptian and Arab elites through increased levels of diplomatic activity. The final section examined a critical time of crisis in the Egyptian regime's regional relations and the aftermath of its rapprochement with Israel, and evaluated the importance of Egyptian migration in fostering cross-regime relations.

Chapters 4 and 5 have argued for a chiefly political rationale behind Egypt's shift in its emigration policy in the early 1970s, driven by the need to establish regime durability in the domestic and international levels, respectively. Yet, one could raise the question of how important economic considerations were in this shift? By highlighting the regime's political rationale, is there a risk of downplaying the importance of key economic problems – unemployment, overpopulation and urbanisation, a currents accounts deficit – that might have contributed to this policy shift? Chapter 6 looks more closely at the case for an economic rationale and identifies how the Sadat and Mubarak regime prioritised political gains, rather than economic ones. While this produced important, short-term political benefits, it was to the long-term detriment of the Egyptian state – arguably, it explains the processes that led to the ousting of President Mubarak in early 2011, known as the January 25 Revolution.

6 | *Egypt's Road to Revolution*

Our density is our destiny.

Gamal Hamdan (1970, 366)

Chapters 4 and 5 highlighted how the post-1970 Egyptian ruling regime employed a permissive labour emigration policy in order to further their domestic and international standing. Yet, a keen reader would raise the important question of whether the introduction of a permissive labour emigration framework by the Egyptian regime in the early 1970s was not a strategic, political calculation, but a rational, economically driven policy shift. If one keeps in mind, for instance, the penurious state of the Egyptian economy in the aftermath of Nasser's death, then the development of a permissive labour emigration framework appears to be an economic necessity rather than a political strategy it constituted a clear means for the ruling regime to combat overpopulation, urbanisation, and unemployment (by encouraging citizens to pursue opportunities abroad), and to bolster its finances through the injection of remittances into the national economy. In this line of argument, the political importance of labour emigration undoubtedly exists, but appears more as an afterthought rather than the driving force behind regime policy. How, therefore, could one determine the ruling regime's priorities at the time, and make a legitimate claim for the determinants of emigration policy being political, rather than economic?

Chapter 6 addresses these objections by critically assessing the argument that Egypt's emigration policy in the post-1970 period was driven by economic considerations. It demonstrates how these constitute a necessary, but not sufficient, condition to explain Egypt's permissive labour emigration policy. Economics, in other words, is not irrelevant, but material reasons are unable to fully explain the rationale of the Egyptian regime's engagement with emigration. While overpopulation, unemployment, and diminishing foreign reserves were identified as the main reasons behind the shift in Egypt's emigration policy, the measures that the regime put forth had little effect – or, in many aspects, adverse effects – on the aforementioned issues. Going back to the study's second assumption, the Egyptian regime's engagement with emigration, therefore, can best be understood as prioritising short-term political goals, rather than long-term economic ones. Not surprisingly, the ruling regime was unprepared for the quantitative and qualitative shift that occurred in the 1990s, as most Arab host states either attempted to nationalise their labour force or shifted their recruitment of migrant labour towards Asians. As detailed in the Introduction, the use of a permissive emigration policy as an instrument of regime legitimation relies upon sufficient economic opportunities abroad; once Libya, Iraq, and the GCC states shifted their immigration policies away from the recruitment of Egyptian workers, the strategy of legitimation stopped bearing fruit. Ultimately, the backfiring of the regime's strategy contributed to the fateful events of 2011.

The chapter is structured around three sections: firstly, it identifies how the Egyptian regime initially approached labour emigration as a solution to three main macroeconomic issues, namely the country's increasingly prominent demographic issues; its chronic under- and unemployment; and, finally, its diminishing foreign reserves and problematic balance-of-payments record. Secondly, it demonstrates how complete deregulation of emigration exacerbated, rather than improved, the economic indicators of each of the aforementioned issues. It explains the negligible effect of population mobility on Egypt's demographic imbalance, emigration's contribution to the worsening of the country's unemployment crisis, and the state's inability to capture migrants' economic remittances or to control the accompanying corruption and inflationary problems. While the regime was acutely aware of these issues and the fact that they could have been avoided via the regulation of cross-border mobility, it opted for complete deregulation instead. Finally, the chapter analyses the various complications this approach engendered, and lays down the ways in which the regime's approach to labour emigration set the ground for the 2011 Egyptian Revolution.

The Liberalisation of Emigration as an Economic Panacea

> We should not be unduly perturbed by the increasing emigration of Egypt's teachers, engineers, physicians, farmers and workers ... We should view

the millions of Egyptians remaining in the country as a burden, which we should reduce by having them emigrate or exported.

Anis Mansur (*al-Akhbar*, 9 April 1975)

I am not opposed to migration, as we are a nation of 45 million people.

Hosni Mubarak (*al-Siyasa*, 26 February 1983)

As Chapter 2 described in detail, in the aftermath of the 1952 Revolution, and particularly since the 1960s, the Egyptian economy has been characterised by three main macroeconomic issues that are of relevance to population mobility: the question of overpopulation and urbanisation, the rising problem of structural unemployment, and a balance-of-payments deficit. All three are issues that the Nasserite regime was confronted with since the 1960s and debated using labour emigration in order to address them. Ultimately, it opted to expand the public sector, instead – a politically driven decision that aggravated these problems further. Unsurprisingly, all three issues resurfaced, more forcefully, following the death of Nasser. For many, the post-1970 shift to a permissive emigration policy has been linked to the regime's attempt to find a solution to these three problems.

Egypt's demographic predicament, for one, became more pressing in the last years of Nasser's rule and increased in intensity under Presidents Sadat and Mubarak. As Zohry accurately describes, 'while the country's population doubled from 9.7 million to 19 million in 50 years (between 1897 and 1947), the next doubling to 38 million people took less than 30 years (from 1947 to 1976). Since then, the population has almost doubled again, totalling 76 million in 2006' (Zohry 2014, 76). This was openly discussed, particularly with regard to overpopulation's deleterious consequences for the state economy as it incurred potential food shortages, lack of development, and a heightened need for housing. 'We have a small cultivable area of land', Sadat declared, 'and a big population that is increasing maybe by the biggest rate in the world' (*Time Magazine*, 19 March 1974). Mubarak would openly state his fears that Egypt's population was growing 'faster than the speed of sound'. The problem was 'horrifying', because people were procreating 'without any consideration or calculation'. 'What will happen when there are 70 million of us, keeping in mind that resources do not increase at the same rate as population? ... What about houses, food, education, medical treatment, and many other needs for [these] millions? Where will we get these things?' (*May Address, DR*

Table 6.1 *Egyptian population growth, 1975–2010*

	1975	1980	1990	2000	2010
Mid-Year Population (millions)	38.6	44.95	56.83	67.64	81.11
Population Growth Rate (Annual %)	2.12	2.45	2.44	1.8	1.97
Fertility Rate (Live Births per Woman)	5.59	5.37	4.35	3.31	2.88
Life Expectancy at Birth (Years)	54.69	58.32	64.55	68.59	70.45
Infant Mortality Rate	154.70	114	67.8	22.3	15.5

Source: World Bank, World Development Indicators

3 May 1988). Mirroring Mubarak's exasperation, Sadat often talked of being kept awake by the thought of the '200 million loaves of native bread he had to provide each morning' to 40 million Egyptians in the mid-1970s, a number that was increasing annually (Vatikiotis 1991, 430).

The effects of overpopulation were exacerbated by the continuing issue of urbanisation and internal migration to the large urban centres, namely Cairo and Alexandria. This took a heavy toll on the cities' infrastructure, transport, and public utilities. Writing in 1973, Waterbury argued that:

For educated, urban Egyptians, acutely aware of the crowding of [Cairo], the major concern is the 'flood' of migrants into the city. Frequently one hears that Cairo and its facilities are designed to handle a population of about 1.5 million, a level exceeded during the Second World War with a massive influx of migrants (606,561 in the period 1937–1947) ... A city suited for a million and a half people is obviously crowded with six million residents. (Waterbury 1973a, 3, 5)

The adverse socio-political effects that such issues would engender for regime durability are underlined by reports of the United States Secretary of State: a 1979 telegram from Cairo Embassy titled 'An Overview of Destabilising Forces in Egypt' read:

The frustrations of living in Cairo and other Egyptian cities increase daily. This is a function of population explosion, of urban migration, and of an infrastructure which was sorely neglected for 25 years. Cairo could comfortably house 2–3 million; it is called upon to shelter some 9 to 10 million. The housing shortage is acute; perhaps as many as a half million Cairenes are camped out in a semi-permanent status in the City of the Dead, with virtually no government services. Cairo's water, sewage, transportation, and telecommunications are all woefully inadequate. (Department of State, 1979)

The regime's concern regarding overpopulation was evident by its coverage across state media, and by the open debate initiated by regime elites on the issue: 'At the bus stop I saw fifteen children', wrote prominent journalist Mohamed Afify. 'They were the product of five women, or, should I say, five human rabbits ... Why doesn't the Egyptian man and wife enjoy love without having so many children. Why not be content with the pleasant overtures of love and avoid the burdensome consequences!' (*al-Gomhuria*, 24 November 1974). On a different occasion, Mubarak declared that 'the dreadful average of the population explosion confronts us with a major challenge that deprives us of reaping the fruit of achievement and consumes the highest proportions of the country's growth rate. The time has come for us to stop – in a scientific and serious pause – and confront this problem' (*DR* 8 November 1983). In a 1989 speech for the National Democratic Party, Mubarak recounted how:

In Luxor I once met a police sergeant who said 'I need a house Mr President'. I asked him 'how many [children] do you have?' He said 13. My God! What he needs is an apartment block ... If each of you needs a whole apartment block to yourself, how can we build a million of them? Not even in a thousand years will we be able to build them ... Yes, we all trust in God, but the Prophet said, 'Do your duty and trust [in God]'. He did not say 'Fool around'. (quoted in *al-Ahram*, 23 July 1989)

In tackling the problem that Mubarak once termed the 'dreadful population explosion [that] consumes all our efforts and exhausts most of the positive developments' (quoted in *R. Cairo*, 6 November 1983), family planning was never seriously considered (cf. Fargues 1997). Its perceived negative political consequences if implemented across the largely conservative context of Egypt made ruling elites reticent about its use (for an ethnographic account of these policies' failures, see Ali 2002). Initially, Sadat established *al-Majlis al-A'lā li-l-Sukkān wa-Tanzīm al-Usra* (the

Figure 6.1 Population growth striking development
(Arab Republic of Egypt, 1991)

Supreme Council for Population and Family Planning), as well as
a Department of Population within the Ministry of Health in 1973. Yet,
family planning was not seen as a sustainable solution: Sadat 'hardly paid
any attention to the problem', argued Ibrahim, not least because family
planning was not viewed favourably by the more religious, or conservative,
Egyptians that Sadat was aiming to co-opt (Ibrahim 2006, 91). Lipman
noted that 'Sadat and his prime ministers hardly even gave lip service to
birth control, despite all their speeches about the demands posed by the
rising population. They did not hide their embarrassment at the dogged,
outspoken support for family planning by the only prominent figure to
make that commitment – Sadat's wife, Jihan' (Lippman 1989, 162). Sadat
eventually settled the matter of family planning by stating that 'successful
birth control requires a certain standard of education, which does not exist
among the majority of our people, particularly in the rural areas' (Sadat
1975, 6). According to Hilmi 'Abd al-Rahman, an adviser to Hegazy:

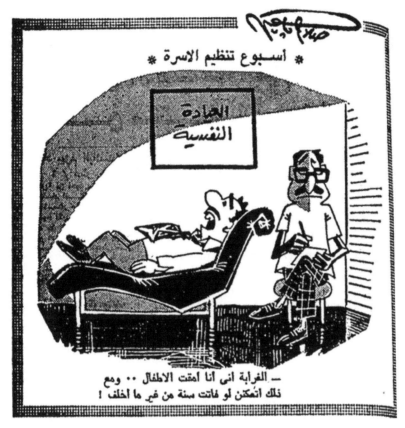

Figure 6.2 Family planning week (*al-Ahram*, 24 April 1973)
'The strange thing is that I hate children ...
but despite that I am all messed up if a year goes by without one!'

The development of the population for the next twenty-five years has already been determined and can only be changed slightly through family-planning efforts. Our population will double in the next twenty-five years with only a 20 percent possibility of variation ... Therefore for the next twenty or twenty-five years the problem in Egypt is mainly to meet the requirements of an increasing population, and if industry and technology develop quickly this will help reduce the population as happened in all advanced societies. (quoted in the *Egyptian Gazette*, 9 February 1975)

As a result, a different solution for overpopulation needed to be identified. Conventional family planning techniques (contraception pills, intrauterine devices, condoms, etc.) were judged a failure, and all the talk shifted 'to further industrialisation, populating the deserts or, importantly, emigration' (Waterbury 1983, 45). In this, ruling elites appeared unanimous that a permissive emigration policy would best tackle overpopulation: 'The high rates of Egyptian population growth at the time dictated a change in the state's emigration laws', Dessouki recalled (*personal interview*). Former Minister Boutros Boutros-Ghali, writing in *al-Ahram*, argued that the 'complicated' problem of overpopulation 'should be tackled through a comprehensive strategy based on family control, the regulation of internal migration, and migration on both the Arab regional and international levels' (*al-Ahram*, 15 November 1975). 'We should not fear surplus in manpower', Hegazy argued in 1974, given that 'Arab, African, and even European countries sought Egyptian manpower' (quoted in *MENA*, 11 May 1974). By 1975, Prime Minister Mamduh Salem declared that emigration was the official target of the nation as a way to provide a durable solution to the issue of overpopulation and serve to benefit neighbouring Arab countries (*al-Akhbar*, 15 August 1975).

Beyond Egypt's demographic problem, the Sadat and Mubarak regime had to contend with the ever-pressing issue of unemployment, particularly for the growing young, trained labour force that was unable to find work in the Egyptian economy. 'Even according to official projections based on inflated estimates by various agencies in the mid-sixties', Ayubi argued, 'the country was, by the early seventies, graduating more than four times the number of engineers it was expected to need until 1980' (Ayubi 1983, 434). According to Mubarak, this was a distinctly political problem: 'unemployment is a bomb that will explode ... sooner or later if we are not prepared to confront it now' (quoted in *al-Ahram*, 23 March 2001). 'Egypt with 20 million people could have been a Mediterranean country, a Greece or Portugal', Boutros-Ghali dryly remarked. 'Egypt with 70 million people will be Bangladesh' (quoted in Lippman 1989, 164).

Indeed, combatting unemployment was one of the prominent issues on the regime's agenda in the post-1970 era (Birks and Sinclair 1979, 299). Unemployment rates were exacerbated by the release of more than a million Egyptians from long-term military service in mid-1974, following the end of the 1973 Arab–Israeli War and as preparations for a rapprochement with Israel were underway (Waterbury 1983, 46; Ibrahim 1982, 66). At the same time, rapid population growth further undermined efforts to curb unemployment: by 1981 there were about 500,000 newcomers to the labour market annually. Even though the

Table 6.2 *Youth unemployment in Egypt, 1991–2010*

Year	Unemployment Rate (% Total Labour Force, ages 15–24)
1991	29.7
1995	32.6
2000	25.5
2005	33.7
2010	26.3

Source: World Bank, World Development Indicators

Figure 6.3 Overpopulation carried by development (*al-Ahram*, 2 September 1994)

official unemployment rate was reduced from 12 per cent in 1986 to less than 9 per cent in the late 1990s, this was negated by population growth: in fact, 'in absolute numbers, unemployment has increased from less than 1 million in the 1980s to consistently over 2 million in recent years' (*MECS 5*, 1980, 414).

The solution of labour emigration quickly became appealing to policy-makers, given the fact that Egypt has the region's largest well-trained deployable force. 'The government encouraged the migration of workers', according to Lippman, aiming at 'reduced domestic unemployment' (Lippman 1989, 108). The regime's rationale appeared to be that labour migration would reduce the size of the labour market and the rate of unemployment in two ways: directly, if those who are unemployed find employment abroad; or, indirectly, if migrants had been employed and were replaced by those unemployed. At the same time, as Nobel laurate and journalist Naguib Mahfouz acknowledged, the excess workers in the government bureaucracy, which place 'limitless burdens on the shoulders of the state', can be amended by training them 'to provide the necessary personnel for employment in the Arab and other world countries' (*al-Ahram*, 1 February 1976).

As a result, the 1978 Five-Year Plan formally identified the encouragement of emigration as a way of combatting Egyptian unemployment (Ministry of Planning, 1978). 'At least a partial solution, a way of easing the pressure', Boutros-Ghali later shared in an interview for the *Washington Post*, is 'for Egypt to "export" Egyptians to other Arab nations' (quoted in *Washington Post*, 27 January 1982). Thus, prospective emigrants to the Arab world were not regarded as an asset by the state. In order to successfully reduce unemployment, Egyptian elites engaged in a concerted effort to "export" labour abroad. As journalist and writer Anis Mansur cynically argued:

We should not be unduly perturbed by the increasing emigration of Egypt's teachers, engineers, physicians, farmers and workers ... We should view the millions of Egyptians remaining in the country as a burden, which we should reduce by having them emigrate or exported. When we do export them, we must teach them to respect the countries where they work, their way of life and political doctrines, in addition to positive and peaceful co-existence. By so doing, Egyptian emigrants will manifest their love of and loyalty to Egypt and that they serve its interests more than those who live and multiple on its land without having any other job but multiplication. (*al-Akhbar*, 9 April 1975)

Figure 6.4 Egyptian migrants as birds (*al-Ahram al-Iqtisadi*, 4 August 2003)
'On your father's life, when you arrive safely,
please send me an employment contract..!'

Finally, the Egyptian regime was faced with a massive balance-of
-payments problem in the aftermath of Nasser's death (Waterbury
1983, 409). Military mobilisation, ISI policies, an inefficient state-
run economy, and even the need to import basic foodstuffs had all
taken their toll on Egypt's balance-of-payments problem. One of
the regime's most dramatic acknowledgements of this problem
came in the immediate aftermath of the 1973 War, when Sadat
admitted that his decision to embark upon a military confrontation
with Israel was not merely a political decision, but a financially
pressing one as well:

I will not hide from you, my sons, that prior to the decision to go to war we had
reached a difficult economic situation. Without economic resistance there
could be no military resistance. Our economic situation, six days prior to the
battle, was so critical that I called a meeting of the National Security Council
and told them we had reached zero. The army cost LE 100 million a month,
and all our tax receipts in one year were LE 200 million, just two months'

expense for the armed forces. There was nothing left for us but to enter the battle, whatever happened. We were in a situation such that if nothing had changed before 1974, we would have been hard put to provide a loaf of bread. After 5 October we received $500 million, which saved our economy and which gave us new life. (quoted in *al-Ahram*, 27 August 1974)

He later declared that:

There were some who advocated fighting, and others who said we were not ready ... At the end I said that I wanted to tell them one thing only – that as of that day we had reach the *marḥalat al-ṣifr* [zero stage] in every sense of the term. What this meant in concrete terms was that I could not have paid a penny toward our debt instalments falling due on 1 January [1974]; nor could I have brought a grain of wheat in 1974. There wouldn't have been bread for the people, that's the least one could say. (quoted in *Al-Usbu' al-'Arabi*, 9 October 1974)

Similar to its treatment of unemployment and overpopulation, the regime turned to labour emigration and economic remittances as the main solution to the state's balance-of-payments issue (Birks and Sinclair 1979, 288). In fact, the importance of attracting remittances has been most frequently cited as the chief economic reason behind Egypt's shift in emigration policy. For Dessouki, 'since the late 1960s, the government has pursued a number of policies which seek to encourage emigrants to invest their savings in Egypt' (Dessouki 1982, 63). By 1977, the Egyptian government put forth its Five-Year economic plan predicting as much as LE 350 million in net returns from incomes abroad, in order to tackle a deficit that was becoming more serious:

By 1975, the deficit on the balance of current accounts had risen to one fifth of GDP, but with the new liberal economic policy no serious action was taken to restrict imports. In the following year the deficit did decline by 39 percent, but mainly as a result of the reopening of the Suez Canal in June 1975, the revival of tourism, and the increase in remittances from Egyptians working abroad. Although in 1976 there was still a deficit of LE 593 million, the World Bank reports expressed optimism with regard to the possibility of eliminating or greatly reducing the deficit early in 1980. But all hope is pinned to these very sources: the Suez Canal, tourism, and remittances from abroad, in addition to the expected increase in oil exports and in private foreign investments. (Amin 1981, 433)

Whereas remittances in 1970 did not exceed $10 million, by 1979 they would amount to more than $2 billion (*al-Ahram al-Iqtisadi*,

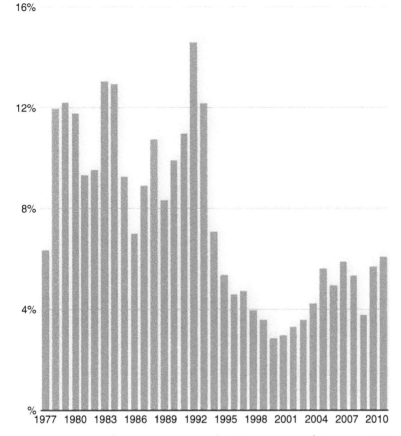

Figure 6.5 Personal remittances received, 1977–2011 (% of Egyptian GDP)
Source: Tsourapas 2015b, 2205

1 January 1980). At the time, it was calculated that the value of remittances exceeded the combined revenue from tourism, the Suez Canal revenues, the value added from the Aswan High Dam, and the economic benefits from the country's cotton exports (Abdel-Fadil 1982, 51). According to data from the Egyptian Central Bank, in the early 1990s migrants' remittances accounted for more than 14 per cent of its GDP (see Figure 6.5). 'The most favourable aspect of the economic scene in the past five years', wrote Birks and Sinclair in 1982, 'has been the surge of foreign exchange flows into Egypt'. This is mostly due to migrants' remittances, the largest source of foreign exchange (Birks and Sinclair

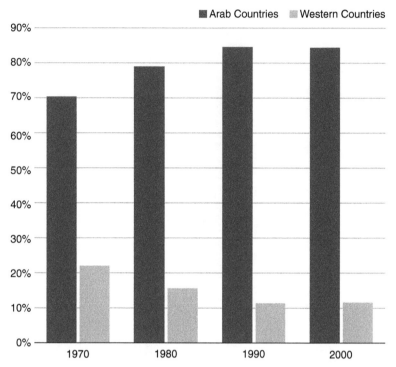

Figure 6.6 Personal remittances by emigrants' host country (% of total)
Source: Tsourapas 2015b, 2206

1982, 40). By 1992, economic remittances would amount to more than 12 per cent of Egypt's GDP. By 2010, migrant workers' remittances continued representing around 3.0 per cent of Egypt's GDP, 'making the migration of [the] labour force the most profitable export for many Arab economies', Egypt included (Fargues 2013, 17).

Overall, therefore, the Egyptian regime under Sadat and Mubarak acknowledged that the Egyptian economy was plagued by long-standing issues related to overpopulation, unemployment, and balance-of-payments deficits. There can be little doubt that the shift in Egypt's emigration policy was put forth by the regime as an ostensible solution to these macroeconomic problems: it was acknowledged at the time, by policy-makers and researchers alike, that 'migrant labour provides Egypt hard currency in the form of worker remittances, and serves as a safety valve for population growth and unemployment' (Lesch 1986, 1). As Ibrahim argued,

Exporting Egyptian labour [became] a new policy evolved to deal with Egypt's economic woes. Here, a self-fulfilling diagnosis-prognosis was at work. Egypt's problems, viewed as overpopulation, surplus labour, low rates of savings and capital formation, indicated that the solution must lie in reducing what Egypt had too much of and increasing what it had too little of. Phrased differently, the economic approach is to export 'negatives' (i.e. surplus population, the unemployed, and the under-employed) and import 'positives' (e.g., remittances, capital, and new technology. (Ibrahim 1982, 66–67)

The Dubious Macroeconomic Effects of Migration Liberalisation

[Remittances] are earnings of private citizens; the governments of the region see little of these riches.

Nazli Choucri (1988, 3)

Remittances in themselves have been a mixed blessing. They have promoted consumer booms and private capital projects such as house-building and funded large dowries for weddings, but they have not increased the health of national economies in Egypt, Yemen, or Jordan.

Beverly Milton-Edwards (2011, 100)

The previous section expanded upon, firstly, three main issues that plagued the Egyptian economy from the mid-1960s onwards, and, secondly, the fact that the liberalisation of emigration was employed in a distinct effort to address them. How effective was emigration policy in resolving these issues, and what can be inferred in terms of its real effect upon Egypt's demographic, unemployment, and balance-of-payments problems? The majority of analyses on this seem to agree with Lippman that '*infitah*, combined with peace and the participation of Egyptian workers in the oil boom of the late 1970s, energised Egypt's stagnant economy' (Lippman 1989, 106). While no one would argue against the fact that foreign currency flowed into Egypt in the billions after 1970, to what extent was migration able to resolve the three main problems discussed above? This section presents a more complex and less optimistic picture – an evaluation of the effects of Egyptian emigration upon each of the three issues demonstrates how full deregulation of population movements not only produced mixed results for the national economy, but also engendered additional economic difficulties for the Egyptian state.

Firstly, in terms of the problem of unemployment and labour surpluses that characterised the Egyptian economy, the regime's decision to fully liberalise its emigration policy did not yield the expected results. Egypt's lack of upward occupational mobility means that the national economy is largely unable to compensate for exports of labour and, as a result, heavy shortages in select economic sectors are frequent. This is due to the fact that Egypt boasts a surplus of unskilled workers, as well as many categories of university graduates, but faces a shortage of skilled workers, as well as of some professional skills. Inevitably, a permissive emigration policy contributed to bottlenecks and 'acute shortages' (Birks and Sinclair 1979, 297), ultimately leading to the odd phenomenon of labour shortages within a labour surplus economy. Roy describes this problem in more detail:

The basic problem with the approach is that there is absolutely no quality control over who goes. The Arab states have long since learned to distinguish between the truly able and productive Egyptian professional and the poorly trained incompetent one. They actively recruit in Egypt and have well-developed means by which to identify the most promising candidates. In this sense, Egypt may be exporting its most needed professionals while retaining the least able and experienced. (Roy 1991, 565)

This issue is linked to broader questions of Egyptian brain drain. Throughout the 1970s and 1980s, 'Egypt's policy-makers allowed for free emigration to Arab countries, despite the shortage of professionals in several sectors at home' (Talani 2010, 67). As Halliday argued, 'it is the most energetic and potentially productive who are likely to leave' (Halliday 1977, 287). 'Many of those who left were common labourers, but others were exactly the people most needed by the expanding domestic economy: middle level managers and technicians, skilled workers and craftsmen' (Lippman 1989, 108). The effects of this complex phenomenon have yet to be determined, hindered in large part by the inability of the Egyptian state to provide detailed statistics in order to assess its magnitude (cf. Feiler 1986; Talani 2010, 69). Broader research on this issue has yet to provide a definitive answer, divided as it is between those who argue that 'the costs entailed by the brain drain are compensated for by the benefits arising from remittances and other savings' (Mabro, quoted in Dessouki 1982, 56), and those who are less optimistic, citing its adverse effects on national development (Ayubi 1983; Zahlan 1981). Yet, if one moves beyond such a broad discussion, there can be little doubt that the deregulation of emigration policy engendered concrete problems within the Egyptian labour sector.

One example of this is the educational sector, where 'emigration of the best teachers, always in strong demand in other Arabic-speaking countries, impedes educational development'. The emigration of 'many teachers (attracted by far higher salaries in the Arab oil countries) has aggravated the shortage of educated personnel, especially in rural areas' (*The New York Times*, 26 December 1976). Despite public warnings from the Minister of Education, Dr Mustafa Kamal Hilmi, that the country suffered from a shortage of 25,000 educators in 1974, some 20,000 teachers were dispatched across 'Arab and friendly countries' in that year alone (*al-Ahram*, 17 June 1974). By 1979, the Ministry of Education would report that it had a shortage of 14,928 teachers in languages alone (*al-Gomhuria*, 30 August 1979). This was well known to Egyptian elites: a report by the National Bank of Egypt argued, in 1979, that 'the main functional categories and professionals which are badly needed in Egypt ... are [those] inclined towards migration'. It estimated that shortages in technicians and skilled workers reached 40–50 per cent (National Bank of Egypt, 1979). By the 1980s, the Ministry of Education was instructed to 'regularly [approve] the annual delegation of over 30,000 teachers to Arab and African countries', to the detriment of already-strained student–teacher ratios (Waterbury 1983, 221). 'This is a very serious problem, not only because education is a basic human need and right, but also because of its effect on economic growth', argued Richards. 'Illiteracy blocks labour-intensive industrial production and helps to strangle the government bureaucracy. The appallingly low literacy levels for rural women surely also contribute to the high fertility rate' (Richards 1984, 329; cf. Ayubi 1995, 298–301). To such criticism, Sadat would respond that 'Egypt will continue to meet the manpower requirements of these countries' (*MENA*, 5 January 1977).

Another notable example was Egypt's construction sector, where labour shortages became a cause for concern, particularly given the surge demand for new housing and infrastructure post-1973, itself a result of the inflow of remittances into the country (LaTowsky 1984):

The occupational immobility prevailing within the rigidly compartmenta-lized domestic labor market has meant that internal readjustments to com-pensate for the exports of particular types of manpower have not been as extensive and successful as in other labor supplying countries, e.g. Jordan. This is the cause of the unexpectedly sudden shortages that have appeared in the numbers of technicians, tradesmen and craftsmen-both among the for-mally and informally qualified. (Birks and Sinclair 1979, 301)

Given a permissive labour emigration policy, 'thousands of Egypt's best craftsworkers and artisans did migrate to the oil states, where they made good salaries and were paid in dollars' (Lippman 1989, 75). According to Richards:

The picture is complicated by the relations between these sections of the labour market: public sector employees take second jobs in the urban private sector, agricultural labourers work on urban construction sites, and so on. But such imperfectly functioning labour markets mean that labour surpluses in some sectors or times (e.g., government services or off-season agriculture) co-exist with shortages elsewhere (skilled construction work or peak-season farm work). The inevitably uneven impact of migration abroad leads to a bewildering pattern of selective bottlenecks, which constrain growth. (Richards 1984, 328)

There is little doubt that this was known to the Egyptian regime. Initially, in February 1971, the Egyptian state had debated regulating the emigration of twelve specialisations, which were deemed 'critical' to the Egyptian state. The latter included graduates of universities, or their equivalent, in the fields of medicine, dentistry, pharmacy, nursing, physical therapy, veterinary medicine, engineering, statistics, and fine arts, as well as some sub-specialisation of commerce, literature, and languages: Arabic, French, English, Spanish, geography, history, and library services. Four committees were authorised to decide on migra-tion requests by individuals in these categories (Atrouzi 1970). This reflected an earlier attempt by Nasser in 1968, which had been cut short due to his death, to prevent mass emigration in sectors that were of particular value to the national economy. Yet, by the end of 1971, an 18-point plan removed such bureaucratic and administrative restric-tions (Ibrahim 1982, 68). Within a few years, all restrictions on migra-tion had been lifted. Indeed, the 'encouragement and full de-regulation of the movement of labour' needs to be interrogated. The reasons why the regime opted for 'random and chaotic emigration' rather than a planned and negotiated export of labour through 'secondment', 'corporate labour contracts', or 'inter-company swap schemes', cannot be explained on economic grounds (cf. Said 1990, 22).

As any regulations regarding Egyptians' emigration were abandoned in favour of a permissive emigration policy, labour shortages became common, resulting in major inflationary pressures and wide wage discrepancies. 'The relative price of labour to capital rose as labour emigration pushed up wages, while accelerating inflation and financial regulations created strongly negative real interest rates', argued Richards. 'Supervisory personnel, so crucial to successful labour-intensive production techniques, were particularly scarce during the emigration boom' (Richards 1991, 1724). In the construction sector, for instance, labour shortages in the 1970s fuelled 'inflationary havoc in the building industry', as daily wages of skilled workers such as bricklayers topped those of architects and civil engineers by 1977 (Shazly 2003, 177–78). As discussed in Chapter 4, this produced the "demonstration effect" that the regime sought, but did so to the detriment of the national economy. In 1987, Lippman drafted a list of 'sample incomes' in Egypt, including those of a primary school teacher (LE 54 per month), a police recruit (LE 13 per month), an assembly line worker (LE 275 per month), and a car parker in Cairo earning a staggering LE 500 per month (Lippman 1989, 86).

This suggests that a plan to combat unemployment by encouraging unregulated temporary emigration served as a short-term solution, at best. It also contributed to the domestic labour markets' chaotic situation, again with the Egyptian regime's consent: a month after the ratification of the 1971 Permanent Constitution, Sadat introduced Presidential Decree 73|71, a law that would allow public sector employees who emigrated in pursuit of employment abroad to be reinstated in their positions in Egypt, if they returned home within a year after their resignation, with any salary increments they missed to be taken into account (Ibrahim 1982, 68; MENA, 9 October 1971). With the consolidated 1983 Migration Law, this was expanded: after 1983, migrants would be reinstated to their old public sector positions (or equivalent ones) if they returned within two years following their resignation. The Law's Article 16 stipulated that even those who had been away for longer than two years could be reappointed if they still qualified for the posting (Lesch 1986, 9). Rather than decreasing, therefore, state-led employment rates continued to soar (particularly once Egyptians began returning en masse from the Gulf states in the late 1980s, as will be discussed in the section below). By the mid-1970s, less than 8 per cent of the Egyptian workforce was employed in the private sector (see Table 6.3). In 1978, the civil service, various state companies, and the public sector employed about 3.2 million Egyptians; by 1986, this figure was about 5 million (Ayubi 1995). Mubarak would try to make light of this unresolved issue:

Bureaucracy exists in all countries. Do not believe that bureaucracy only exists in your country. There is also extensive bureaucracy in the United States ... We do not deny that there is bureaucracy. No one can deny that. Whoever can end it completely will be a hero. I will give him the highest medal in the state and pay him 5,000 pounds a month in violation of the law. Let him show me this cleverness and how he will do it. (1987 speech, quoted in *al-Ahram*, 14 October 1986)

If the argument that the Sadat and Mubarak regimes expected to tackle the long-standing unemployment problem through permissive emigration appears problematic, emigration policy's utility in combatting Egypt's demographic and urbanisation issues is equally unconvincing. In terms of urbanisation, the continuing inefficiencies within Egypt's agricultural sector exacerbated the problem of urbanisation from the mid-1980s onwards (cf. Ibrahim 1982, 13–16). At the time, the Minister of Agriculture

Table 6.3 *Estimate of employment in Egypt*

Sector	Number	Percentage
Agriculture	6,490,000	50.7%
Government	1,740,000	13.6%
Public Sector	1,210,000	9.4%
Private Sector	950,000	7.4%
Armed Forces	342,500	2.7%
Unemployed	1,479,000	11.5%
Total	12,811,500	100.0%

Source: Birks and Sinclair 1979, 290

had called emigration 'one of the major crises facing Egyptian agriculture' (Taylor 1984, 4). But even earlier, Egyptian agriculture was especially affected by the construction boom of 1973–79 (expanding at 20 per cent per year), during which some half a million agricultural workers left the sector: 'Very small farmers, who formerly had often worked for wages from time to time, seem to have withdrawn from wage labour participation to devote themselves full-time to on-farm livestock production. Resulting increases in agricultural real wages, along with labour market imperfections, have engendered widespread complaints of a "labour shortage"' (Richards 1984, 328).

At the same time, the high probability of migrants' return to Egypt precluded the use of migration as a solution to Egypt's demographic problem. By definition, the encouragement of "temporary migration" as a solution to Egypt's demographic problem does not constitute an economically sound policy. Under Sadat, the population grew at an average annual pace of 2.9 per cent. By 1981, the population of 43 million was rising by about 100,000 a month. At the same time, the rural exodus continued, with roughly 20 per cent of all Egyptians living in Cairo by 1980. According to a 1979 US Secretary of State report on Egypt to Congress, 'the backlog in housing exceeds 1.5 million units, and another 1.5 million are needed each decade to keep up with current population growth' (quoted in Lippman 1989, 145). This placed an extraordinary burden on public services and housing: by April 1981 there was a shortage of 1.5 housing units (*MECS 5*, 1980, 414). The 1987–92 Five-Year Plan proposed a target of 1 million additional housing units, but such plans were deemed unrealistic as, officials admitted, 'location is a vital question. The entire Nile Valley is already too crowded' (quoted in Lippman 1989, 146). This echoed Nasserite policy-makers' rejection of migration as a demographic solution in earlier times: 'oh we've heard a lot about that one over the years, exporting to the *fellahin* to the Sudan and so forth', Egyptian experts declared. But 'how many might migrate? A million? There are a million Egyptians born every year' (Waterbury 1973b, 11). Overall, as Mubarak admitted in 1988, Egypt's population was 'multiplying so fast, we are even beating marathon contestants' (*DR*, May 3 1988).

Beyond the negative effects of emigration upon the state's demographic and unemployment issues, the impact of migrants' remittances on the Egyptian national economy was also dubious, at best. Much like overpopulation and unemployment, the reliance on remittances is not a viable long-term developmental solution. For one, the calculations of migrants' economic remittances as a percentage of Egypt's GDP are misleading, given that 'economic remittances represent private citizens' earnings, rather than governmental income' (Choucri 1988, 3).[1] Economic remittances represent money that will constitute either citizens' savings or consumption. At the same time, moving beyond this key issue, the Egyptian state has been unable to calculate the exact extent of economic remittances (Hallwood 1987). The Egyptian Central Bank produces official data on remittances classified into financial transfers (i.e. transfers from abroad, but, also, foreign currency declared upon arrival to Egypt by returning migrants, and converted into Egyptian pounds) and real remittances. These figures underestimate the extent of economic remittances for three reasons: first, the foreign exchange earnings that finance part of the imports could derive not from work abroad, but from tourism; second, Egyptian earnings in foreign currency might be remitted, but are not always declared; and finally, even if some of this undeclared income is converted into Egyptian pounds (and, thus, appear as part of imports), it could also continue being deposited in foreign currency accounts or in foreign banks in Egypt, and remain untraceable (Amin and Awni 1986, 58).

According to a January 1986 estimate by Muhammad Marzouk Hamed, Undersecretary in the Ministry of Migration, actual remittances totalled $10 billion, of which only $2 billion was transmitted through legal routes (*al-Ahram*, 29 January 1986). To amend these calculation errors and to provide a more accurate picture of remittances, the *National Specialized Councils* attempted to estimate actual remittances by Egyptian workers abroad in 1983. In the published report, the earnings of Egyptian migrants were estimated by multiplying the estimated number of migrants by their average wage (estimated as falling between average wages in Saudi Arabia, representing 'high-wage' countries, and Iraq, representing 'low-wage' countries). It arrives at an estimate of remittances by calculating the Egyptians' propensity to save (falling between that of Bangladeshi and Pakistani workers in the same region) of about 56 per cent, or 'more than half' of migrants' income (National Specialized Councils, 1983).

Table 6.4 *Official remittances by Egyptians working abroad (in LE millions)*

Year	Financial Transfers	Declared Imports Financed by Own-Exchange System	Total Remittances
1974	124	16	140
1975	164	93	257
1976	364	167	531
1977	384	265	649
1978	654	587	1,241
1979	666	883	1,549
1980	818	1,070	1,888
1981	591	936	1,527
1982	931	1,396	2,327

Source: Central Bank of Egypt Bulletin, 1983

Table 6.5 *Estimates of total earnings, savings, and remittances of Egyptians abroad*

Year	Numbers of Egyptians Abroad (in thousands)	Average Wage Abroad (in LE)	Total Earnings (in LE millions)	Total Expenditures (in LE millions)	Total Savings (in LE millions)	Total Remittances (in LE millions)
1974	500	1,600	800	352	448	255
1975	550	2,526	1,389	661	778	457
1976	600	3,386	2,032	894	1,138	681
1977	659	4,382	2,888	1,271	1,617	1,040
1978	725	5,244	3,802	1,673	2,129	1,762
1979	796	5,342	4,253	1,871	2,382	2,208
1980	875	5,880	5,145	2,264	2,881	2,856
1981	931	6,079	5,660	2,491	3,169	2,505

Source: National Specialized Councils, 1983, 81

The inability to measure the exact amount of remittance inflows into Egypt was coupled with the relinquishing of control over foreign exchange, of taxation on remittances, and of duties upon imported goods. Put differently, the decision to adopt a fully non-regulated emigration policy prevented the Egyptian state from benefitting even to a small extent from workers' remittances. Initially, under Nasser, Egyptians working abroad were obliged to transfer a certain proportion of their incomes back to their country in a free currency: 10 per cent for married migrants, and 25 per cent for single migrants (Roy 1991, 556). Control over foreign exchange was gradually relaxed, until it was fully eliminated in May 1974 (*al-Ahram*, 30 May 1974). In 1971, a 50 per cent bonus was given to remittances returned through the official banking system (a 35 per cent bonus had been decided in 1968), in order to increase savings (Lesch 1986, 5). In 1973, a 'parallel money market' was established that allowed Egyptians to not declare their source of foreign exchange. The "own exchange" policy was established by decree in 1974, which allowed Egyptians to import consumption and capital goods with foreign exchange from earnings abroad and absolve any licence requirements up to LE 5,000 through the intermediary of the Central Bank (*Rose al-Yūsuf*, 15 September 1975). By March 1974, Hegazy affirmed to the Peoples' Assembly that 'the door would be wide open to Egyptians working abroad to participate in industrial, housing, and other schemes ... in order to encourage them to invest their savings and funds in their homeland. No individual in this category will be questioned about the source of his funds as is being done now' (*MENA*, 30 March 1974). In April 1974, expatriates were legally able to open accounts in convertible currencies in Egyptian banks, 'with full freedom to transfer from these accounts any restrictions' (*al-Gomhuria*, 18 April 1974). In June 1975, all restrictions on foreign exchange dealings were abolished (*al-Gomhuria*, 5 June 1975). In 1977, the regime replaced Law No. 43|1974, which originally granted certain tax exemptions only to foreigners, with Law No. 32|1977, which provided tax exemptions to both Egyptian and non-Egyptian citizens (Dessouki 1982, 64; Talani 2010, 65). As a result, Egyptian migrants' financial remittances began enjoying a fully tax-free status (Choucri 1977, 16), which implied that remittances had no effect upon the balance-of-payments problem that Egypt was facing.

As a result of the deregulation process, another issue arose that further prevented the Egyptian state from benefitting economically from workers' remittances: Egyptian moneychangers began offering expatriates more advantageous exchange rates for their foreign currency than any state-owned bank could legally offer. Using data

obtained from the Egyptian Central Bank, *al-Ahram al-Iqtisadi* published a report that concluded that 'investment and business banks'
extracted 565.2 per cent, or $5.65 for every dollar deposited, and the
joint/commercial banks extracted $22.42. Thus, the dollar reaped
a tenfold return, mainly in the form of Egyptian remittances from the
Gulf (Moore 1986, 644). Sami Ali Hassan, the so called "dean" of
moneychangers, was able to turn more than $2 billion from remittances
of Egyptians in the Gulf (*al-Ahram al-Iqtisadi*, 1 October 1984). Hassan
was later convicted of bribing officials in the Lebanese Jammal Trust
Bank to provide him with guarantees against which he borrowed local
currency from three 'free-wheeling' banks, namely the *Egypt African
Bank*, the *Faisal Islamic Bank*, and the *al-Ahram Bank* – all of which
were exposed to this scheme. It was only when the Lebanese bank proved
unable to honour its guarantees that the scheme was exposed, with its
president also convicted (Moore 1986, 644):

> There have been occasions when the government has sought to enforce more
> strictly the transfer of funds from abroad in order to deflate the volume of
> funds passing through unofficial foreign exchange channels. In May 1981,
> a series of regulations were decreed, the most significant of which was a new
> requirement that those bringing foreign exchange into the country for
> deposit had to produce a customs receipt. The reaction was immediate,
> with foreign currency deposits dropping by almost $1 billion within
> a matter of weeks. These regulations were quickly modified, and subse-
> quently dropped altogether. (Roy 1991, 556)

The regime has attempted to harness these remittances via a variety
of schemes, from the issuance of special bonds to the establishment of
banks that offer advantageous terms to Egyptians abroad (Birks and
Sinclair 1979, 302). But it was only in 1989, when strapped for cash,
that the Egyptian state attempted to tax migrant activity abroad. Law
228|1989 imposed a flat tax on Egyptian civil servants working abroad.
In 1993, the Supreme Constitutional Court ruled that taxing Egyptians
abroad is unconstitutional, given that it neither agreed with the principle of fair distribution (the regime did not grade it according to income
brackets), nor was it equitable, given that it only applied to the public
sector rather than employees of the private sector. The regime replied
that the ruling applied only to those who had filed the suit, and
continued reaping about 240 million Egyptian pounds over the
1989–93 period. The Mubarak regime introduced Law 208|1994,

Table 6.6 *Sources and uses of foreign exchange of the "al-Infitah" banks, June 1981*

| | Commercial (in LE millions) | al-Infitah Banks | |
		Investment & Business (in LE millions)	Totals (in LE millions)
Foreign Exchange Deposits	743.7	708.1	1,451.8
Current Accounts	131.6	96.3	
Savings Accounts	485.0	529.6	
Blocked Accounts	127.1	82.2	
Residents' Accounts	723.9	648.4	1,372.3
Foreigners' Accounts	19.8	59.7	79.5
Net placements in foreign exchange with banks outside Egypt	443.9	337.4	781.3
Net placements abroad as a percentage of deposits	59.7%	47.6%	53.8%
Net placements as per cent of Egyptian residents' deposits	61.3%	52.0%	56.9%
Net placements as per cent of foreigners' deposits	2,241.9%	565.2%	982.8%

Source: al-Ahram al-Iqtisadi, 25 February 1985

which amended both problems; however, the Supreme Constitutional Court in 1998 argued that 'the law violated the principle of fairness, this time because the tax applied to salaried employees only and not to experts on special contracts' (Soliman 2011, 114). Again, the Mubarak regime claimed that a Court ruling could not be applied retroactively in the area of taxation (*al-Ahram*, 4 January 1998).

All things considered, the intricacies of Egypt's labour emigration in the post-1971 period undermine the argument that this policy was clearly determined by macroeconomic factors. While its origins are undoubtedly also economic – with labour emigration aiming to curtail overpopulation and unemployment, and to increase foreign currency into state coffers – the logistics of the policy's development and implementation highlight a number of irregularities: in terms of migration

resolving Egypt's demographic problem, why did it not combine migration with family planning clinics and services in order to combat overpopulation? In terms of its unemployment problem, why didn't the
regime regulate the emigration of specific employment groups in order
to ensure that the domestic market was not distorted, and that the
Egyptian state's needs remained fulfilled? Why did it, for instance,
continue dispatching thousands of teachers across the Arab world
when Egypt's needs for additional educators were made abundantly
clear? Finally, in terms of the inflow of workers' remittances, why did it
choose to foster consumption, and to not even intervene at a later point
in order to curtail the massive inflationary issues caused by it? Why,
despite a massive bureaucratic apparatus and a strong tradition in
detailed statistical bookkeeping, was the Egyptian state unable to
calculate the extent of workers' remittances?

    One answer, simply put, could be poor economic management. For
instance, *The Economist* reported the 'often repeated story that [Sadat]
dozes off whenever the cabinet starts discussing economic matters'
(*The Economist*, 29 January 1977).[2] But this is unconvincing.
The long institutional history of the Egyptian state does not lend
credence to the hypothesis that the massive shift towards a pro-
migration policy was, in any way, whimsical. On top of this, even if
one were to argue that the state's poor economic management of
migration does not negate its initial interest in improving its finances,
this is a largely anachronistic argument; it neglects the fact that the
liberalisation of migration, in 1971, predated the hike in remittances,
which occurred after the October War, by at least three years. As Birks
and Sinclair have argued, the oil price rises of 1973 'could not have
been conceived of even a few years earlier' (Birks and Sinclair 1979,
287).

    Instead, the policy shift was arguably driven by a short-term political
rationale, as discussed in Chapter 5 and 6: a permissive labour emigration policy that dispatched hundreds of thousands of Egyptians abroad
served the regime's immediate political goals, both domestically and
internationally. As a result, little consideration was given to the (unlikely, at the time) possibility that these Egyptians would return – either
voluntarily or not. Moreover, the long-term economic risks of
a permissive labour emigration policy appeared not to have been
adequately considered by regime elites – or to have been sidestepped.
Yet, Arab states' initial drive to recruit Egyptian workers in the 1970s

was not to last: as will be detailed in the section below, the gradual
decrease in the recruitment of Egyptian workers negated the political
benefits of Egypt's permissive emigration policy, and helped pave the
way for the January 25 Revolution.

The Egyptian Migration Crises and the 2011 Revolution

> – Colonel Gaddafi in Libya is deporting twenty thousand Egyptian
> workers. How are you going to respond . . .?
>
> – Well . . . we don't take the situation so seriously. We are ready to absorb
> our workers; they can find work here, or in other Arab countries.
>
> Interview of Anwar Sadat to Der Spiegel (26 March 1976)

The previous section examined labour emigration's effects on the
Egyptian economy, highlighting in particular how it failed to provide
a long-term solution to the three main economic problems it had sought
to address: overpopulation, unemployment, and a lack of foreign currency reserves. Instead, a permissive policy produced domestic labour-
market imbalances and inflationary pressures, which the regime did not
aim to address in any concerted manner. After all, market imbalances
and inflationary pressures constituted additional ways of encouraging
Egyptians to emigrate (tying into the themes of Chapter 4), while the
absence of any regulatory framework regarding employment abroad
served the interests of the Arab oil-producing states, which were initially eager to recruit massive numbers of Egyptian labour (as discussed
in Chapter 5).

The ruling regime appeared content in the post-1971 framework of
a permissive emigration process and the short-term political benefits it
gained; in fact, Egyptian emigration policy has not changed since 1971.
However, the long-term economic repercussions soon became apparent.
It is tempting to argue that the shift in Egypt's emigration policy paved
the way for the events of the January 25 Revolution by accentuating
socio-economic imbalances and further undermining any "social contract" that existed under the Nasserite era. While this would merit
a separate analysis on its own, two issues arguably contributed to the
2011 events, which the ruling regime did not take sufficiently into
account. Firstly, the impermanent nature of Egyptian labour emigration
across the Middle East increased socio-economic and political tensions
for the ruling regime as Egyptian migrants were faced with deportation

at regular intervals. Secondly, the oil-producing states' shifts in their labour immigration policies since the 1980s, whereby they both reduced the numbers of foreign workers in favour of domestic ones, and began recruiting Asian, rather than Arab labour, created further domestic socio-economic and political unrest.

As noted in Chapter 5, Egyptian labour emigration to the Arab world is largely characterised by its transient nature and the absence of any rights (Fargues 2013; Talani 2010), as a result of both the securitisation of migration in the Gulf and the bifurcation of Egyptian policy. Ibrahim calculated that Egyptians in Kuwait worked for only 3.6 years, on average, before returning to Egypt. The vast majority of state officials interviewed for this project expected that all Egyptian regional migrants would eventually return to Egypt. This is supported by the fact that Egyptians were also encouraged to take on positions abroad that were distinctly short-term (Ibrahim 1982, 44). Egyptians were also encouraged to serve as 'replacement' labour, such as when 'the filling of a vacancy created by the movement of a migrant who has left his country for a job opportunity abroad by the immigration of a national of another country' (Feiler 2003). Egyptians migrants, for instance, moved into Sudan as temporary workers in the post-1975 period. This was also the case in Jordan after 1973; by March 1977, 'Egyptian workers were arriving at a monthly rate of 10,000' (Birks and Sinclair 1980, 87). At the same time, the Egyptian state has been notoriously lacking in protecting these migrants' rights abroad, and in taking a stance against host states' violations: 'Migrants have no legal protection, no political rights, and no rights to organize, publish or strike', writes Halliday. 'Like serfs or slaves, they are usually tied to one particular employer and the Saudi press is replete with advertisements by contractors publishing details of migrant laborers who have fled from their place of work' (Halliday 1984, 4).

The history of human rights' abuses within Gulf states has been frequently identified, but less attention has been paid to the frequent deportations facing Egyptian populations across the Arab world, notably in Libya and Iraq.[3] Historically, Libya has been a preferred destination for Egyptian workers seeking opportunity abroad. While the statistics are notoriously unreliable, by conservative estimates roughly 229,500 Egyptians were working in Libya in 1975. That number had risen to 250,000 by 1980. The death of Nasser and subsequent rise of Sadat, however, contributed to the gradual deterioration of bilateral relations and turmoil for Egyptian migrants in Libya. When Sadat abandoned plans for the Federal Arab Republic between Egypt, Libya, and Syria in 1973, Gaddafi deported hundreds of Egyptian migrants, many of whom were tortured and unceremoniously dumped at the border. While Egyptians continued to flood into Libya, daily life for them grew harder – sometimes including unpleasant encounters with Libyan military personnel. As *al-Ahram* noted, the wife of an Egyptian doctor travelling back to Egypt was stopped in Salloum, where 'a Libyan customs officer inspected her suitcases and tossed her underwear provocatively before his companions. When she upbraided him, he beat her, broke her glasses and insulted her with words of abuse that outraged some Egyptian soldiers who happened to be there at the Customs House. The two sides might have clashed' (*al-Ahram*, 28 August 1974). A few months later, in April 1975, Gaddafi expelled a few hundred more Egyptians. Mufrih Nasr Isma'il, a migrant from Fayyoum, died in an incident of police brutality in Derna. On April 24, there occurred several instances of 'barbarous' Libyan torture of Egyptians, including sleep deprivation and beatings with 'sticks, whips and pipes' (*MENA*, 24 April 1975).

The Sadat regime never framed the maltreatment of Egyptians in Libya as a human rights violation. In fact, official media downplayed the extent of the abuses in order to avoid shutting down the valuable route of labour export. Musa Sabri, an *al-Ahram* journalist and confidant of President Sadat, wrote on 24 April: 'Really, I do pity [Gaddafi], and I am worried for the Libyan people ... The members of the Libyan Revolutionary Council should have searched for a way to treat their sick brother'. Instead, the regime treated the expulsions as a distinctly political issue, approaching other Arab countries that might host the workers who had left Libya. Following a visit by Sadat to Saudi Arabia, *al-Ahram* reported that the kingdom 'was ready to absorb all the Egyptian migrants working in Libya who now wish to leave', though without spelling out the details. The key was to project confidence – Egyptian newspapers made sure to mention that foreign governments' requests for labourers 'exceed the number of Egyptian workers in Libya' (*al-Ahram*, 24 April 1975).

Similar statements were issued in March 1976, when Libyan authorities began denying admission to Egyptians carrying only identity cards and expelled more than 3,000 such migrants. Again, the

Table 6.7 *Employment in Libya by economic sector and nationality, 1975*

Sector	Libyans		Non-Nationals		Total	Libyans' Share of All Employment
	Number	Percentage	Number	Percentage		
Agriculture	115,500	25.4	17,600	7.9	133,100	86.8
Mining, Quarrying, and Petroleum	12,100	2.7	5,500	2.5	17,600	68.8
Manufacturing	19,100	4.2	13,800	6.2	32,900	58.1
Electricity, Gas, and Water	9,400	2.1	3,600	1.6	13,000	72.3
Construction	34,600	7.6	118,000	53.0	152,600	22.7
Trade, Restaurants, and Hotels	40,800	9.0	7,700	3.5	48,500	84.1
Transport, Storage, and Communication	47,200	10.4	6,200	2.8	53,400	88.4
Finance, Insurance, and Real Estate	6,100	1.3	1,600	0.7	7,700	79.2
Public Administration, Education, Health, and Other	169,600	37.3	48,700	21.8	218,300	77.7
Total	454,400	100.0	222,700	100.0	677,100	67.1

Source: Birks and Sinclair 1980, 162

Table 6.8 *Percentage of Arab migrant workers in Libya, by country of origin, 1972–1976*

Country or Area of Origin	1972	1973	1974	1976
Egypt	49.3	60.4	62.3	66.8
Tunisia	19.0	18.3	18.5	15.1
Syrian Arab Republic	5.3	5.7	6.3	5.7
Jordan	4.8	3.9	3.3	3.2
Palestine	5.8	4.0	3.4	3.0
Lebanon	12.6	5.3	4.1	2.5
Sudan	n/a	n/a	n/a	2.2
Morocco	n/a	n/a	n/a	1.1
Other	3.2	2.4	2.1	0.4
Total	100	100	100	100

Source: Birks and Sinclair 1980, 161

Egyptians were driven to the border and simply left there. The Matrouh governorate in Egypt declared a state of emergency, while Sayyid Fahmi, the Egyptian Minister of Interior, directed additional trains and buses to the border for the migrants' pickup. *Akhbar el-Yom* reported on 20 March that at least one worker died, while a second, Yunis 'Abd al-'Al, was completely paralysed and left unable to speak as a result of head injuries. At the same time, there were several reports of male Egyptian migrants being forced to enter the Libyan armed forces – later evidence showed similar attempts to press-gang Egyptians in Iraq – or to renounce Egyptian citizenship in favour of becoming Libyan. On 5 October 1976, *al-Ahram* reported that some 2,500 Egyptians had been arrested in Derna and sent to recruiting stations. The men were subsequently tortured before being released to the Egyptian border authorities at Marsa Matrouh. Sadat continued to gloss over the abuses themselves, repeating instead that Egyptians working in Libya could be employed in other Arab countries. In an interview on 26 March with *Der Spiegel*, Sadat argued that he didn't 'take the situation so seriously. We are ready to absorb our workers; they can find work here, or in other Arab countries.'

Egyptian–Libyan relations reached their lowest point when a four-day border war broke out between the two countries from 21–24 July 1977. Border skirmishes escalated to limited Egyptian air attacks

Figure 6.7 'Gaddafi the murderer' (*al-Akhbar*, 24 April 1975)
'Egyptian Worker Killed in Libya | The Leader's Victories ... '

on Soviet-built installations within Libya. While tensions persisted for months afterwards, by November Libya had begun issuing entry visas to Egyptians once more, ushering in a few quiet years for Egyptians

Figure 6.8 The speech of President Anwar Sadat (*al-Ahram*, 2 May 1975)
The President's 1st May Speech | The airwaves say: 'The Speech of President Anwar Sadat.' The man on the left, Colonel Gaddafi, is blocking the ears of the Libyan people, watched by the world. 'OK, I've blocked his ears ... But I still want someone to block mine! ... '

there. Even then, however, the Egyptian Minister of Education, Mustafa Kamal Hilmi, pointed out in the People's Assembly that the majority of Egyptian teachers in Libya had requested an early end to their secondment, and had applied to return to Cairo. Despite previous periods of turmoil, 6,909 teachers had been sent to Libya for the 1976–77 academic year. Yet, their numbers dramatically decreased given the deterioration of the two states' relations leading to the border war, coupled with the continuing violence against Egyptians; by 1983, the Egyptian Ministry of Education's secondment programme in Libya was effectively terminated (Messiha 1980, 3).

Sporadic incidents occurred in the ensuing years, but no more mass deportations occurred – perhaps the economic embargo imposed upon Egypt by the rest of the Arab world in the aftermath of the Camp David Accords deterred Gaddafi from further unilateral action. It was only in 1985 that the Libyan regime, facing severe economic problems given the slump in the price of oil, decided again to dispense with the 'huge army' of 'non-productive' foreigners. At least 20,000 Egyptians were deported during August and September of that year, with some estimates putting the number of deportees as high as 100,000 out of a community of 250,000 (*The New York Times*, 18 August 1985). The Egyptians were allowed to take only half their earnings, and were 'stripped of their electrical appliances and often even household goods at the border'. This mass expulsion followed a raft of measures against foreign labourers, including pay cuts and cancellation of contracts. Egyptian and other Arab workers were allowed to remit only 300 dinars per person per year, as opposed to the 90 per cent of total income they had been able to send home in 1975. In fact, foreign workers in Libya were not permitted to make any financial transfers at all during the first half of 1985.

Mubarak challenged Gaddafi to admit that he had 'exhausted his country's wealth on adventurism and terrorist acts which he [took] pride in supporting and financing everywhere'. Libyan state radio, the *Voice of the Great Arab Homeland*, issued a sharp rejoinder: Egypt rejected the establishment of a united pan-Arab state. Its citizens, therefore, were foreigners, and the Libyan state was by no means responsible for finding them jobs. Gaddafi denounced as 'monkeys' the Arab heads of state who had 'sold themselves' to Washington. The deported Egyptian workers were complicit because they had refused to become Libyan citizens and had transferred their savings out of Libya, thereby bolstering the Egyptian regime and the Camp David agreement (Fawat 1985). The expulsion of Egyptian workers was, again, part of a broader confrontation between the two regimes that included an Egyptian troop mobilisation along the border and the Libyan hijacking of an Egyptian airliner in 1985.

By 1989, Egypt had re-normalised its relations with the Arab world, and a new rapprochement emerged with Libya. Libya agreed to reopen its labour market to Egyptian workers, and in August 1989 alone, about 70,000 Egyptians were reported to have crossed into Libya. By March 1990, Libya agreed to reimburse the previously deported

Egyptians for financial losses, allotting $6 million to Egypt; $4 million was to be given immediately to 6,000 expelled workers, out of 18,000 complaints on file with the Egyptian Ministry of Labour. In the spirit of collaboration, Libya was happy to take in additional Egyptian labourers who had been forced to flee the Gulf amidst the turbulence of the 1990–91 Gulf war. This process culminated in the December 4 signing of ten *takamul* [integration] bilateral agreements on economic matters. The warming of relations, however, was only temporary, as by 1995 some 7,000 Egyptians were again expelled, this time in retaliation for the strengthening of Egyptian–Israeli relations (Feiler 1991).

Like Libya, Iraq had enjoyed a long tradition of attracting Egyptian professionals since its establishment, but it became a major destination for unskilled Egyptians in the post-1970 era. This was aided by the fact that Iraq allowed Arabs to enter without a visa or work permit, as per the Ba'ath Party's pan-Arabist leanings (Lesch 1986, 7). Yet the 1988 ceasefire with Iran created a number of problems for Egyptian migrants, as the early promises of Taha Yasin Ramadan al-Jizrawi that Egyptians would be given priority in the recruitment for recon-struction projects were not kept (Feiler 1991, 140). The socio-economic pressures from the demobilisation of Iraqi soldiers who returned to find Egyptian workers either occupying most employment positions or competing with them for any opening led to harsh mea-sures against Egyptians in Iraq. This was coupled with Saddam Hussein's wish to challenge a newly consolidated Egypt. As a result, violent attacks by the returning Iraqi soldiers were not uncommon: 1,052 bodies were flown in from Baghdad in the first ten months of 1989, many with bullet holes and other marks of violence, while reports of police brutality, and mass attacks against Egyptians were quite common. In late 1989, 10 extra flights per day were ordered for the following few months between Iraq and Egypt in order to 'cope with the exodus' (*The New York Times*, 15 November 1989). At the same time, in an effort to tackle the country's severe economic pro-blems, the state began delaying payments to foreign workers, and, in October, imposed a ceiling on the amount of remittances they were allowed to send home, from 40 Iraqi dinars to anywhere between 10 to 30 Iraqi dinars (*al-Gomhuria*, 9 November 1989). This, according to Ramadan, was 'related to certain economic conditions' that Egypt should accept. By mid-November, the number of Egyptians in the country was estimated at 1 million, while delayed remittances were estimated at $350 million (*MENA*, 16 November 1989). Egypt was forced to accept a compromise payment of $50 millions by the end of the year.

The Iraq–Kuwait War marked another turning point in the politicised nature of intra-Arab migration. The invasion of Iraq into Kuwait on 2 August 1990, and Saddam Hussein's proclamation of Kuwait as Iraq's 19th Province, was condemned at the United Nations' Security Council [UNSC], which demanded the withdrawal of Iraqi forces. Importantly, Yemen, serving as a UNSC non-permanent member, abstained from voting; the Yemenis believed that an Arab solution, rather than an international one, was needed. The Saudis did not appreciate this, and also disagreed with the Palestine Liberalisation Organisation's Yasser Arafat's ostensible support for Iraq. Hosni Mubarak, on the other hand, was not only vocal in denouncing the Iraqi aggression, but also spearheaded a military operation to amend the invasion (Feiler 1991, 134–35). As a result, by 1990 Egypt was faced with an extreme wave of return migration from Iraq and Kuwait given the regional instability, as 'more than half a million migrants returned to Egypt within two months of the invasion' (Feiler 1991, 134–35). The exodus was also catalysed by the targeting of migrants as payback for Mubarak's lack of support for Saddam Hussein. Out of a community of 150,000–250,000 Egyptians in Kuwait, by 22 August 1990 roughly 5,000 to 8,000 were arriving from Aqaba to Nuweiba daily: 'The Iraqis, they were our brothers, but now after two weeks everything has changed', one returning migrant told *The New York Times*, reporting stories of rape and theft. Fleeing Kuwait, Egyptians said they 'had to sleep at night in desert camps, and Iraqi soldiers, they came in the night and searched our pockets' (*The New York Times*, 22 August 1990).

Once in Jordan, Egyptians fleeing from Kuwait and Iraq also had to face Palestinians, who were also disgruntled at Mubarak's foreign policy choices:

[Palestinians in Jordan] cursed them, kicked and screamed at them and charged the refugees extortionate prices for food and water, because Egypt had sided against Saddam Hussein. 'The Palestinian people, not the Jordanians, they attacked and hit us … When we walked in public, they shouted very bad things about Egypt and about President Hosni Mubarak.

We Egyptians, we cannot stand for this, so we answered back, and the Palestinians hit us. They were kicking, beating and attacking us in the streets, they were so furious with Mubarak.' Mansour Hassan Ahma said, as he lifted his full-length shirt to show the scars on his legs. 'They said, "You are a dirty nation". As bad as the Iraqi people are, they are better than the Palestinians.' (*The New York Times*, 22 August 1990)

The massive exodus created serious problems for the Egyptian state. During the Gulf crisis alone, the International Monetary Fund calculated Egypt's losses as $27 billion (*al-Akhbar*, 11 January 1991), while *Le Monde* calculated a loss of $3 billion in remittances, and $7,500 in support each for returnee (*Le Monde*, 12 April 1991). The unemployment problem in Egypt was exacerbated by as much as 25 per cent, with the International Labor Organisation calculating some 3 million Egyptians as unemployed (*al-Ahram Weekly*, 11 April 1991). Already in the mid-1980s, the Egyptian government was struggling to find employment even for the modest number of returnees from the Gulf: the Ministry of Emigration let migrants participate in soil-improvement projects, whereby they would later be allocated one-fourth of the reclaimed land (*Rose al-Yūsuf*, 23 June 1986), while the Egyptian government tried – unsuccessfully – to find new labour markets in South America and Africa for these return migrants (*al-Ahrar*, 16 August 1985). But Egypt was unprepared for the massive return wave from Iraq and Kuwait. For Vatikiotis, this highlighted

the absence of any official Egyptian state policy on the emigration of Egyptian workers to the Arab states, or anywhere else for that matter. The government had made no provision for any legislative or policy measures to ensure the protection of citizens abroad, especially in Iraq. In the Gulf in particular, the country's consular services were woefully under-represented. As large numbers of Egyptians began to return from Iraq, ruined, abused and destitute, in late 1989, negotiations between Cairo and Baghdad to agree a mutual policy regarding Egyptian migrant labour in Iraq were held in Cairo in a series of hurriedly arranged meetings between a stream of visiting Iraqi ministers and President Mubarak. The opposition attacked the President and the Atef Sidqy government for having failed to provide acceptable rules to regulate the migration of Egyptian workers seeking employment in the Arab states and other countries overseas, as well as their protection in circumstances such as those which arose in Iraq. (Vatikiotis 1991, 432)

Indeed, one of the responses of the Mubarak regime to the economic needs of returning migrants due to the Iraq–Kuwait War was to pledge to employ 100,000 of them in the Egyptian bureaucratic apparatus (*The New York Times*, 26 August 1990). A strong indication of regime unpreparedness was that, in scrambling to provide housing and employment opportunities for these returnees, 'senior figures in the Mubarak regime' were hoping to encourage the 'more permanent settlement of Egyptian communities in Africa, a possibility reminiscent of the establishment of the Lebanese community in West Africa 50–75 years ago' (Vatikiotis 1991, 433). This mirrors earlier attempts by Prime Minister Kamal Hassan Ali to introduce measures 'designed to direct returning workers and their families to new settlement areas, mainly in thinly-populated desert regions'. Unfortunately, for the regime, 'there are already signs that few returnees will want to take on the task of pioneering new desert communities. As a result, pressure on the overtaxed housing market of the major cities is likely to increase' (*The Middle East*, January 1986).

Beyond a variety of expulsions that Egyptian labour communities abroad faced, the Egyptian regime did not take into consideration the fact that Egyptians abroad might be forced to return due to future

Table 6.9 *Geographical distribution of Egyptian regional migrants, 1990 and 1993 (%)*

Country	1990	1993
Iraq	44.1	6.9
Saudi Arabia	29.3	45.9
Kuwait	9.3	9.0
Jordan	6.5	9.4
United Arab Emirates	4.3	2.9
Libya	3.0	22.9
Yemen	1.6	0.9
Qatar	1.0	1.1
Oman	0.6	0.6
Sudan	0.2	0.2
Bahrain	0.1	0.2
Total	100	100

Source: Farrag 1998, 73

falling oil prices, competition by South Asian and Asian labour, or the
wish of host states to nationalise their work force. In fact, all three
scenarios occurred as early as the mid-1980s, although the process of
nationalisation is ongoing (Haddad 1987, 249; Kapiszewski 2006).
Only the mid-1980s slump in oil prices, for instance, led to the return
of more than 300,000 Egyptians in 1986 alone (*The Middle East*,
January 1986). The recruitment of Egyptian workers is, ultimately,
tied to the fluctuation of oil prices and the priorities of the oil-
producing Arab host states. One of these priorities has been finding
employment for nationals, at the expense of migrant labour.
As Kapiszewski observes:

What makes the situation more difficult is the fact that that the excep-
tionally favorable situation which the nationals have enjoyed for decades
has started to change. A growing number of them have experienced
difficulties in finding the kind of employment they have been looking
for. The public sector, in which most nationals used to find employment,
has already become saturated, while the private sector has remained too
competitive for the great majority of them. As the unemployment among
nationals began to grow, which was a phenomenon unheard of in the
past, the GCC governments decided to embark on the formulation of
labor market strategies to improve this situation, to create sufficient
employment opportunities for nationals, and to limit the dependence on
the expatriate labor (the so-called localization, nationalization or indi-
genization of labor, depending on the country referred to as: Saudization,
Omanization, Emiratization, etc.). (Kapiszewski 2006, 5)

At the same time, this was also affected by a move away from Arab
immigrant labour towards cheaper Asian immigrant labour, which
affected the Egyptian regime's internal legitimacy. Beyond being
a cheaper form of labour, Asian immigrants are believed to be more
efficient and manageable and easier to lay off (Girgis 2002, 29). Thus,
the recruitment of workers from India and Pakistan, but also the
Philippines, Thailand, Bangladesh, Sri Lanka, and Indonesia, gradually
replaced the predominance of Arab migrants. Logistically, as well,
Asian recruitment agencies were able to provide a continuous flow of
labour into the GCC states, in particular, in sectors that the Arab
countries perceived as lacking in specialisation (Choucri 1983).
Finally, Asian workers tended not bring their families with them to
the Gulf, thereby further reducing Gulf states' anxieties about permanent settlers. As a result, Arab labourers in GCC states decreased from

Table 6.10 *Arab share in foreign populations, 1975–2002*

	1970	1985	1996	2002
Bahrain	22%	15%	12%	15%
Kuwait	80%	69%	33%	30%
Oman	16%	16%	11%	6%
Qatar	33%	33%	21%	19%
Saudi Arabia	26%	19%	10%	13%
United Arab Emirates	26%	19%	10%	13%
Gulf Cooperation Council	72%	56%	31%	32%

Source: Kapiszewski 2006b, 9

72 per cent in 1970 to only 32 per cent in 2002; non-Arab labourers grew from 12 per cent of all workers in the Gulf in 1970 to 41 per cent in 1980, and to 63 per cent in 1985 (Russel and Teitelbaum 1992). As has been observed by a number of researchers, the recruitment of Egyptian labour, particularly over the past 15 years, has decreased considerably, as 'migration flows to the Gulf "matured": inflows decelerated and the decline in the proportion of Arabs continued'. It has been estimated that, in 2010, out of 12.5 million migrants in the GCC, more than 7 million of them are Asian rather than Arab labourers (Cammett et al. 2015, 504).

   The Mubarak regime attempted to bypass this issue by promoting the export of female labour, a strategy that backfired: this has been particularly clear during the 'maids' crisis of mid-2007, when it was revealed that Aisha Abdel Hady, the Minister of Manpower and Migration, was to strike a deal with Saudi Arabia to provide 120,000 female maids. *Al-Usbu' al-'Arabi* wrote:

The signing of an understanding with a number of Saudi businessmen to export 120,000 Egyptian girls and ladies to work as maids in Saudi homes, but under the name of 'housekeeper' . . . is a serious incident in the history of Egypt . . . As for the minister in question, she bragged about having been able, and for the first time, to provide new job opportunities for Egyptian girls in Saudi Arabia and allow them to work as maids and cooks, and to embellish the content of the understanding, the term nurses was added. . . . It is worth mentioning in this regard that the only way through which women were able to work in the palaces of the Saudis is by marrying businessmen in exchange for sums of money that were considered by the simple parents of the bride as being huge sums. The poor woman was then surprised to discover that she travelled there to be a slave and not a wife . . . and returned a few months later utterly disappointed and maybe even pregnant with a futureless child. (Al-Usbu' al-'Arabi, 1 June 2007)

Aswani underlined the mass indignation regarding this governmental decision:

Can we expect Aisha Abdel Hady to defend the dignity and rights of Egyptians as she should in her role as minister of manpower? The answer is absolutely not. Thousands of Egyptians who work in the Gulf states are robbed of their due by their sponsors, are mistreated and humiliated, and are often detained and flogged unjustly. They wait for the government of their country to defend their rights, but Aisha Abdel Hady, who kisses hands [she was seen on TV kissing the hand of Suzanne Mubarak], does nothing for them. On the contrary, two years ago Aisha Abdel Hady announced she had made an agreement with the Saudi authorities to provide thousands of Egyptian maids to work in Saudi homes. This extraordinary deal shocked Egyptians, first, because Egypt has hundreds of thousands of highly qualified people who are more eligible to obtain contracts to work in the Gulf; second, because sending Egyptian women to work as maids is incompatible with the most basic rules of national dignity and puts them at risk of being humiliated or sexually abused; third, because many Egyptian women have intermediate or advanced qualifications but under pressure of poverty and unemployment are forced to agree to work as maids; and, fourth, because the Saudi authorities, who are strict in all religious matters and require that women be accompanied by a close male relative when they go to the country on pilgrimage or umra, did the opposite this time and asked for Egyptian maids to go to Saudi Arabia unaccompanied. (Aswani 2011, 24)

In the last years of Mubarak's rule, the ruling regime struggled to maintain control of public finances, as the opportunities for mass labour emigration gradually diminished. Egyptians who had the means to do so would opt for permanent migration to North America, Europe, and Australia – a phenomenon beyond the scope of this study. Egyptians that were desperate enough would try to pursue irregular migration, across the Mediterranean, to Italy or Greece. The vast majority of the population, however, had to endure unemployment and rising rates of inflation without any recourse to pursuing employment abroad. Unlike the opportunities afforded to their parents in the 1970s and 1980s, the younger generation of Egyptians were unable to relocate to the Gulf with ease: by the 1990s, the unregulated *makatib al-tawzīf* (non-governmental recruitment agencies) would court Arab employers who had travelled to Egypt to secure contracts for Egyptian workers. The agencies, then, sold these contracts at exorbitant prices to Egyptians desperate to emigrate abroad. Indicatively, in the early 2010s, a work permit for Saudi Arabia was priced at 20,000 EGP, while permits for Kuwait were sold for 30,000 EGP each. By then, the liberalisation of Egyptian labour emigration policy was of little benefit to the Mubarak regime.

Conclusion

Issues of economics have frequently been put forth, by Egyptian policymakers and researchers alike, as the main driver behind the Egyptian regime's liberalisation of its migration. These arguments revolve around the poor economic condition of the Egyptian state at the end of Nasser's rule, and the attempts by Sadat and Mubarak to employ emigration as a 'quick fix' for the country's demographic, unemployment, and balance-of-payments problems. Yet, this chapter has highlighted how the argument that liberalisation of Egypt's emigration policy was purely a means towards the improvement of state finances is unconvincing, for it raises a number of questions.

In fact, analysing the economics of Egyptian emigration from 1970 until 2011 confirms a short-term political rationale of the Egyptian ruling regime, which failed to take into account, or plan for, the long-term economic consequences of its policy. A permissive labour emigration policy was aimed to contribute to short-term regime survival – as Chapters 4 and 5 demonstrated – but the extent to which it was economically sustainable in the long run is questionable. The expectation that the Egyptian state would be perennially able to outsource its economic woes by exporting hundreds of thousands of migrants to its Arab neighbours proved tenuous. For one, some Arab states, such as Libya and Iraq, perceived Egypt's dependence on migration as an opportunity to destabilise the ruling regime; deportations of Egyptians would occur whenever bilateral relations deteriorated. Even allied powers such as Saudi Arabia would eventually reduce their dependence on Egyptian migrants as per their security and economic priorities. The fact that the Egyptian state scrambled to respond to successive waves of return migrants demonstrates the ruling regime's lack of long-term planning.

Overall, a close analysis of Egypt's shift to a permissive labour emigration policy reveals how it ultimately contributed to the deterioration of the national economy, intense social unrest, and dissatisfaction with the political system – factors that led to the outbreak of the January 25 Revolution. Sadat was initially able to use this policy to enhance the regime's legitimation tactics, facilitate its low-intensity repression, and strengthen its co-optation strategies – so long as out-migrant flows continued. In the decades leading up to 2011, as Arab host states closed their borders to mass migration, the use of labour emigration for regime survival became gradually more difficult. Within the overall deteriorating economic situation in Egypt in the last years of Mubarak's rule, once the harsh long-term economic effects of the shift to a permissive emigration policy materialised, the very foundations of the post-1952 ruling regime would be under threat.

7 | Conclusion

Egyptian manpower is our most precious capital.
Prime Minister Abdel Aziz Hegazy (*al-Ahram*, 27 October 1974)

How does labour emigration policy affect regime survival in non-democratic contexts? In the case of modern Egypt, in particular, what was the relationship between labour emigration and authoritarianism? Within the broader field of political science, the relationship between labour emigration and authoritarian durability has yet to be established as a separate field of inquiry: on the one hand, despite a voluminous literature on the politics of non-democratic regimes, comparative politics scholars expect that non-democratic regimes seek to limit their citizens' mobility for the purposes of political control. As a result, the phenomenon of migration, which by definition traverses state boundaries, has yet to be systematically examined as a determinant of authoritarianism. Within the field of migration studies, on the other hand, studies on immigration politics have traditionally overshadowed research on emigration policies. The latter, when examined, tend to draw on liberal democratic or transitional states, rather than authoritarian ones. In the Middle Eastern context, research on migration has highlighted the economic factors that determine migratory policy dynamics, mainly in the post-1973 context. Egyptian emigration policy has historically been contextualised within the aftermath of the 1973 "oil shock" that led to an influx of immigrants into the oil-producing countries of the Arab world, thereby producing much-needed economic remittances for the Egyptian state. But such approaches do not address why Egypt also subsidised the regional emigration of Egyptian professionals in the 1952–70 era. Overall, was Egypt's emigration policy confined to economic aims, or did it also have distinctly political aims? How was emigration policy employed for the consolidation of authoritarian rule in Egypt under President Nasser, as well as under Presidents Sadat and Mubarak?

In addressing this research question, this study relied on a theoretical framework based on the comparative politics literature on authoritarianism, to which it introduced key research agendas within the fields of migration and diaspora politics, international relations, Middle East studies, and the politics of development. In order to evaluate the effect of emigration policy on authoritarian politics, the study has been based on two key assumptions: first, labour emigration policy operates within a continuum between two endpoints: a restrictive and a permissive policy, respectively. The former involves the implementation of varying sets of obstacles that aim to prevent labour emigration, while the latter is based on a liberal framework that allows, or even encourages, citizens' pursuit of employment opportunities abroad. In the Egyptian case, Nasser adopted a restrictive policy, with the exception of a secondment policy regulating high-skilled professionals' regional, short-term emigration. Under Sadat and Mubarak, Egypt would shift to a permissive labour emigration policy.

A second assumption refers to a particular rationale of non-democracies, which arguably prioritise regime survival at the expense of any other state goals. An authoritarian regime is more likely to develop policies that produce short-term political gains that enable ruling elites to remain in power. This implies that measures that may be economically beneficial in the long term, but involve heavy immediate political costs, are unlikely to be implemented. By taking this into account in the Egyptian case, this study has produced a more accurate understanding of the Nasserite regime's decision to pursue a restrictive labour emigration policy at times of high unemployment and intense overpopulation, while also subsidising an elaborate, costly programme of high-skilled Egyptians' regional emigration. At the same time, the study has been able to produce a more nuanced understanding of the Sadat and Mubarak period: the adoption of a permissive emigration policy might have exacerbated certain economic indicators, but it also produced distinct short-term benefits for the ruling regime.

The study's main argument is that the Egyptian regime's use of emigration policy, in both case studies (the Nasser and the post-Nasser periods), constituted an instrument that formed part of the regime's survival strategies, rather than a tool for the state's long-term socio-economic development. In both the Nasser and post-Nasser periods, the regime resisted multiple calls to reform emigration policy, despite the heavy toll that it was inflicting on the Egyptian state economy. The Egyptian case, therefore, demonstrates how scholars of emigration and diaspora politics need to begin disaggregating the state: in contrast to mainstream approaches based on liberal democratic cases, the interests of an authoritarian regime and the state are not synonymous. At least insofar as authoritarian regimes are concerned, economic considerations appear to constitute a necessary, but not a sufficient, condition for explanations of either a restrictive or a permissive policy.

In the Nasserite era, as was explored in Chapters 2 and 3, emigration policy was employed for short-term political gain both domestically and internationally: domestically, a restrictive emigration policy was employed to support the regime's legitimation strategy, to complement its high-intensity repressive tactics towards political opponents, and to co-opt Egyptian elites in the direction of ISI and state-led economic growth. Internationally, the policy of secondment aimed at aiding the development of Arab states, strengthening relations with Arab regimes across the Middle East, and, therefore, serving as an instrument of external legitimation for the Free Officers regime. Yet, in both cases, the regime's emigration policy choices were not a panacea. Not only were a number of political opponents – particularly members of the Egyptian Muslim Brotherhood – able to flee abroad, but any attempts at legitimacy were undermined by the deteriorating economic condition of the Egyptian state: domestically, high unemployment rates undermined the appeal of a restrictive emigration policy, as Egyptians became eager to explore economic opportunities abroad. The Egyptian regime's choice of state-led economic growth was undermined by the problem of overpopulation. While there exists no publicly available data on the cost of Egypt's secondment programme, the subsidisation of regional emigration undoubtedly also incurred significant cost for the national economy.

Chapters 4 and 5 explored a similar political rationale by the Sadat and Mubarak regimes, which imposed a fully permissive labour emigration policy. Domestically, this policy aimed to generate short-term political gain for the ruling regime's stability: it aimed to enhance the new regime's legitimation agenda, both materially and discursively, by supporting the ideological move towards de-Nasserisation; it formed an instrument of low-intensity opposition management; and it aimed to co-opt Egyptian elites – who later came to be known as the *fat cats* – into the liberal economic model of development. Internationally, emigration functioned as an instrument of external legitimation for the ruling regime's standing in the region, as Egypt sought closer ties to the oil-rich Arab countries. Again, however, the regime's emigration policy strategy was unsuccessful in ensuring long-term developmental or economic benefits. Despite being ostensibly driven by economic priorities such as the reduction of unemployment, the tackling of overpopulation, and the desire to address the country's deficit through an influx of remittances, the full shift to a permissive labour emigration policy aggravated Egypt's economic indicators.

As Chapter 6 explained, the absence of any regulatory frameworks (which were seen as potentially contradicting the regime's emphasis on economic liberalisation), as well as the political wish to satisfy the Arab countries' labour needs at the expense of Egyptian development, prevented emigration from benefitting Egypt in the 1970–2011 period. Therefore, the argument that Egypt's emigration policy shift was economically driven, or mainly aimed at improving macroeconomic or developmental indicators, is unconvincing. In terms of the Egyptian domestic political economy, the laissez-faire approach to labour emigration proved problematic: aside from contributing to rising economic disparities and aggravating issues of urbanisation and unemployment, the permissive emigration policy did not allow the state to tax, or benefit in any way, from the huge influx of economic remittances. Importantly, the insistence that the Egyptian state no longer intervene politically in the process of migration left state mechanisms unable to respond to the plight of and deportations faced by its citizens across the Arab world in the post-1970 era. Despite the fact that thousands of Egyptians were being periodically harassed, tortured, deported, or even killed abroad from the mid-1970s onwards in Libya, Iraq, Kuwait, Jordan, and elsewhere, no solution was forthcoming. When faced with such crises, the ruling regime would scramble to find employment for such deportees in the Egyptian public sector or provide temporary housing – it would attempt to address the problem's effects, rather than its causes. At the same time, the gradual reduction of oil-producing states' recruitment of Egyptian workers undermined the legitimacy of the ruling regime and its permissive emigration policy. Ultimately, this contributed to a pile-up of grievances that culminated in the 2011 uprisings against the Mubarak regime.

How applicable are this study's findings beyond the Egyptian case? Arguably, it is not difficult to identify similar processes of authoritarian regimes' employing emigration policies towards their consolidation of political power. Authoritarian regimes have often employed restrictive emigration policies that aim to complement their stability. Restrictions on emigration have complemented a ruling regime's legitimation strategies – as occurred in the Soviet Union or across the Eastern bloc under the Cold War, when the rejection of labour emigration to the West contained a normative aspect, namely the rejection of liberal democracy and capitalism. Similarly, regimes prevented citizens' emigration for repressive purposes – most recently, in July 2016, the Turkish prime minister prohibited travel abroad for thousands of public sector educational staff, as he tried to consolidate his political rule in the aftermath of a failed military coup d'état. Such restrictions also impact upon the broader co-optation strategies of a ruling regime – in Latin America and elsewhere, restrictions on emigration have been identified as complementing a ruling regime's emphasis on self-sufficiency, ISI, and state-led economic growth, which by definition rely on the support of economic elites. Finally, there is an international component to non-democracies' restrictive emigration policies, which frequently allow for the circulation of high-skilled professionals across select countries in order to strengthen cross-regime relations and enhance the ruling regime's external legitimacy. Similar to Egyptian professionals' short-term emigration across the Arab world, Russian professionals were dispatched across Eastern Europe in the 1945–90 era, or Cubans across Latin American and sub-Saharan states. In all these instances, the motivation is not mainly, or even primarily, economic; the rationale is guided by a political quest towards regime legitimacy, whether domestically or internationally.

On the other hand, the politics behind the permissive labour emigration policy that Egypt pursued under Sadat and Mubarak can shed light on how population mobility has been employed in the past by other non-democratic regimes. The introduction of a permissive emigration policy by the Sadat regime to underline a normative shift in regime ideology towards liberalism is reminiscent of similar attempts by the Chinese ruling regime during the post-1978 economic reforms. The minimisation of political dissent in the aftermath of Sadat's Corrective Revolution is comparable to the aftermath of the Russian Revolution, which incurred the exodus of more than

900,000 'White Émigrés'. Similar processes occurred in the aftermath
of the 1959 Cuban Revolution, and the 1979 Iranian Revolution –
phenomena of dubious economic utility for the state, but with distinct
political advantages for the new regime. Labour migration to Western
Europe was adroitly employed as a co-optation strategy of domestic
elites by the Tito regime in Yugoslavia, in Morocco under King Hasan
II, and in post-independence Tunisia, all from the 1960s onwards.
The international aspect of this – the promotion of cross-regime relations through labour migration – is evident in the relations between
Arab states and Pakistan or, to a smaller extent, North Korea and the
GCC states. Chinese diplomacy in sub-Saharan Africa also typically
includes agreements on labour migration. Authoritarian regimes' cooperation with international powers in the field of population mobility
and control is also commonplace – examples include the relations
between the European Union and Gaddafi's Libya or Ben Ali's Tunisia.

On a broader, theoretical level, this study has addressed key issues
within a select number of research agendas. It contributes to the literature on the politics of labour migration by shifting attention away from
immigration policies within the Global North or the emigration policies of thoroughly studied liberal cases, such as India, the Philippines,
and Mexico. It focuses on how two non-democratic regimes engaged
with labour emigration within the Egyptian context, and paves the way
for a new research agenda discounting the expectation that non-
democracies do not engage with the issue of emigration – or, that
they engage with it solely in a restrictive manner by building on
research on the migration–development nexus, particularly aspects of
brain drain and brain gain. It brings aspects of Hirshman's exit versus
voice framework into its theorisation, but highlights how it is linked
with low-intensity repression, which is only one of the ways through
which authoritarianism and labour emigration interact. It also speaks
to a rising body of research that examines the effects of labour emigration through the prism of economic remittances, and highlights how
a ruling non-democratic regime would prioritise short-term political
benefits over long-term economic gains.

At the same time, this study speaks to the well-established literature
on authoritarianism and non-democratic politics within political
science, and adds an under-studied dimension to this body of research.
Labour emigration constitutes part of a broader set of strategies that
non-democratic regimes employ to maintain power, and aim to use for

legitimation purposes across the domestic and international levels. Labour emigration is aimed at complementing a regime's ideological elements, at adding another layer to its management of political dissent, and at co-opting a labour force into its developmental strategy. Importantly, the legitimacy goals of non-democracies are served by labour emigration within both a restrictive and a permissive framework. Similar to Nasserite Egypt, a number of non-democracies have historically restricted labour emigration for political reasons: East Germany and the Warsaw Pact countries throughout the better part of the Cold War prevented labour emigration to the West; Fascist Italy and Nazi Germany implemented tightly controlled exit visa regimes for their citizens; Cuba did so before 2013; and so on. At the same time, much like Sadat and Mubarak's regime employed a permissive framework to enhance its legitimacy, so have regimes across the world – from China in the aftermath of Mao's death and Tito's Yugoslavia, to sub-Saharan African states and Singapore's People's Action Party.

The agenda on the interplay between labour migration and authoritarianism invites numerous strands of future research: for one, it is important to examine the conditions under which an authoritarian regime selects a specific emigration policy. Beyond examining how specific emigration policies affect authoritarianism, as this book has done, the impact of specific authoritarian regimes on emigration policy-making is also important: are some autocracies more likely to develop permissive, rather than restrictive, labour emigration policies? What are the determining factors of such a policy orientation? At the same time, a more ambitious research agenda would involve the conceptualisation of how autocracies engage with various forms of cross-mobility. Beyond labour emigration, when do autocracies develop permissive or restrictive immigration policies? How does permanent migration impact upon these policies? In essence, what is the interplay between emigration, immigration, and diasporas within an autocratic context? The field of labour migration offers fascinating range of possibilities for future research for comparative political scientists of autocratic regimes.

Overall, through its focus on modern Egypt from 1952 to 2011, this study has demonstrated the various ways through which emigration may function as a strategic tool towards the political survival of non-democratic regimes. Over this sixty-year period, labour emigration policy was employed on different registers – the domestic and the international – and accrued distinct political benefits for the ruling regime in each one, and considerable economic costs for the Egyptian state. The argument that population mobility and authoritarianism exhibit distinct linkages can be applied to a variety of non-democratic contexts which employ either restrictive or permissive policies. Although the study's inductive approach did not allow extensive focus on these cases, it has demonstrated that the use of migration by authoritarian regimes would appear to be the norm, rather than the exception.

Notes

1 Introduction

1. Egyptians also emigrated beyond the Arab world, particularly to Europe, North America, and Australia. However, this type of mobility to liberal democratic contexts of the West (which the Egyptian state considers "permanent migration") is driven by different sets of mechanisms that are more closely linked to the development of diaspora policies, rather than labour emigration policies (for a review of this policy bifurcation, see Tsourapas 2015b). As a result, they are not analysed in this book.
2. A strand of literature also puts forth "culturalist" arguments behind the absence of democratisation, particularly in the Middle Eastern context, by attempting to link religion or broader Muslim traditions to authoritarianism. These persistent, albeit flawed, arguments have been successfully debunked in the aftermath of Said's *Orientalism* (2014), and are not discussed.
3. It is dubious, for instance, whether Nasser's book *Egypt's Liberation: The Philosophy of the Revolution* (1955) should be ascribed to him or to ghost-writer Heikal. Sadat's biography, *In Search of Identity* (1978), has been 'widely ridiculed for its self-serving distortion and twisted history' (Kays 1984, 109). Heikal's numerous books on Egyptian politics have also been accused of producing a biased, particularly damning account of the Sadat era.
4. The memoirs of Sadat's Foreign Minister, Mohamed Ibrahim Kamel, for instance, recount the difficulty he had in understanding Sadat's personality: a secretive man, Sadat 'never got rid of the mentality, methods and techniques commonly associated with a member of an underground organisation secretly scheming to carry out a plot either for the assassination of a traitor, or for the overthrow of a regime', Kamel argues. 'This trait continued to largely dominate his character, even after he became President' (Kamel 1986, 121–22).
5. The same has been identified for decisions on Egypt's emigration policy (Dessouki 1982; Amin and Awni 1986).

6. Although formal statistics are rarely made available, elites would occasionally disclose partial data to the Egyptian press.

2 'Egyptians Don't Emigrate'

1. In fact, as late as 1988, Syria enacted a law that prevented Syrian engineers from emigrating before they had been employed in the public sector for at least five years (see Tsourapas 2018d).
2. It is interesting to note that Egyptian elites would identify population growth as being responsible for the lack of hygiene and the various disorderly crowds from the mid-nineteenth century onwards (see Mitchell 1988).

3 Exporting the Free Officers' Revolution

1. The Jordanian Minister of Education was a third signatory to the treaty, which was ratified in 1958.
2. The Lebanese newspaper *Commerce du Levant* estimated about 60,000 Egyptian farmers to have also moved to Syria, although these figures appeared exaggerated to the British.
3. The decrease of Syrian officers and subsequent introduction of Egyptians in the country's armed forces caused clashes between Syrian and Egyptian army personnel, resulting in the death of seven Egyptian officers in Aleppo. See FO 371/134374.
4. There is significant overlap between the regime's use of emigration in its regional relations and its repressive apparatus. Indicatively, as Nasser told the American ambassador that communist and Ba'ath opposition was 'manageable' because he had succeeded in 'destroying the political character of the Army through transfers and retirements and the stationing of Egyptian officers in the Northern region' (Podeh 1999, 114).
5. This pattern was oddly reminiscent of the Napoleonic invasion of Egypt, some 150 years earlier.

4 'Our Most Precious Asset'

1. The internal political workings of the Egyptian regime in the 1970–71 period are considered only in passing as they are not the main focus of this study. For more elaborate examinations, see: Kandil (2012, 99–111); Cooper (1982, 64–82); Ansari (1986, 153–70); Beattie (2000, 39–92).
2. Another relevant argument frequently raised is that the liberalisation of emigration benefitted the regime politically because it allowed for the

most restless elements of the social body to emigrate, rather than protest against the Egyptian regime (see, for instance, Ibrahim 1983: 93), thereby serving as a "safety valve" against domestic opposition activism.

3. This study acknowledges that terminology matters – in this case, whether to term the Muslim Brotherhood as an Islamist or Islamic fundamentalist group. It employs "Islamist" for purposes of ease, but recognises that this can be a potentially problematic term (albeit generating a discussion beyond the focus of this study). See Volpi (2010).

4. Quoted in Ghannam (2002, 29). Very similar statements were made in President Sadat's two-hour interviews on Egyptian television, which were reproduced in their entirety in *al-Ahram* (26 December 1979 and 26 December 1980).

5 'The Rich Hive Invaded by Foreign Bees'

1. It could be argued that this is also linked to Sadat's decision to abolish the statistical count of Egyptian emigrants, as discussed in Chapter 4.

2. Indeed, as early as 1967, the Arab League tried to broker a multilateral labour agreement, but it was ratified solely by Iraq (Collyer 2004, 11).

3. Cairo interviewees argued that it was also Washington's insistence that Gulf countries did not begin mass deportations of Egyptian workers – an argument backed by Haddad (Haddad 1987, 248) – but this cannot be verified.

4. There undoubtedly exists a relationship between Egyptian military actors and their empowerment through the liberalisation of Egyptian emigration policy – particularly through the creation of new relations with military elites across the GCC – as has been pointed out to me in multiple interviews. Unfortunately, the lack of any publicly available data on this does not allow further elaboration at this stage.

6 Egypt's Road to Revolution

1. For the author's graph on this, see Figure 6.5.

2. Interestingly, similar arguments were raised against the Free Officers group. 'There is little evidence that Nasser and his officer colleagues gave much thought to economics before coming to power and some would say decidedly insufficient thought thereafter', notes Waterbury. 'None had any economic training and only two, Khalid Muhi al-Din and Yussef Sadiq, because of their Marxism, were attuned to questions of political economy' (Waterbury 1983, 49).

3. In the post-2011 era, Jordan has also engaged in the deportation of Egyptian migrants for political gain (Tsourapas 2018b).

Appendix Primary Sources Index

Record Repositories

- The National Archives [TNA] – London
  - BW114 British Council: Registered Files, Persian Gulf
  - CO 1015 Colonial Office: Central Africa and Aden: Original Correspondence
  - CO 1035 Colonial Office: Intelligence and Security Departments: Registered Files
  - FCO 39 Foreign Office, North and East African Department and Successors
  - FCO 93 Foreign Office, Near East and North African Department
  - FCO 141 Foreign & Commonwealth Office: Records of Former Colonial Administrations
  - FO 141 Egypt: Embassy and Consular Archives: Correspondence
  - FO 371 Foreign Office: General Political Correspondence
  - FO 407 Foreign Office: Confidential Print Egypt and the Sudan
  - FO 464 Foreign Office: Confidential Print Arabia
  - FO 414 Foreign Office: Confidential Print North America
  - FO 481 Foreign Office: Confidential Print Iraq
  - FO 484 Foreign Office: Confidential Print Lebanon

- General Records of the Department of State – Washington DC
  - Department of State, INR/IL Historical Files, Box 11, Cairo. Secret; Roger. 1979
- Freedom of Information Act Electronic Reading Room, Central Intelligence Agency – Washington, CV
  - Interagency Intelligence Memorandum, *Egypt: Sadat's Domestic Position.* 1976. NIO 76–025
  - National Intelligence Daily Cable, 17 December 1977; CG NIDC 77/292 C

- *Egypt: Regional Issues and Relationships, An Intelligence Assessment,* 1983
- *Egypt and the Arab States: Reintegration Prospects, An Intelligence Assessment.* 1986
- National Archives & Record Administration [NARA] – Washington DC
- Service of Diplomatic & Historical Archives – Athens
- Archives of the Department of Secondment, Egyptian Ministry of Education – Cairo
- Archives of the Egyptian Ministry of Manpower and Migration – Cairo

Edited Collections of State Papers

- *Foreign Relations of the United States,* 1952–54. Vol. IX, The Near and Middle East, Part 1 & 2. Washington: Government Printing Office, 1986
- *Foreign Relations of the United States,* 1958–1960. Vol. XIII, Arab-Israeli Dispute; United Arab Republic; North Africa. Washington: Government Printing Office, 1992
- United Arab Republic, *Statistical Pocket-Book,* 1952–1962. Cairo: Ministry of Information, 1963
- Arab Republic of Egypt, *Statistical Yearbook,* 1952–1980. Cairo: Ministry of Information, 1981

Unofficial Collections of Documents

- *President Gamal Abdel Nasser's Speeches and Press Interviews* (multiple volumes). Cairo, Egyptian Ministry of Information: 1958–63
- *Speeches and Interviews of President Mohamed Anwar el Sadat* (multiple volumes). Cairo, Egyptian Ministry of Information: 1970–81
- *Middle East Contemporary Survey [MECS]* (multiple volumes). Tel Aviv: Moshe Dayan Center for Middle Eastern and African Studies

Reports

- National Bank of Egypt. *Economic Bulletin.* Multiple Volumes (1948–2010)
- USAID 'Food for Peace' programme (PL-480). 1954

- Daily Report: Middle East and Africa [DR], US Foreign Broadcasting Information Service (1974–88)
- INP Research Report. *Employment Problems in Rural Areas, Report B: Migration in the United Arab Republic.* December 1965
- Arab Republic of Egypt, Central Agency for Public Mobilisation and Statistics, *Population Movements Across the Borders,* 1969
- People's Assembly; Legislative Council, *The Law for Arab and Foreign Investment and Free Zones* (n.d)
- AID V. 8, Egyptian Labor Migration, Progress Report, 1 June 1977–1 September, 1977
- Ministry of Planning. 1978. *Wathiqat Al-Khitta Al-Khamsiyya.* Cairo: Ministry of Planning
- National Specialized Councils. *The Economics of Savings of Egyptians Abroad,* Arab Center for Research and Publishing, 1983
- Arab Republic of Egypt, Central Agency for Public Mobilisation and Statistics. *Population Movements Across the Borders,* 1969. Cairo
- Arab Republic of Egypt, National Population Information Centre, *Special Issue,* 4 October 1991
- UAR/INP/ILO (1965–68). Research Report on Employment Problems in Rural Aras, Cairo: Institute of National Planning

Private Papers and Oral History Sources

- St Anthony's College, Middle East Centre – Oxford
  - Elisabeth Monroe's Papers – 'Egyptian Efforts to Dominate the Arab World' (4/57)
- American University of Cairo, Rare Books and Special Collections Library – Cairo
  - Anis Mansour's Papers
- Concord Oral History Program
  - Joseph Coolidge Wheeler
- London School of Economics and Political Science – London
  - Professor Fred Halliday's Papers

Unpublished PhD Dissertations

- Aboulsayan, Ahmed. 2000. *Oil, Economic Growth and Structural Change in the Libyan Economy: 1960–1990.* Unpublished PhD dissertation. SOAS, University of London

- al-Najjar, Zaynab. 1972. *Enrolment in the Division of Public Service and Emigration: Is There a Conflict of Organisational Objectives?* Unpublished PhD dissertation. American University of Cairo
- Asmar, Marwan Rateb. 1990. *The State and Politics of Migrant Labour in Kuwait.* Unpublished PhD dissertation. University of Leeds
- Attia, Attia Abd El-Moneim M. 1973. *Egypt's Foreign Policy in Africa with Particular Reference to Decolonisation and Apertheid within the United Nations.* Unpublished PhD dissertation. St John's University, New York
- Barsalou, Judith Marie. 1985. *Foreign Labor in Sa'udi Arabia: The Creation of a Plural Society.* Unpublished PhD dissertation. Columbia University, New York
- Doran, Michael Scott. 1997. *The Politics of Pan-Arabism: Egyptian Foreign Policy, 1945–48.* Unpublished PhD dissertation. Princeton University, New Jersey
- Dorman, W. Judson. 2007. *The Politics of Neglect. The Egyptian State in Cairo, 1974–98.* Unpublished PhD dissertation. SOAS, University of London
- El-Solh, Camillia F. 1985. *Egyptian Migrant Peasants in Iraq. A Case-Study of the Settlement Community in Khalsa.* Unpublished PhD dissertation. University of Oxford
- Hibshi, Mohamed Ali. 1975. *The Development of Teacher Education in Saudi Arabia, 1928–1972.* Unpublished PhD dissertation. University of London, Institute of Education
- Huyette, Summer Scott. 1983. *Political Adaptation in Sa'udi Arabia: A Study of the Council of Ministers.* Unpublished PhD dissertation. Columbia University, New York
- Rahmy, Ali Abdel Rahman. 1981. *The Egyptian Foreign Policy in the Arab World – Intervention in Yemen: 1962–1967, Case Study.* Unpublished PhD dissertation. University of Geneva

Media Sources (in Arabic)

- *al-Ahram*
- *al-Ahram al-Iqtisadi*
- *al-Akhbar*
- *Akhbar el-Yom*
- *al-Gomhuria*

- *Al-Usbu' al-'Arabi*
- *al-Siyasa* (Kuwait)
- *al-Siyasa al-Dawliyya*
- *Rose al-Yūsuf*

Media Sources (in English, French, German, Greek)

- *al-Ahram Weekly* (Egypt)
- *Arab Observer* (Egypt)
- *British Broadcasting Corporation [BBC] Radio* (United Kingdom)
- *Cairo Today* (Egypt)
- *CBS News* (United States)
- *Central Intelligence Agency Weekly Summary* (Washington DC)
- *Der Spiegel* (Germany)
- *Egyptian Gazette* (Egypt)
- *Executive Intelligence Review* (United States)
- *Financial Times* (United Kingdom)
- *Le Monde* (France)
- *Middle East Economic Digest [MEED]* (United Kingdom)
- *Middle East News Agency [MENA]* (Egypt)
- *Middle East Report* (United States)
- *Newsweek* (United States)
- *Radio Cairo* (Egypt)
- *Saudi News Agency* (Saudi Arabia)
- *Sunday Times* (France)
- *The Economist* (United Kingdom)
- *The Guardian* (United Kingdom)
- *The New York Times* (United States)
- *The Middle East* (London)
- *The Middle East Times* (Lebanon)
- *The Times* (United Kingdom)
- *Time Magazine* (United States)
- *Washington Post* (United States)

Author's Interviews

1 Amin, Kareem – Head of Cabinet, Assistant Foreign Minister for Consular Affairs and Egyptians Abroad, *Ministry of Foreign Affairs, Arab Republic of Egypt.* Cairo, 20 February 2014

2 Azzam, Ahmed – Diplomat, *Ministry of Foreign Affairs, Arab Republic of Egypt*. Cairo, 7 December 2013 & 19 March 2014

3 Ashry, Nahed Hassan – Minister of Manpower and Migration (2014–), *Arab Republic of Egypt*. Cairo, 24 February 2014

4 Awad, Ibrahim – Director, *Center for Migration & Refugee Studies, American University of Cairo*. Cairo, 15 September 2013 & 1 May 2014

5 Badran, Ibrahim Gamil – Minister of Health (1976–78), *Arab Republic of Egypt* & President (1978–80), *Cairo University*. Cairo, 21 January 2014

6 Baumgart, Susanne – Regional Head for Language Services, *Goethe Institut*. Cairo, 10 December 2013

7 El Behary, Hend – Journalist, *Al-Masry al-Youm*. Cairo, 16 April 2014.

8 Dessouki, Ali E. Hillal – Minister (1999–2004), Ministry of Sports and Youth, *Arab Republic of Egypt*. Cairo, 13 April 2014

9 Eddin Ibrahim, Saad – Director, *Ibn Khaldun Center for Development Studies*. Cairo, 21 October 2013

10 Ghomeim, Ahmed Faruq – Professor of Economics, *Cairo University*. Cairo, 21 October 2013

11 Glavanis, Pandeli – University Senate Chair, *American University of Cairo*. Cairo, 18 September 2013

12 Abd al-Hady, Aisha – Minister of Migration (2006–2011); Minister of Manpower and Migration, *Arab Republic of Egypt*. Cairo, 2 April 2014

13 Hegazy, Abd El Aziz Muhammad – Minister of Treasury (1968–1970); Minister of Finance and Trade (1973–1974); Prime Minister (1974–1975), *Arab Republic of Egypt*. Cairo, 27 April 2014

14 Korany, Bahgat – Professor of Political Science, *American University of Cairo* & Deputy Chairman (1990–1999), *Association of Egyptian Scientists in Canada*. Cairo, 16 February 2014

15 LaTowsky, Robert J. – Independent Consultant, USAID & Ministry of Education, *Arab Republic of Egypt*. Cairo, 30 April 2014

16 Mahdy, Iman – Researcher, *Information and Decision Support Center (IDSC) – The Egyptian Cabinet*, Cairo, 16 April 2014

17 El Sayyid, Mustapha Kamel – Professor Emeritus, *Cairo University*. Cairo, 3 February 2014

18 Roman, Howaida – Researcher, *National Center for Social Research*. Cairo, 2 October 2013

19 Zohry, Ayman – Adviser, *International Labor Organization.*
    Cairo, 12 January 2014
20 Anonymous (4) – Senior Diplomats, *Ministry of Foreign Affairs,*
    Arab Republic of Egypt. Cairo, 11 December 2014,
    16 December 2014, & 22 January 2015
21 Anonymous (3) – Senior Officials, *Ministry of Migration &*
    Manpower, Arab Republic of Egypt. Cairo, 4 & 13 February 2014
22 Anonymous (3) – Senior Diplomats, *European Union Delegation*
    to Egypt. Cairo, 17 & 19 April 2014

Bibliography

Abdalla, Ahmed. 2008. *The Student Movement and National Politics in Egypt: 1923–1973*. Cairo: American University in Cairo Press.

'Abd al-Faḍīl, Maḥmūd. 1980. 'Athar Hijrat al-Ammāla 'alā al-Buldān al-Nafṭiyya 'alā tafāwut dukhūl al-Afrād wa-Anmāṭ al-istihlāk al-infāq fī-l-buldān al-Muṣaddira li-l-'Ammāla' [The effect of labour migration to oil-producing countries one the dispersal of personal income and ways of using money in labour-exporting countries]. *al-Nafṭ wa-l-Ta'āwun al-'Arabī* 1 (5): 87–111.

1982. *Al-Nafṭ Wa-Al-Waḥdah Al-'arabīyah [Oil and Arab Unity]*. Cairo: Dār al-Mustaqbal al-'Arabī.

Abdel-Malek, Anouar. 1968. *Egypt: Military Society: The Army Regime, the Left, and Social Change under Nasser*. New York: Random House.

Abou-El-Fadl, Reem. 2015. 'Neutralism Made Positive: Egyptian Anti-Colonialism on the Road to Bandung'. *British Journal of Middle Eastern Studies* 42 (2): 219–40.

Achcar, Gilbert. 2004. *Eastern Cauldron: Islam, Afghanistan, Palestine, and Iraq in a Marxist Mirror*. New York: Monthly Review Press.

2010. *The Arabs and the Holocaust: The Arab-Israeli War of Narratives*. New York: Metropolitan Books.

Adamson, Fiona. 2006. 'Crossing Borders: International Migration and National Security'. *International Security* 31 (1): 165–99.

2018. 'Sending States and the Making of Intra-Diasporic Politics: Turkey and Its Diasporas in Europe'. *International Migration Review (Forthcoming)*.

Adamson, Fiona, and Madeleine Demetriou. 2007. 'Remapping the Boundaries of "State" and "National Identity": Incorporating Diasporas into IR Theorizing'. *European Journal of International Relations* 13 (4): 489–526.

Ahmed, Faisal Z. 2012. 'The Perils of Unearned Foreign Income: Aid, Remittances, and Government Survival'. *American Political Science Review* 106 (1): 146–165.

Ahmed, Ramadan A. 2003. 'Egyptian Migrations'. In *Migration: Immigration and Emigration in International Perspective*, edited by Leonore Loeb Adler and Uwe P. Gielen, 311–27. Westport: Praeger.

Al-Abd, Abdel-Maguid. 1971. 'Human Wealth'. In *Readings in the Growth of Human Resources*. Beirut: Markaz Dirāsāt al-Waḥdah al-'Arabīyah.

Al-Awadi, Hesham. 2005. 'Mubarak and the Islamists: Why Did the "Honeymoon" End?' *Middle East Journal* 59 (1): 62–80.

Albrecht, Holger. 2013. *Raging against the Machine: Political Opposition under Authoritarianism in Egypt*. Syracuse: Syracuse University Press.

Alemán, José, and Dwayne Woods. 2014. 'No Way Out: Travel Restrictions and Authoritarian Regimes'. *Migration and Development* 3 (2): 285–305.

Al-Fahim, Mohamed Abduljalil. 1995. *From Rags to Riches: Story of Abu Dhabi*. London: The London Centre of Arab Studies.

Ali, Kamran Asdar. 2002. *Planning the Family in Egypt: New Bodies, New Selves*. Austin: University of Texas Press.

Al-Rasheed, Madawi. 2010. *A History of Saudi Arabia*. 2nd edn. New York: Cambridge University Press.

Ambrosio, Thomas. 2010. 'Constructing a Framework of Authoritarian Diffusion: Concepts, Dynamics, and Future Research'. *International Studies Perspectives* 11 (4): 375–92.

Amin, Galal A. 1981. 'Some Economic and Cultural Aspects of Economic Liberalization in Egypt'. *Social Problems* 28 (4): 430–41.

　1989. 'Migration, Inflation and Social Mobility: A Sociological Interpretation of Egypt's Current Economic and Political Crisis'. In *Egypt under Mubarak*, edited by Charles Tripp and Edward Roger John Owen, 103–21. London: Routledge.

　1995. *Egypt's Economic Predicament: A Study in the Interaction of External Pressure, Political Folly, and Social Tension in Egypt, 1960–1990*. New York: E. J. Brill.

　2011. *Egypt in the Era of Hosni Mubarak: 1981–2011*. Cairo: American University of Cairo Press.

Amin, Galal A., and Elizabeth Taylor Awni. 1986. *Hijrat Al-amālah Al-Miṣrīyah: Dirāsah Naqdīyah Lil-Buhūth Wa-Al-Dirāsāt Al-Khāṣṣah Bi-Hijrat Al-amālah Al-Miṣrīyah Ilá Al-Khārij [Egyptian Labor Migration: A Critical Study of Research and Studies on the Migration of Egyptian Workers Abroad]*. Ottawa: Markaz al-Buhūth lil-Tanmiyah al-Dawlīyah.

Ansari, Hamied. 1986. *Egypt, the Stalled Society*. Albany: State University of New York Press.

Arab Republic of Egypt. 1971. *The Constitution of the Arab Republic of Egypt*. Cairo: Ministry of Planning.

Arendt, Hannah. 1951. *The Origins of Totalitarianism*. New York: Harcourt Brace and Company.

Aswani, Alaa. 2011. *On the State of Egypt: A Novelist's Provocative Reflections.* Translated by Jonathan Wright. Cairo: American University in Cairo Press.

Atia, Mona. 2013. *Building a House in Heaven: Pious Neoliberalism and Islamic Charity in Egypt.* Minneapolis: University of Minnesota Press.

Atrouzi, M. Fahmi el. 1970. *Emigration Procedures and the Laws and Decree Regulations.* Cairo: Alam al Kitab.

Ayubi, Nazih N. M. 1980. *Bureaucracy and Politics in Contemporary Egypt.* St. Antony's Middle East Monographs 10. London: Ithaca Press.

—— 1983. 'The Egyptian "Brain Drain": A Multidimensional Problem'. *International Journal of Middle East Studies* 15 (4): 431–50.

—— 1991. *The State and Public Policies in Egypt Since Sadat.* Political Studies of the Middle East Series, no. 29. Reading: Ithaca Press.

—— 1995. *Over-Stating the Arab State: Politics and Society in the Middle East.* London: I. B. Tauris.

Babiracki, Patryk. 2015. *Soviet Soft Power in Poland Culture and the Making of Stalin's New Empire, 1943–1957.* Chapel Hill: The University of North Carolina Press.

Badella, Alessandro. 2014. 'American Hubris: US Democracy Promotion in Cuba after the Cold War (Part 1)'. *The International Journal of Cuban Studies* 6 (2): 157–88.

Badry, Hala. 2010. *Matar 'ala Baghdad: Riwayah [Rain Over Baghdad: A Novel].* Damascus: Dār al-Madá lil-Thaqāfah wa-al-Nashr.

Baer, Gabriel. 1964. *Population and Society in the Arab East.* New York: Praeger.

Baganha, Maria Ioannis. 2003. 'Portuguese emigration after World War II'. *Contemporary Portugal, Politics, Society and Culture*, edited by António Costa Pinto, 139–58. New York: Columbia University Press.

Baker, Raymond William. 1978. *Egypt's Uncertain Revolution under Nasser and Sadat.* Cambridge: Harvard University Press.

Balfour-Paul, Glen. 1991. *The End of Empire in the Middle East: Britain's Relinquishment of Power in Her Last Three Arab Dependencies.* Cambridge: Cambridge University Press.

Beach, Derek, and Rasmus Brun Pedersen. 2013. *Process-Tracing Methods: Foundations and Guidelines.* Ann Arbor: University of Michigan Press.

Beattie, Kirk J. 2000. *Egypt during the Sadat Years.* New York: Palgrave.

Beblawi, Hazem, and Giacomo Luciani. 1987. *The Rentier State.* London: Croom Helm.

Beinin, Joel. 1990. *Was the Red Flag Flying There?* London: I. B. Tauris.

—— 1992. 'Exile and Political Activism: The Egyptian-Jewish Communists in Paris, 1950–59'. *Diaspora: A Journal of Transnational Studies* 2 (1): 73–94.

2005. *The Dispersion of Egyptian Jewry: Culture, Politics, and the Formation of a Modern Diaspora.* Cairo: American University in Cairo Press.

Belaid, Sadok. 1988. 'Role of Religious Institutions in Support of the State'. In *Beyond Coercion: The Durability of the Arab State,* edited by A. I. Dawisha and I. William Zartman, 147–63. London: Croom Helm.

Belgrave, Sir Charles Dalrymple. 1960. *Personal Column.* London: Hutchinson.

Bellin, Eva. 2004. 'The Robustness of Authoritarianism in the Middle East: Exceptionalism in Comparative Perspective'. *Comparative Politics* 36 (2): 139–57.

2012. 'Reconsidering the Robustness of Authoritarianism in the Middle East: Lessons from the Arab Spring'. *Comparative Politics* 44 (2): 127–49.

Bertocchi, Graziella, and Michael Spagat. 2001. 'The Politics of Co-Optation'. *Journal of Comparative Economics* 29 (4): 591–607.

Bhagwati, Jagdish N. 1976. 'Taxing the Brain Drain'. *Challenge* 19 (3): 34–38.

Birks, J. S., and C. A. Sinclair. 1979. 'Egypt: A Frustrated Labor Exporter?' *Middle East Journal* 33 (3): 288–303.

1980. *International Migration and Development in the Arab Region.* Geneva: International Labour Office.

1982. 'Employment and Development in Six Poor Arab States: Syria, Jordan, Sudan, South Yemen, Egypt, and North Yemen'. *International Journal of Middle East Studies* 14 (1): 35–51.

Bodin, Jean. 1576. *Les Six Livres de la République.* Paris: Jacques du Puys.

Boix, Carles, and Susan C. Stokes. 2003. 'Endogenous Democratization'. *World Politics* 55 (4): 517–49.

Botman, S. 1988. *The Rise of Egyptian Communism, 1939–1970.* Contemporary Issues in the Middle East. Syracuse: Syracuse University Press.

Boucher, Anna, and Justin Gest. 2014. 'Migration Studies at a Crossroads: A Critique of Immigration Regime Typologies'. *Migration Studies* 3 (2): 182–98.

Boutros-Ghali, Boutros. 1997. *Egypt's Road to Jerusalem: A Diplomat's Story of the Struggle for Peace in the Middle East.* New York: Random House.

Brand, Laurie A. 2006. *Citizens Abroad: Emigration and the State in the Middle East and North Africa.* Cambridge: Cambridge University Press.

2013. *Jordan's Inter-Arab Relations: The Political Economy of Alliance-Making.* New York: Columbia University Press.

2014. *Official Stories: Politics and National Narratives in Egypt and Algeria*. Stanford: Stanford University Press.

Brettell, Caroline B. 1979. 'Emigration and its Implications for the Revolution in Northern Portugal'. In *Contemporary Portugal: The Revolution and Its Antecedents*, edited by Lawrence S. Graham and Harry M. Makler, 281–98. Austin: University of Texas Press.

Brownlee, Jason. 2004. 'Ruling Parties and Durable Authoritarianism'. CDDRL Working Papers. Stanford.

Brubaker, Rogers. 1990. 'Frontier Theses: Exit, Voice, and Loyalty in East Germany'. *Migration World* 18 (3/4): 12–17.

Byman, Daniel, and Jennifer Lind. 2010. 'Pyongyang's Survival Strategy: Tools of Authoritarian Control in North Korea'. *International Security* 35 (1): 44–74.

Cammett, Melani Claire, Ishac Diwan, Alan Richards, and John Waterbury. 2015. *A Political Economy of the Middle East*. 4th edn. Boulder: Westview Press.

Carroll, Raymond. 1982. *Anwar Sadat*. New York: F. Watts.

Castles, Stephen, Mark J. Miller, and Hein De Haas. 2014. *The Age of Migration*. 5th edn. New York: Guilford Press.

Castles, Stephen, and Raúl Delgado Wise. 2008. *Migration and Development: Perspectives from the South*. Geneva: International Organization for Migration.

Chalcraft, John. 2010. 'Monarchy, Migration and Hegemony in the Arabian Peninsula'. *LSE Kuwait Programme on Development, Governance and Globalisation in the Gulf States*.

Chami, Ralph, Adolfo Barajas, Thomas Cosimano, Connel Fullenkamp, Michael Gapen, and Peter Montiel. 2008. *Macroeconomic Consequences of Remittances*. Washington, DC: International Monetary Fund.

Choucri, Nazli. 1977. 'The New Migration in the Middle East: A Problem for Whom?' *International Migration Review* 11 (4): 421–43.

1986. 'The Hidden Economy: A New View of Remittances in the Arab world'. *World Development* 14 (6): 697–712.

1988. 'Migration in the Middle East: Old Economics or New Politics?'. *Journal of Arab Affairs* 7 (1): 1–18.

Cleland, Wendell. 1936. *The Population Problem in Egypt; A Study of Population Trends and Conditions in Modern Egypt*. Lancaster: Science Press.

Collier, David. 2011. 'Understanding Process Tracing'. *Political Science and Politics* 44 (4): 823–30.

Collyer, Michael. 2004. 'The Development Impact of Temporary International Labour Migration on Southern Mediterranean Sending

Countries: Contrasting Examples of Morocco and Egypt'. Brighton: Sussex Centre for Migration Research: 1–54.

Cooley, John K. 1982. *Libyan Sandstorm*. New York: Holt, Rinehart, and Winston.

Cooper, Mark N. 1982. *The Transformation of Egypt*. London: Croom Helm.

Coury, Ralph M. 1982. 'Who "Invented" Egyptian Arab Nationalism? Part 1'. *International Journal of Middle East Studies* 14 (3): 249–81.

Cremeans, Charles Davis. 1963. *The Arabs and the World; Nasser's Arab Nationalist Policy*. New York: Praeger.

Dalachanis, Angelos. 2017. *The Greek Exodus from Egypt – Diaspora Politics and Emigration, 1937–1962*. New York: Berghahn Books.

Davenport, Christian. 2007. 'State Repression and Political Order'. *Annual Review of Political Science* 10 (1): 1–23.

Davidson, Christopher M. 2008. *Dubai: The Vulnerability of Success*. New York: Columbia University Press.

Dawisha, A. I. 1975. 'Intervention in the Yemen: An Analysis of Egyptian Perceptions and Policies'. *Middle East Journal* 29 (1): 47–63.

1985. 'Arab Regimes, Legitimacy and Foreign Policy'. *The International Spectator* 20 (2): 3–10.

De Haas, Hein. 2005. *Morocco's Migration Transition: Trends, Determinants and Future Scenarios*. The Netherlands: Global Commission on International Migration.

2010. 'Migration and Development: A Theoretical Perspective'. *International Migration Review* 44 (1): 227–64.

Dekmejian, R. Hrair. 1971. *Egypt under Nasir; A Study in Political Dynamics*. Albany: State University of New York Press.

Délano, Alexandra. 2011. *Mexico and Its Diaspora in the United States: Policies of Emigration Since 1848*. New York: Cambridge University Press.

Dessouki, Ali E. Hillal. 1981. 'Policy Making in Egypt: A Case Study of the Open Door Economic Policy'. *Social Problems* 28 (4): 410–16.

1982. 'The Shift in Egypt's Migration Policy: 1952–1978'. *Middle Eastern Studies* 18 (1): 53–68.

Dib, George. 1978. 'Migration and Naturalization Laws in Egypt, Lebanon, Syria, Jordan, Kuwait, and the United Arab Emirates. Part I: Migration Laws'. *Population Bulletin of the Economic Commission for Western Asia* 15: 33–62.

Doran, Michael Scott. 1999. *Pan-Arabism before Nasser: Egyptian power politics and the Palestine Question*. Oxford: Oxford University Press.

Dowty, Alan. 1989. *Closed Borders: The Contemporary Assault on Freedom of Movement*. New Haven: Yale University Press.

Dunning, Thad. 2008. *Crude Democracy: Natural Resource Wealth and Political Regimes*. Cambridge: Cambridge University Press.

Economist Intelligence Unit. 1979. *Quarterly Economic Review: Egypt*. London.

Emsley, J. 2008. *Molecules of Murder: Criminal Molecules and Classic Cases*. Cambridge: Royal Society of Chemistry.

Erdmann, Gero, André Bank, Bert Hoffmann, and Thomas Richter. 2013. 'International Cooperation of Authoritarian Regimes: Toward a Conceptual Framework'. GIGA Working Paper Series 229. GIGA German Institute of Global and Area Studies.

Escribà-Folch, Abel, Covadonga Meseguer, and Joseph Wright. 2015. 'Remittances and Democratization'. *International Studies Quarterly* 59 (3): 571–86.

Esposito, John L. 1998. *Islam and Politics*. 4th edn. Syracuse: Syracuse University Press.

Fahim, H. M. 2015. *Dams, People and Development: The Aswan High Dam Case*. New York: Pergamon Policy Studies.

Faist, Thomas. 2008. 'Migrants as Transnational Development Agents: An Inquiry into the Newest Round of the Migration–Development Nexus'. *Population, Space and Place* 14 (1): 21–42.

Fargues, Philippe. 1997. 'State Policies and the Birth Rate in Egypt: From Socialism to Liberalism'. *Population and Development Review* 23 (1): 115–38.

2013. 'International Migration and the Nation State in Arab Countries'. *Middle East Law and Governance* 5 (1–2): 5–35.

2014. 'The Fuzzy Lines of International Migration. A Critical Assessment of Definitions and Estimates in the Arab Countries'. *A Critical Assessment of Definitions and Estimates in the Arab Countries (June 1, 2014)*. Robert Schuman Centre for Advanced Studies Research Paper No. RSCAS 71.

Farquhar, Michael. 2017. *Circuits of Faith: Migration, Education and the Wahhabi Mission*. Stanford: Stanford University Press.

Farrag, Mayar. 1998. 'Emigration Dynamics in Egypt'. In *Emigration Dynamics in Developing Countries*, edited by Reginald T. Appleyard, 44–88. Aldershot: Ashgate.

Fawat, Ibrahim. 1985. 'Libya: Economic Crisis, Political Expulsions'. *AfricAsia* 22: 32–34.

Feiler, Gil. 1986. 'The Number of Egyptian Workers in the Arab Oil Countries, 1974–1983: A Critical Discussion'. Tel Aviv: The Dayan Center.

1991. 'Migration and Recession: Arab Labor Mobility in the Middle East, 1982–89'. *Population and Development Review* 17 (1): 134–55.

2003. *Economic Relations Between Egypt and the Gulf Oil States, 1967–2000: Petro-Wealth and Patterns of Influence.* Brighton: Sussex Academic Press.

Fergany, Nader. 1983. *Al-Hijrah Ilá Al-Naft: Ab'ād Al-Hijrah Lil-'amal Fī Al-Buldān Al-Naftiyah Wa-Atharuhā 'alá Al-Tanmiyah Fī Al-Waṭan Al-'arabī [Migration to Oil: Dimensions of Labour Migration in Oil Countries, and Its Impact on Development in the Arab World].* Beirut: Markaz Dirāsāt al-Wahḍah al-'Arabīyah.

1988. *In Pursuit of Livelihood: A Field Study on Egyptian Migration for Work in the Arab Countries [in Arabic].* Beirut: Center for Arab Unity Studies.

Ferris, Jesse. 2013. *Nasser's Gamble: How Intervention in Yemen Caused the Six-Day War and the Decline of Egyptian Power.* Princeton: Princeton University Press.

Fitzgerald, David. 2006. 'Inside the Sending State: The Politics of Mexican Emigration Control'. *International Migration Review* 40 (2): 259–93.

2009. *A Nation of Emigrants: How Mexico Manages Its Migration.* Berkeley: University of California Press.

Flower, R. 2011. *Napoleon to Nasser: The Story of Modern Egypt.* New Orleans: Garrett County Press.

Frank, Andre Gunder. 1966. 'The Development of Underdevelopment'. *Monthly Review* 18 (4): 17–31.

Gadalla, Saad M. 1978. *Is There Hope? Fertility and Family Planning in a Rural Egyptian Community.* Cairo: American University in Cairo Press.

Gamlen, Alan. 2008. 'The Emigration State and the Modern Geopolitical Imagination'. *Political Geography* 27 (8): 840–56.

Garza, Rodolfo de la and Myriam Hazan. 2003. *Looking Backward Moving Forward: Mexican Organizations in the US as Agents of Incorporation and Dissociation.* Claremont: The Tomas Rivera Policy Institute.

George, Alexander L., and Andrew Bennett. 2005. *Case Studies and Theory Development in the Social Sciences.* Cambridge: MIT Press.

Gerges, Fawaz A. 1994. *The Superpowers and the Middle East: Regional and International Politics, 1955–1967.* Boulder: Westview Press.

2012. *Obama and the Middle East: The End of America's Moment?* New York: Palgrave Macmillan.

Gerschewski, Johannes. 2013. 'The Three Pillars of Stability: Legitimation, Repression, and Co-Optation in Autocratic Regimes'. *Democratization* 20 (1): 13–38.

Ghannam, Farha. 2002. *Remaking the Modern: Space, Relocation, and the Politics of Identity in a Global Cairo.* Los Angeles: University of California Press.

2013. *Live and Die Like a Man: Gender Dynamics in Urban Egypt.* Stanford: Stanford University Press.

Gilbar, Gad G. 1997. *Population Dilemmas in the Middle East: Essays in Political Demography and Economy.* London: Frank Cass.

Girgis, Maurice. 2002. 'The GCC factor in future Arab labor migration.' Paper presented at the Fourth Mediterranean Forum, Amman, Jordan, October.

Glasius, Marlies. 2018. 'Extraterritorial Authoritarian Practices: A Framework'. *Globalizations* 15 (2): 179–97.

Gordon, J. 2012. *Nasser: Hero of the Arab Nation.* London: Oneworld Publications.

Gordon, Joel. 1992. *Nasser's Blessed Movement Egypt's Free Officers and the July Revolution.* New York: Oxford University Press.

Graz, Liesl. 1992. *The Turbulent Gulf: People, Politics and Power.* 2nd edn. London: I. B.Tauris.

Greenhill, Kelly M. 2010. *Weapons of Mass Migration: Forced Displacement, Coercion, and Foreign Policy.* Ithaca: Cornell University Press.

Grzymala-Busse, Anna. 2011. 'Time will tell? Temporality and the Analysis of Causal Mechanisms and Processes'. *Comparative Political Studies* 44 (9): 1267–97.

Haber, Stephen, and Victor Menaldo. 2011. 'Do Natural Resources Fuel Authoritarianism? A Reappraisal of the Resource Curse'. *American Political Science Review* 105 (1): 1–26.

Haddad, Yvonne Y. 1987. 'Islamic "Awakening" in Egypt'. *Arab Studies Quarterly* 9 (3): 234–59.

Hahn, Peter L. 1991. *The United States, Great Britain, and Egypt, 1945–1956: Strategy and Diplomacy in the Early Cold War.* Chapel Hill: University of North Carolina Press.

Halliday, Fred. 1977. 'Migration and the Labour Force in the Oil Producing States of the Middle East'. *Development and Change* 8 (3): 263–91.

1984. 'Labor Migration in the Arab World'. *Middle East Research and Information Project Report* 123: 3–10.

Hallwood, Paul. 1987. 'Labor Migration and Remittances Between OPEC Members and Non-Oil LDCs'. *Middle East Review* 19 (3): 39–48.

Hamdan, Gamal. 1970. *Egypt's Identity. A Study in the Genius of the Place.* Cairo: National Library of Egypt.

Hamdy, Mostafa, ed. 1964. 'Manpower Requirements for the United Arab Republic for the Period 1960-1985' (in Arabic). *Institute of National Planning*, Memo No. 431, May 1964

Handoussa, Heba, and Nemat Shafik. 1993. 'The Economics of Peace: The Egyptian Case'. In *The Economics of Middle East Peace: Views from the Region*, edited by Stanley Fischer, Dani Rodrik, and Elias H. Tuma, 19–54. Cambridge: Massachusetts Institute of Technology Press.

Hansen, Bent, and Samir Muhammad Radwan. 1982. *Employment Opportunities and Equity in a Changing Economy: Egypt in the 1980s: A Labour Market Approach*. Geneva: International Labour Office.

Hawley, Donald. 2007. *The Emirates: Witness to a Metamorphosis*. Wilby: Michael Russell.

Hear, Nicholas Van. 1998. *New Diasporas: The Mass Exodus, Dispersal and Regrouping of Migrant Communities*. London: University College London Press.

Heikal, Mohammed Hasaneyn. 1956. 'An African Policy for Egypt'. *The Egyptian Economic & Political Review*. 21–24.

   1983. *Kharīf Al-Ghaḍab: Qiṣṣat Bidāyat Wa-Nihāyat 'aṣr Anwar Al-Sādāt*. Beirut: Sharikat al-Maṭbū'āt.

Herbst, Jeffrey. 1990. 'Migration, The Politics of Protest, and State Consolidation in Africa'. *African Affairs* 89 (355): 183–203.

Heydemann, Steven, and Reinoud Leenders. 2011. 'Authoritarian Learning and Authoritarian Resilience: Regime Responses to the "Arab Awakening"'. *Globalizations* 8 (5): 647–53.

Hinnebusch, Raymond A. 1985. *Egyptian Politics under Sadat: The Post-Populist Development of the Authoritarian-Modernizing State*. Cambridge: Cambridge University Press.

Hirschman, Albert O. 1970. *Exit, Voice, and Loyalty: Responses to Decline in Firms, Organizations, and States*. Cambridge: Harvard University Press.

   1978. 'Exit, Voice, and the State'. *World Politics* 31 (1): 90–107.

   1993. 'Exit, Voice, and the Fate of the German Democratic Republic: An Essay in Conceptual History'. *World Politics* 45 (2): 173–202.

Hirst, David, and Irene Beeson. 1981. *Sadat*. London: Faber and Faber.

Hofstadter, Dan. 1973. *Egypt and Nasser*. New York: Facts on File.

Hollifield, James F. 2004. 'The Emerging Migration State'. *International Migration Review* 38 (3): 885–912.

Hollifield, James F. 2012. 'Migration and International Relations'. In *The Oxford Handbook of the Politics of International Migration*, edited by Marc R. Rosenblum and Daniel J. Tichenor, 345–82. Oxford: Oxford University Press.

Hollifield, James F., and Caroline F. Brettell, eds. 2015. *Migration Theory: Talking Across Disciplines*. 3rd edn. New York: Routledge.

Hopwood, Derek. 1991. *Egypt, Politics and Society, 1945–1990*. 3rd edn. London: HarperCollins Academic.

Hourani, Albert Habib. 1947. *Minorities in the Arab World. Issued under the Auspices of the Royal Institute of International Affairs*. London: Oxford University Press.

2013. *A History of the Arab Peoples*. London: Faber & Faber.

Hudson, Michael C. 1977. *Arab Politics: The Search for Legitimacy*. New Haven: Yale University Press.

Huntington, Samuel P. 2006. *Political Order in Changing Societies*. New Haven: Yale University Press.

Ibrahim, Ibrahim, ed. 1983. *Arab Resources: The Transformation of a Society*. London: Routledge.

Ibrahim, Saad Eddin. 1982. *The New Arab Social Order: A Study of the Social Impact of Oil Wealth*. Westview's Special Studies on the Middle East. Boulder: Westview.

2006. 'State, Women, and Civil Society: An Evaluation of Egypt's Population Policy'. In *Arab Society: Class, Gender, Power, and Development*, edited by Nicholas S. Hopkins and Saad Eddin Ibrahim, 3rd edn., 85–104. Cairo: American University in Cairo Press.

Ibrahim, Sunallah. 2001. *Zaat*. Cairo: The American University in Cairo Press.

Ishow, Habib. 1996. *L'irak, Paysanneries, Politiques Agraires Et Industrielles Au XXe Siècle: Contribution À La Réflexion Sur Le Développement*. Paris: Publisud.

Ismael, Tareq Y., and Rifa'at El-Sa'id. 1990. *The Communist Movement in Egypt, 1920–1988*. Syracuse: Syracuse University Press.

Israeli, Raphael. 1985. *Man of Defiance: A Political Biography of Anwar Sadat*. London: Weidenfeld & Nicolson.

Issawi, Charles Philip. 1963. *Egypt in Revolution – An Economic Analysis*. London: Oxford University Press.

James, Laura M. 2006. *Nasser at War: Arab Images of the Enemy*. Basingstoke: Palgrave Macmillan.

Jankowski, James P. 2002. *Nasser's Egypt, Arab Nationalism, and the United Arab Republic*. Boulder: Lynne Rienner Publishers.

Kamel, Mohamed Ibrahim. 1986. *The Camp David Accords: A Testimony*. London: KPI Limited.

Kandil, Hazem. 2012. *Soldiers, Spies, and Statesmen: Egypt's Road to Revolt*. London: Verso.

2015. *Inside the Brotherhood.* Cambridge: Polity Press.

Kanovsky, Eliyahu. 1997. *Iran's Economic Morass: Mismanagement and Decline under the Islamic Republic.* Washington Institute for Near East Policy.

Kapiszewski, Andrzej. 2001. *Nationals and Expatriates: Population and Labour Dilemmas of the Gulf Cooperation Council States.* Reading: Ithaca Press.

2006. 'Arab Versus Asian Migrant Workers in the GCC Countries'. *United Nations Expert Group Meeting on International Migration and Development in the Arab Region.* Beirut.

Kapur, Devesh. 2010. *Diaspora, Development, and Democracy: The Domestic Impact of International Migration from India.* Princeton: Princeton University Press.

Kapur, Devesh, and John McHale. 2003. 'Migration's New Payoff'. *Foreign Policy* 139: 48–57.

Kassem, Maye. 2004. *Egyptian Politics: The Dynamics of Authoritarian Rule.* Boulder: Lynne Rienner Publishers.

Kays, Doreen. 1984. *Frogs and Scorpions: Egypt, Sadat and the Media.* London: Frederick Muller.

Kazamias, Alexander. 2009. 'The Myth of the Nasserite "Purge" of the Greeks from Egypt'. *Journal of the Hellenic Diaspora* 35 (2): 14–34.

Kepel, Gilles. 1985. *The Prophet and Pharaoh: Muslim Extremism in Egypt.* London: Al Saqi Books.

Kerr, Malcolm H. 1978. *The Arab Cold War: Gamal 'abd Al-Nasir and His Rivals, 1958–1970.* 3rd edn. London: Oxford University Press.

Kerr, Malcolm H., and al-Sayyid Yasin, eds. 1982. *Rich and Poor States in the Middle East: Egypt and the New Arab Order.* Boulder: Westview Press.

Khalili, Laleh. 2007. *Heroes and Martyrs of Palestine: The Politics of National Commemoration.* Cambridge: Cambridge University Press.

Khater, Akram Fouad. 2001. *Inventing Home: Emigration, Gender, and the Middle Class in Lebanon, 1870–1920.* Berkeley: University of California Press.

King, Stephen Juan. 2009. *The New Authoritarianism in the Middle East and North Africa.* Indianapolis: Indiana University Press.

Kissinger, Henry. 1979. *White House Years.* Boston: Little, Brown.

Koinova, Maria. 2009. 'Diasporas and Democratization in the Post-Communist World'. *Communist and Post-Communist Studies* 42 (1): 41–64.

Koinova, Maria and Gerasimos Tsourapas. 2018. 'How Do Countries of Origin Engage with Migrants and Diasporas? Multiple Actors and

Comparative Perspectives'. *International Political Science Review* 39 (3): 311–21.

Kosinski, Leszek A. 1978. 'Yugoslavia and International Migration'. *Canadian Slavonic Papers / Revue Canadienne Des Slavistes* 20 (3): 314–38.

Lackner, Helen. 1978. *A House Built on Sand: A Political Economy of Saudi Arabia*. London: Ithaca Press.

LaTowsky, Robert. 1984. 'Egyptian Labor Abroad: Mass Participation and Modest Returns'. *Middle East Research and Information Project Report* 123: 11–18.

Lesch, Ann Mosely. 1986. 'Egyptian Labor Migration: Economic Trends and Government Policies'. *American Universities Field Staff Report, Africa*, 38.

Levitsky, Steven R., and Lucan A. Way. 2011. *Competitive Authoritarianism: Hybrid Regimes after the Cold War*. New York: Cambridge University Press.

———2012. 'Beyond patronage: Violent Struggle, Ruling Party Cohesion, and Authoritarian Durability'. *Perspectives on Politics* 10 (4): 869–89.

Linz, Juan J. 1964. 'An Authoritarian Regime: The Case of Spain'. In *Cleavages, Ideologies, and Party Systems: Contributions to Comparative Political Sociology*, edited by Erik Allardt and Yrjö Littunen, 291–342. Helsinki: Transactions of the Westermarck Society.

Linz, Juan J, and Alfred Stepan. 1996. *Problems of Democratic Transition and Consolidation: Southern Europe, South America, and Post-Communist Europe*. Baltimore: The Johns Hopkins University Press.

Lippman, Thomas W. 1989. *Egypt after Nasser: Sadat, Peace, and the Mirage of Prosperity*. New York: Paragon House.

Lipset, Seymour Martin. 1959. 'Some Social Requisites of Democracy: Economic Development and Political Legitimacy'. *The American Political Science Review* 53 (1): 69–105.

Luna-Martinez, Jose de. 2005. *Workers' Remittances to Developing Countries: A Survey with Central Banks on Selected Public Policy Issues*. Washington, DC: World Bank Publications.

Lust-Okar, Ellen. 2010. *Structuring Conflict in the Arab World: Incumbents, Opponents, and Institutions*. Cambridge: Cambridge University Press.

Mahdavy, Hussein. 1970. 'The Patterns and Problems of Economic Development in Rentier States: The Case of Iran'. In *Studies in the Economic History of the Middle East*, edited by M. A. Cook, 428–67. Oxford: Oxford University Press.

Mansfield, Peter. 1965. *Nasser's Egypt*. Middlesex: Penguin Books.

March, Andrew F. 2003. 'From Leninism to Karimovism: Hegemony, Ideology, and Authoritarian Legitimation'. *Post-Soviet Affairs* 19 (4): 307–36.

Martin, Philip L. 1991. *The Unfinished Story: Turkish Labour Migration to Western Europe: With Special Reference to the Federal Republic of Germany*. Vol. 84. International Labour Organization.

Massey, Douglas S. 1999. 'International Migration at the Dawn of the Twenty-First Century: The Role of the State.' *Population and Development Review* 25 (2): 303–22.

Matthews, Roderic D., and Matta Akrawi. 1949. *Education in Arab Countries of the Near East: Egypt, Iraq, Palestine, Transjordan, Syria, Lebanon*. Washington, DC: American Council on Education.

McDermott, Anthony. 1988. *Egypt from Nasser to Mubarak: A Flawed Revolution*. London: Routledge.

Meseguer, Covadonga, and Katrina Burgess. 2014. 'International Migration and Home Country Politics'. *Studies in Comparative International Development* 49 (1): 1–12.

Messiha, Suzanne A. 1980. *Export of Egyptian School Teachers to Saudi Arabia and Kuwait: A Cost-Benefit Analysis*. Cairo: American University in Cairo.

Messina, Anthony M., and Gallya Lahav. 2006. *The Migration Reader: Exploring Politics and Policies*. London: Lynne Rienner Publishers.

Milton-Edwards, Beverley. 2011. *Contemporary Politics in the Middle East*. 3rd edn. Cambridge: Polity Press.

Misnad, Sheikha. 1985. *The Development of Modern Education in the Gulf*. London: Ithaca Press.

Mitchell, Richard P. 1969. *The Society of the Muslim Brothers*. London: Oxford University Press.

Mitchell, Timothy. 1988. *Colonising Egypt*. Cambridge: Cambridge University Press.

Moench, Richard U. 1988. 'Oil, Ideology and State Autonomy in Egypt'. *Arab Studies Quarterly* 10 (2): 176–92.

Mohie El-Din, A. 1980. 'External Migration of Egyptian Labour'. Mission on Employment Strategy in Egypt. International Labour Organisation.

Mohie-Eldin, Amr, and Ahmed Omar. 1978. 'The Emigration of Universities' Academic Staff'. Unpublished Paper. Cambridge, MA: MIT/Cairo University Technology Planning Program 37.

Moore, Clement Henry. 1986. 'Money and Power: The Dilemma of the Egyptian Infitah'. *Middle East Journal* 40 (4): 634–50.

Morris, Benny. 2004. *The Birth of the Palestinian Refugee Problem Revisited*. Cambridge: Cambridge University Press.

Moss, Dana M. 2016. 'Transnational Repression, Diaspora Mobilization, and the Case of the Arab Spring'. *Social Problems* 63 (4): 480–98.

Mossallam, Alia. 2014. "We Are the Ones Who Made This Dam 'High'!' A Builders' History of the Aswan High Dam'. *Water History* 6 (4): 297–314.

Mountjoy, A. B. 1972. 'Egypt: Population and Resources'. In *Populations of the Middle East and North Africa: A Geographical Approach*, edited by John Innes Clarke and W. B. Fisher, 291–314. London: University of London Press.

Mufti, Malik. 2012. 'The United States and Nasserist Pan-Arabism'. In *The Middle East and the United States: History, Politics, and Ideologies*, edited by David W. Lesch and Mark L. Haas, 5th edn., 147–50. Boulder: Westview Press.

Munz, Rainer, and Myron Weiner, eds. 1997. *Migrants, Refugees, and Foreign Policy – US and German Policies towards Countries of Origin*. Oxford: Berghahn Books.

Nasser, Gamal Abdel. 1955. *Egypt's Liberation: The Philosophy of the Revolution*. Washington, DC: Public Affairs Press.

1966. *On Africa*. Cairo: Ministry of National Guidance, Information Administration.

Naujoks, Daniel. 2013. *Migration, Citizenship, and Development: Diasporic Membership Policies and Overseas Indians in the United States*. New Delhi: Oxford University Press.

Nutting, Anthony. 1972. *Nasser*. London: Constable.

O'Ballance, Edgar. 1971. *The War in the Yemen*. London: Faber.

Obeidi, Amal. 1999. *Political Culture in Libya*. Richmond: Curzon.

O'Donnell, Guillermo A. 1973. *Modernization and Bureaucratic-Authoritarianism: Studies in South American Politics*. Berkeley: Institute of International Studies.

Østergaard-Nielsen, Eva, ed. 2003. *International migration and sending countries: Perceptions, Policies and Transnational Relations*. Houndmills: Palgrave MacMillan.

Oweiss, I. M. 1980. 'Migration of Egyptians'. *L'Egypte Contemporaine* 71 (381): 201–12.

Owen, Roger. 2012. *The Rise and Fall of Arab Presidents for Life*. Cambridge: Harvard University Press.

Owen, Roger, and Sevket Pamuk. 1999. *A History of Middle East Economies in the Twentieth Century*. Cambridge: Harvard University Press.

Pappe, Ilan. 2007. *The Ethnic Cleansing of Palestine*. Oxford: Oneworld Publications.

Peretz, Pauline. 2015. *Let My People Go: The Transnational Politics of Soviet Jewish Emigration During the Cold War*. Vol. 1. Trans. Ethan Rundell Somerset: Taylor and Francis.

Pfaff, Steven. 2006. *Exit-Voice Dynamics and the Collapse of East Germany: The Crisis of Leninism and the Revolution of 1989*. Durham: Duke University Press.

Podeh, Elie. 1999. *The Decline of Arab Unity: The Rise and Fall of the United Arabic Republic*. Brighton: Sussex Academic Press.

Posusney, Martha Pripstein, and Michele Penner Angrist, eds. 2005. *Authoritarianism in the Middle East: Regimes and Resistance*. Boulder: Lynne Rienner.

Qubain, Fahim Issa. 1966. *Education and Science in the Arab World*. Baltimore: Johns Hopkins Press.

Quinlivan, James T. 1999. 'Coup-Proofing: Its Practice and Consequences in the Middle East'. *International Security* 24 (2): 131–65.

Rahmy, Ali Abdel Rahman. 1983. *The Egyptian Policy in the Arab World: Intervention in Yemen, 1962–1967: Case Study*. Lanham: University Press of America.

Reid, Donald M. 1990. *Cairo University and the Making of Modern Egypt*. *Cambridge Middle East Library 23*. Cambridge: Cambridge University Press.

Richards, Alan. 1984. 'Ten Years of Infitah: Class, Rent, and Policy Stasis in Egypt'. *The Journal of Development Studies* 20 (4): 323–338.

——— 1991. 'The Political Economy of Dilatory Reform: Egypt in the 1980s'. *World Development* 19 (12): 1721–30.

Rodriguez, Robyn Magalit. 2010. *Migrants for Export: How the Philippine State Brokers Labor to the World*. Minneapolis: University of Minnesota Press.

Rostow, Walt Whitman. 1960. *The Stages of Economic Growth: A Non-Communist Manifesto*. Cambridge: Cambridge University Press.

Rousillon, Alain. 1985. 'Migration Ou Développement: Quelle Stratégie Migratoire Pour l'Égypte De L' 'Ouverture Économique'?' In *Migrations et Changements Sociaux Dans l'Orient Arabe*, edited by André Bourgey, Philippe Gorokhoff, and Nancy Michel, 131–67. Beirut: Presses de l'Institut français du Proche-Orient.

Roy, Delwin A. 1991. 'Egyptian Emigrant Labor: Domestic Consequences'. *Middle Eastern Studies* 27 (4): 551–82.

Russell, Sharon Stanton, and Michael S. Teitelbaum. 1995. *International migration and international trade*. Washington, DC: The World Bank.

Sadat, Anwar. 1974. *The October Working Paper*. Cairo: Ministry of Information, State Information Service.

1975. *Speeches and Interviews by President Anwar El Sadat.* Cairo: Ministry of Information, State Information Service.

1978a. *Al-Bahth 'an Al-Dhat.* Cairo: Modern Egyptian Library.

1978b. *In Search of Identity: An Autobiography.* New York: Harper & Row.

1981. *The Basic Relationship of the Human Being: His Relationship to God, Himself, Others, the Universe, and Things.* Cairo: General Agency for Information.

Sadat, Camelia. 1985. *My Father and I.* New York: Macmillan.

Sadat, Jihan. 2002. *A Woman of Egypt.* New York: Simon & Schuster.

Said, Edward W. 2014. *Orientalism.* Anniversary Edition. New York: Vintage Books.

Said, Mohamed El Sayed. 1990. 'The Political Economy of Egyptian Migration, 1974–1989'. 'Regional Papers' Series no. 36. Cairo: The Population Council.

Sakr, Naomi. 2013. *Transformations in Egyptian Journalism.* London: I. B. Tauris.

Saleh, Saniyah 'Abd al-Wahhab. 1979. *Attitudinal and Social Structural Aspects of the Brain Drain: The Egyptian Case.* American University in Cairo: Cairo Papers in Social Science.

Sassen, Saskia. 1988. *The Mobility of Labor and Capital: A Study in International Investment and Labor Flow.* Cambridge: Cambridge University Press.

Sayyid-Marsot, Afaf Lutfi. 2007. *A History of Egypt: From the Arab Conquest to the Present.* 2nd edn. Cambridge: Cambridge University Press.

Schlumberger, Oliver. 2007. *Debating Arab Authoritarianism: Dynamics and Durability in Nondemocratic Regimes.* Stanford: Stanford University Press.

Schmidt, Dana Adams. 1968. *Yemen: The Unknown War.* London: Bodley Head.

Seccombe, Ian J. 1983. 'Labour Migration to the Arabian Gulf: Evolution and Characteristics 1920–1950'. *British Journal of Middle Eastern Studies* 10 (1): 3–20.

Sedgwick, Mark. 2010. 'Measuring Egyptian Regime Legitimacy'. *Middle East Critique* 19 (3): 251–67.

Sela, Avraham. 1998. *The Decline of the Arab-Israeli Conflict: Middle East Politics and the Quest for Regional Order.* Albany: State University of New York Press.

Sell, Ralph R. 1988. 'Egyptian International Labor Migration and Social Processes: Toward Regional Integration'. *International Migration Review* 22 (3): 87–108.

Shazly, Saad. 2003. *The Crossing of the Suez*. San Francisco: American Mideast Research.

Shukri, Ghali. 1981. *Egypt: Portrait of a President, 1971–1981: The Counter-Revolution in Egypt, Sadat's Road to Jerusalem*. Middle East Series. London: Zed Press.

Sika, Nadine. 2015. 'Highly Skilled Migration and Development in Egypt'. In *Migration from the Africa and the Middle East – Skilled Migrants, Development and Globalization*, edited by Philippe Fargues and Alessandra Venturini, 151–65. London: I. B. Tauris.

Silvera, Alain. 1980. 'The First Egyptian Student Mission to France under Muhammad Ali'. *Middle Eastern Studies* 16 (2): 1–22.

Simmons, Beth, and Zachery Elkins. 2005. 'On Waves, Clusters and Diffusion: A Conceptual Framework'. *Annals of the American Academy of Political and Social Science* 598: 33–51.

Singerman, Diane. 1995. *Avenues of Participation: Family, Politics, and Networks in Urban Quarters of Cairo*. Princeton Studies in Muslim Politics. Princeton: Princeton University Press.

Sirrs, O. L. 2010. *A History of the Egyptian Intelligence Service: A History of the Mukhabarat, 1910–2009*. Cass Series on Intelligence and Military Affairs: Studies in Intelligence Series. Oxon: Routledge.

Soest, Christian von. 2015. 'Democracy Prevention: The International Collaboration of Authoritarian Regimes'. *European Journal of Political Research* 54 (4): 623–38.

Soliman, Samer. 2011. *The Autumn of Dictatorship: Fiscal Crisis and Political Change in Egypt under Mubarak*. Stanford: Stanford University Press.

Springborg, Robert. 1989. *Mubarak's Egypt: Fragmentation of the Political Order*. Boulder: Westview Press.

Stacher, Joshua. 2012. *Adaptable Autocrats: Regime Power in Egypt and Syria*. Stanford: Stanford University Press.

Szyliowicz, Joseph S. 1973. *Education and Modernization in the Middle East*. Ithaca: Cornell University Press.

Takriti, Abdel Razzaq. 2013. *Monsoon Revolution: Republicans, Sultans, and Empires in Oman, 1965–1976*. Oxford: Oxford University Press.

Talani, Leila Simona. 2010. *From Egypt to Europe: Globalisation and Migration across the Mediterranean*. London: Tauris Academic Studies.

Talani, Leila Simona, and Simon McMahon, eds. 2015. *Handbook of the International Political Economy of Migration*. Northampton: Edward Elgar Publishing.

Tansey, Oisín. 2016. *International Politics of Authoritarian Rule*. Oxford: Oxford University Press.

Tarouty, Safinaz El. 2016. *Businessmen, Clientelism, and Authoritarianism in Egypt.* New York: Springer.

Taylor, Elizabeth. 1984. 'Egyptian Migration and Peasant Wives'. *Middle East Research and Information Project Report* 124: 3–10.

Teitelbaum, Michael S. 2001. 'International Migration: Predicting the Unknowable'. In *Demography and National Security*, edited by Myron Weiner and Sharon Stanton Russell, 21–37. New York: Berghahn Books.

Al-Tali'a. 1969. 'The Road to the Cairo of the Future'. *Al-Tali'a* 5 (2): 76–101.

Tilly, Charles. 1992. *Coercion, Capital and European States: AD 990 – 1992.* Cambridge, MA: Wiley-Blackwell.

Todaro, Michael P. 1969. 'A Model of Labor Migration and Urban Unemployment in Less Developed Countries'. *The American Economic Review* 59 (1): 138–48.

Tripp, Charles. 2007. *A History of Iraq.* 3rd edn. Cambridge: Cambridge University Press.

Tsourapas, Gerasimos. 2014. 'Notes from the Field: Researching Emigration in Post-2011 Egypt'. *American Political Science Association Migration & Citizenship Newsletter* 2 (2): 58–62.

2015a. 'The Politics of Egyptian Migration to Libya'. *Middle East Research and Information Project.* www.merip.org/mero/mero031715.

2015b. 'Why Do States Develop Multi-Tier Emigrant Policies? Evidence from Egypt'. *Journal of Ethnic and Migration Studies* 41 (13): 2192–2214.

2018a. 'Authoritarian Emigration States: Soft Power and Cross-Border Mobility in the Middle East'. *International Political Science Review* 39 (3): 400–16.

2018b. 'Labor Migrants as Political Leverage? Migration Interdependence and Coercion in the Mediterranean'. *International Studies Quarterly* 62 (2): 383–395.

2018c. 'The Peculiar Practices of Authoritarian Emigration States'. *British Academy Review* 32: 22–24.

2018d. 'Theorizing State-Diaspora Relations in the Middle East: Authoritarian Emigration States in Comparative Perspective'. *Mediterranean Politics.* DOI: 10.1080/13629395.2018.1511299

United Arab Republic. 1964. *Al-Ta'līm Al-'ālī : Mushkilātuh Wa-Usus Takhtītih.* Cairo: Wizārat al-Ta'līm al-'Ālī.

United Arab Republic Information Department. 1958. *Nasser's Speeches and Press – Interviews.* Cairo: UAR Information Department.

Van Evera, Stephen. 1997. *Guide to Methods for Students of Political Science.* Ithaca: Cornell University Press.

Van Hear, Nicholas. 1998. *New Diasporas: The Mass Exodus, Dispersal and Regrouping of Migrant Communities.* London: University College London Press.

Vassiliev, Aleksei Mikhailovich. 1997. *The History of Saudi Arabia.* London: Saqi Books.

Vatikiotis, P. J. 1978. *Nasser and His Generation.* London: C. Helm.

1991. *The History of Modern Egypt: From Muhammad Ali to Mubarak.* 4th edn. Baltimore: Johns Hopkins University Press.

Volpi, Frederic, ed. 2010. *Political Islam.* London: Routledge.

Wahbah, Murad. 1994. *The Role of the State in the Egyptian Economy: 1945–1981.* Vol. 24. Reading: Ithaca Press.

Wang, Shaoguang, and Angang Hu. 1999. *The Political Economy of Uneven Development: The Case of China.* Armonk: M. E. Sharpe.

Waterbury, John. 1972. 'Manpower and Planning II: The Burden of Dependency'. *American Universities Field Staff Report,* Northeast Africa Series, 17 (3): 1–17.

1973a. 'Cairo: Third World Metropolis'. *American Universities Field Staff Report,* Northeast Africa Series, 18 (5): 1–23.

1973b. 'Egyptian Elite Perceptions of the Population Problem'. *American Universities Field Staff Report,* Northeast Africa Series, 18 (3): 1–17.

1975. 'Chicken and Eggs: Egypt's Population Explosion Revisited'. *American Universities Field Staff,* Northeast Africa Series, 20 (1): 1–15.

1979. *Hydropolitics of the Nile Valley.* Contemporary Issues in the Middle East. Syracuse: Syracuse University Press.

1983. *The Egypt of Nasser and Sadat: The Political Economy of Two Regimes.* Princeton: Princeton University Press.

1985. 'The 'Soft State' and the Open Door: Egypt's Experience with Economic Liberalization, 1974–1984'. *Comparative Politics* 18 (1):65–83.

1997. 'From Social Contracts to Extraction Contracts: The Political Economy of Authoritarianism and Democracy'. In *Islam, Democracy, and the State in North Africa,* edited by John Pierre Entelis, 141–76. Indianapolis: Indiana University Press.

Weber, Max. 2009. *From Max Weber: Essays in Sociology.* Oxon: Routledge.

Wedeen, Lisa. 1999. *Ambiguities of Domination: Politics, Rhetoric, and Symbols in Contemporary Syria.* Chicago: University of Chicago Press.

Weinbaum, Marvin G. 1985. 'Egypt's 'Infitah' and the Politics of US Economic Assistance'. *Middle Eastern Studies* 21 (2): 206–22.

Weiner, Myron, and Sharon Stanton Russell, eds. 2001. *Demography and National Security.* New York: Berghahn Books.

Weiner, Myron, and Michael S. Teitlebaum. 2001. *Political Demography, Demographic Engineering.* New York: Berghahn Books.

Wheaton, William C. 1979. 'Public Policy and the 'Shortage' of Housing in Egypt'. Paper Prepared for the CU/MIT Technology Adaptation Program. Cairo.

Wickham, Carrie Rosefsky. 2005. *Mobilizing Islam: Religion, Activism and Political Change in Egypt.* New York: Columbia University Press.

2013. *The Muslim Brotherhood: Evolution of an Islamist Movement.* Princeton: Princeton University Press.

Wisensale, Steven K., and Amany A. Khodair. 1998. 'The Two-Child Family: The Egyptian Model of Family Planning'. *Journal of Comparative Family Studies* 29 (3): 503–16.

Woodward, Susan L. 1995. *Socialist Unemployment: The Political Economy of Yugoslavia, 1945–1990.* Princeton: Princeton University Press.

Wynn, Wilton. 1959. *Nasser of Egypt: The Search for Dignity.* Clinton: Colonial Press.

Zahlan, A. B., ed. 1981. *The Arab Brain Drain: Proceedings of a Seminar Organised by the Natural Resources, Science and Technology Division of the United Nations Economic Commission for Western Asia, Beirut 4–8 February 1980.* London: Ithaca Press.

Zaki, R. 1980. *The Inflation Problem in Egypt.* Cairo: Egyptian Public Book Authority.

Zohry, Ayman. 2014. 'Migration and Development in Egypt'. In *Migration from the Middle East and North Africa to Europe: Past Developments, Current Status and Future Potentials,* edited by Michael Bommes, Heinz Fassmann, and Wiebke Sievers, 75–98. Amsterdam: Amsterdam University Press.

Zohry, Ayman, and Barbara Harrell-Bond. 2003. *Contemporary Egyptian Migration: An Overview of Voluntary and Forced Migration.* Sussex: Development Research Centre on Migration, Globalisation and Poverty.

Zollner, Barbara. 2007. 'Prison Talk: The Muslim Brotherhood's Internal Struggle during Gamal Abdel Nasser's Persecution, 1954 to 1971'. *International Journal of Middle East Studies* 39 (3): 411–33.

Index

For EU product safety concerns, contact us at Calle de José Abascal, 56–1°, 28003 Madrid, Spain or eugpsr@cambridge.org.

www.ingramcontent.com/pod-product-compliance
Ingram Content Group UK Ltd.
Pitfield, Milton Keynes, MK11 3LW, UK
UKHW020333140625
459647UK00018B/2125